AF411783

Machiavelli's Legacy

Machiavelli's Legacy

The Prince After Five Hundred Years

Edited by

Timothy Fuller

PENN

UNIVERSITY OF PENNSYLVANIA PRESS

PHILADELPHIA

Published by
University of Pennsylvania Press
Philadelphia, Pennsylvania 19104-4112
www.upenn.edu/pennpress

Printed in the United States of America on acid-free paper
1 3 5 7 9 10 8 6 4 2

Library of Congress Cataloging-in-Publication Data
Machiavelli's legacy : *The Prince* after five hundred years /
edited by Timothy Fuller.
    pages cm
Includes bibliographical references and index.
ISBN 978-0-8122-4769-5 (alk. paper)
    1. Machiavelli, Niccolò, 1469–1527. Principe.   2. Political
science—Philosophy.   I. Fuller, Timothy, 1940– editor.
JC143.M4M3228 2016
320.1—dc23
                                                2015025668

CONTENTS

Introduction

TIMOTHY FULLER

Machiavelli is, next to Plato, perhaps the most famous political thinker in our tradition, and also among the most controversial. The term "Machiavellian" is in common use today, no doubt employed by many who know little if anything about his life or writings. The term carries with it a sinister overtone going back at least to Shakespeare's portrayal of an evil King Richard III who calls himself a "Machiavel." But in the course of centuries the reception and interpretation of Machiavelli's thought has become complicated, the source of numerous scholarly disputes. Is he a "teacher of moral evil"? Or is he, without endorsing them, providing a sober and detached view of the actualities of human conduct, thereby becoming a catalyst for the modern social sciences? Is he the advocate of absolute princely power or the defender of republican government? Is *The Prince* a handbook for rulers or is it a satire on princely rule, intended to warn the public about princes? Is he calling for a great act of founding a new order implying a vision of what we have come to know as the modern state? Does his discussion of "Fortuna" suggest that human ingenuity must always be defeated by historical contingency, or is there room for human choice and action to create a new order which might restore, in a new form, the lost greatness of Roman antiquity? Was *The Prince* written in hope of release from exile and in search of employment from the Medici in the Florentine government? Or was it written for the "attentive reader" who would see a much larger purpose?

Among the questions widely debated among students of political philosophy today, a central question is, What is "modernity"? What do we mean when we use this term? At what point might we say modernity came to sight? What distinguishes the "modern" from the "ancient"? Is the character of politics in our time markedly different—for better or worse—from politics in earlier times? Such debates quickly and inevitably bring Machiavelli to the forefront. He is taken to instantiate the emergence of a distinctly modern understanding of the human condition and of politics, fostering a dramatic change in human self-understanding.

There is as well much debate about a "crisis" of modern Western civilization. This results in part from the destructiveness of the twentieth century, which called into question the belief in progress toward perpetual peace and prosperity. But there is also widespread concern for what may be called a spiritual crisis, a crisis of meaning, a fear that we do not know what the right order of society is or whether the West can any longer provide the model for the future of the world. We are aware of infinite variety which encourages cultural and moral relativism at the same time that that variety is defended as a source of the freedom for us to make up our own purposes and to pursue them.

But what then is the right use of our freedom thus understood? Freedom comes to be associated with creativity rather than with the effort to conform our character to the right order of things. Is "right order" simply whatever orders can establish themselves and prolong their historical presence? Do we mean to say that our purpose is to define our own purposes and then pursue them? Does this mean that outside of whatever commitments we may happen to make and establish as conventional wisdom, anything and everything is permitted? This is itself an ancient argument, well known to Plato (for example, in the *Gorgias*). But whereas Plato's Socrates offers the possibility of resisting this argument, Machiavelli embraces it when he tells us in chapter 6 of *The Prince*, speaking of the legendary founders of political orders: "And as one examines their actions and lives, one does not see that they had anything else from fortune than the opportunity, which gave them the matter enabling them to introduce any form they pleased." In short, he is arguing that the order we have is not to be judged by its conformity to a hypothetical transcendent order, but by its capacity to persist through time, reflecting the creative genius of those who brought it into being as a fortress against the chaotic and violent forces of nature.

One will see in the essays that follow differing responses to these and other issues the reader of Machiavelli must confront. Together these essays constitute a set of distinct voices in dialogue on Machiavelli's legacy.

Harvey C. Mansfield, William R. Kenan Jr. Professor of Government at Harvard, is an internationally known translator of, and commentator on, Machiavelli's thought. In "Machiavelli's Effectual Truth," he provides an excellent summary of the controversies in interpreting Machiavelli's thought, and summarizes his own position within that controversy. In this respect, Mansfield's essay provides most valuable guidance for the reader who wants to examine Machiavelli's legacy. Beyond this, however, Mansfield presents a detailed account of Machiavelli's criticism of the legacy of Greek philosophy and Christian thought. In doing so, he shows that Machiavelli intended to replace the dualistic legacy (the distinction between the divine and the human) of Greek and Christian thought with a vision of a unified field of experience—distinguishing fact from imagination—within which he argued we must take our bearings. For Machiavelli, the "human whole" is all there is. To comprehend fully what is visible requires us to set aside the quest for what is invisible. As Mansfield points out, Machiavelli's term "effectual truth" has been little studied. His essay elaborates on the magnitude of what Machiavelli meant by effectual truth. In doing so, he shows the deep divide between the ancient legacies and the Machiavellian legacy, a legacy that is realized in increasingly radical departures from what was once taken to be the perennial wisdom. Mansfield reminds us of what the ancient Greek and Christian legacies were (and are); he thus opens the way to a more profound assessment of the claims Machiavelli made to be in possession of the effectual truth, recognizing that there are competing legacies within the Western tradition. In light of the ravaging experiences of the twentieth and twenty-first centuries, we are called upon to ask how effective this effectual truth has been.

Maurizio Viroli, professor of government at the University of Texas, in "The Redeeming Prince," presents us with a very different Machiavelli. For him, Machiavelli has created the myth of a redeemer anticipating the unification of Italy, which came to pass only in the nineteenth century. In this view, the final chapter of *The Prince*, exhorting the unification of Italy, is the key to understanding Machiavelli's thought, not the "effectual truth" of chapter 15, which, in this version, is an instrument in service of the visionary ideal. Viroli argues that the constant theme of Machiavelli's writings is liberation from foreign domination. Viroli knows that this is not the predominant way of interpreting Machiavelli's thought, but he provides extensive references to the whole of Machiavelli's writings in defense of his argument. This includes his insistence that *The Prince* is a rhetorical performance from start to finish, and that, according to the prevailing rules of rhetorical argument, the most vital point comes at the conclusion (whereas, for example, Mansfield finds the most vital point at the center).

Viroli knows that scholars have argued that the final "Exhortation" was written several years after the body of the work was composed in 1513. He launches an argument to defend the view that the "Exhortation" is not only consistent with the rest of *The Prince*, but is internally consistent with having been written close to the time of the rest of the work, perhaps in January 1514. He argues further, against the view that Machiavelli wrote to gain the favor of the Medici, that the text contains much to annoy them, offering advice that they would not have found congenial. This would be consistent with Machiavelli's suggestion that he wrote *The Prince* for "whoever can understand it." Finally, Viroli shows that by 1515 Machiavelli was in a state of depression, doubtful of grand proposals, and thus in a mood not conducive to the writing of the "Exhortation" by that time. For Viroli, Machiavelli was not a realist but a visionary, a prophetic voice for the future greatness of Italy.

Finally, Viroli argues that learning "how not to be not good" when necessary appears in all true founders, including Moses. In this respect, there is, one might say, a realistic element in an otherwise visionary endeavor which, according to Viroli, is to use princely rule now in order to establish republican order in the long run. Thus for Viroli the theme of Italian "redemption" is key to understanding Machiavelli's legacy.

Catherine Heidt Zuckert, Nancy Reeves Dreux Professor of Political Science at the University of Notre Dame, explores Machiavelli's "revolution in thought." She, too, refers to his mixed reputation, to the question of the "effectual truth." But she points out that learning how not to be good when necessity requires it is not the same as learning how to be "entirely bad." Machiavelli's "realism" about human nature, she remarks, is already elaborated in Thucydides and in the Christian doctrine of original sin. Ancient descriptions of the wickedness of human beings can be just as graphic as those we find in Machiavelli. Within that tradition the emphasis was on achieving the rule of an aristocratic few who might be capable of bringing a certain nobility to the unseemly aspects of politics.

Zuckert thinks the true novelty in Machiavelli is what she calls a "democratic bias." In *The Prince* this comes out in his advice that the prince seek support among the people against the "great." Since the people in general seek not to be ruled, while the great seek to rule, the prince offers the prospect of liberation from control by the great in an alliance with the people. This implies, further, that in return for the allegiance of the people the prince will limit his intervention in their lives while, at the same time, learning how to be rhetorically persuasive, relying less on direct coercion and more on clothing his necessary actions in a moralizing vocabulary. The danger is that an adept prince may gain the very sort of control the people do not wish to have exercised over them, granting favors that increase their dependency such that their capacity to resist (to avoid being ruled) will be severely diminished. The counter to this must then lie in the great and ambitious, whose interest it becomes to defend the people against the ruler. Whether Machiavelli is defending the prince or the ambitious, in each case the goal is to protect the people's desire not to be ruled within the limits of what the security of the state may require. While the democratic bias may be attractive, Zuckert finally wonders if denying to public service its nobility has, in the long run, debased the political life, depriving it of that luster of which Aristotle spoke.

Arlene W. Saxonhouse is Caroline Robbins Professor of Political Science and Women's Studies at the University of Michigan. Her essay, "Machiavelli's Women," brings forward another distinct dimension of Machiavelli's thought. She finds in his portrayal of women a deeper and more radical challenge to traditional thought than we had hitherto identified. To get at this, Saxonhouse examines Machiavelli's correspondence in detail, finding a disturbing picture of sexual ambiguity tending to undermine hierarchies of defined status, and pointing to transcending the limits of nature. His famous discussion of the opposition between fickle Fortuna and the manly man who seeks to overcome her by force is challenged in the letters by accounts of his repeated submission to feminine charms. She connects these reports with more well known passages in which Machiavelli describes women who have all the attributes of manliness.

All this, Saxonhouse argues, reveals Machiavelli's intent to delegitimate all hierarchical conceptions of order, to bring down "the great chain of being"; he is engaged in nothing less than transforming the whole imaginative structure within and through which human beings had interpreted the world from time immemorial. Machiavelli's thought is, then, a gateway into an unbounded modernity in which an unchained imagination is our only resource.

David Wootton is anniversary professor of history at the University of York. "Machiavelli and the Business of Politics" analyzes the term "state" as Machiavelli and others in the sixteenth and seventeenth centuries, up until Hobbes, understood it. Wootton finds a significant range of connotations referring variously to the ruler, to the ruled, from the regime to power politics, and so on. There is here uncertainty as to the goal or end served by politics, suggesting that the purpose of human life may be to make up our own purposes and to hope for felicity insofar as we can realize the ends we choose. This characteristic shows itself both in individuals and in states. Machiavelli identifies various goals ranging from the pursuit of pleasure in individuals to the pursuit of honor or glory in statecraft. This reminds one of the Machiavellian assertion that there are two desires: to rule and to avoid being ruled. What disappears is an objective standard for assessing the multiplicity of ways in which the fulfillment of these two desires will be defined and pursued. The "state" for Machiavelli cannot yet have a clear and settled definition, since the various pursuits of life will affect what the term meant to those who were using it in his time. The notion of the modern constitutional state, having a meaning independent from the particular goals of individuals who may occupy the offices of such a state, is still to come; the state is not yet depersonalized. Moreover, Machiavelli avoids the use of the word "political" insofar as it suggests the classical concept of the polity as symbolizing an ideal of human relations.

Wootton goes on to analyze *ragione*, "reason," finding it also to have multiple meanings, including "law" and "business," suggesting the task of reasoning sensibly in various modes of interaction, or acting according to the logic of the activity that engages you. "Reason of state," then, means the "logic of power politics." But to the extent that Machiavelli expresses goals, such as redeeming the greatness of Italy, he also is the harbinger of the pursuit of grand projects for remaking the world—satisfying both the aspirations of rulers and the desires of the ruled—which became such a powerful impetus in European politics at a later date. In these terms, Machiavelli is both a realist and an idealist; his politics is a business as well as a search for nobility as we define that for ourselves.

David C. Hendrickson, distinguished scholar of American diplomatic history and foreign policy, traces the reception of Machiavelli in the theorizing of international relations. On the one hand, he examines Machiavelli's contribution to the concept of "reason of state," which proposes that the ethic of statecraft differs from the ethic of ordinary life; but he also shows that the term "Machiavellian" has become disconnected from intimate knowledge of what Machiavelli actually wrote—it has taken on a life of its own and is used as a term of abuse against one's enemies. Analytically, on the other hand, Machiavelli's is a call to understand what you are getting into if you go into politics. Appearance and reality there cannot be separated, and you have to be prepared to accept the ordeal this imposes or you will indeed fail and come to ruin. In this respect, Machiavelli is to be applauded for refusing to be taken in by conventional pieties; he is not to be blamed for pointing out what is going on as if, in pointing it out, he is the source of the problem.

Moreover, the ancients had no illusions on this score. Read Thucydides or book 2 of Saint Augustine's *City of God*, which describes the real manner in which the Romans created their empire in words that are not second to Machiavelli's in their brutality. Machiavelli himself, having read the ancients carefully, says that the ancients tended to conceal what they knew of this reality, but he is going to bring it out full force. We see here a Machiavelli who could justify—or "rationalize"—lying in politics, but who himself claimed to be telling the truth about lying at the same time. One could see him as a critic of the evils of politics even as he seems to be praising the capacity of the statesman for using that evil to achieve ambitious goals.

Hendrickson also brings to our attention the reception of Machiavelli in the Scottish Enlightenment. Adam Smith's critique of Machiavelli indicates that between the sixteenth and the eighteenth centuries, a virtue of "politeness" came to sight, bespeaking the desire to amend the world, to overcome the brutality Machiavelli's analysis forced us to recognize. In this respect, Machiavelli could be a catalyst for the movement to transcend or reform the world he described. Smith and Hume too were profoundly aware also of a dramatic change in European life spawned by the rise of the commercial society in which competitive economic interactions, as alternatives to resort to force, increasingly played a role in changing the moral sentiments in modernity. The resort to force was increasingly defined as an aberration in human relations rather than as a natural and inevitable fact of human conduct. One could say that Machiavelli's legacy paradoxically excited what we have come to know as the Kantian response.

However, as Hendrickson also shows, Machiavelli did not merely endorse the resort to force. He went to considerable length to analyze different strategies for using force in terms of their useful or self-defeating characteristics. In this respect, Machiavelli was not merely "Machiavellian," and his analysis of conquest or alliance is most pertinent to discussing issues of foreign policy today. Hendrickson shows how Washington and Jefferson, for instance, understood the need of distinguishing among various approaches to the use of force. Finally, Hendrickson examines what he finds to be striking parallels between Roman expansion and U.S. expansion in the twentieth century.

As with the other commentators here, Thomas E. Cronin, McHugh Professor of American Institutions and Leadership at Colorado College, reflects as an Americanist on the paradoxes of Machiavelli's thought and legacy. Cronin systematizes Machiavelli's views on leadership with a view to illuminating the paradoxes of leadership as we experience them today. Like Hendrickson, Cronin sees the issue of the American founding—how to create a strong government without destroying liberty—as the experience of issues of leading and leadership which Machiavelli's analysis anticipated. Cronin knows that the claim of the founders was to invent a constitutional system that would redeem us from the Machiavellian problem if we could choose a government by reflection and deliberation rather than suffer a government to emerge by accident and force. But we should remember that they were acutely aware of the "Machiavellian problem" as they searched for an antidote to it.

Like Catherine Zuckert, Cronin thinks that the advice to learn how to be not good when necessary does not equate to advice to cultivate evil or dwell in the resort to force. Rather, he advises to recognize when the resort to force is unavoidable; to do what is necessary does not mean to do more than necessity requires. Cronin summarizes those maxims of Machiavelli which prompt one to think that Machiavelli teaches moral evil, but insists that, in doing so, Machiavelli is also instructing the reader, and the would-be leader, what to expect; this is as much advice about anticipating and minimizing the risks as it is about risk taking. Cronin's conclusion is that we need not succumb to the brutal elements of Machiavelli's teaching in order to learn important lessons from those elements.

Clifford Orwin, professor of political philosophy at the University of Toronto, offers a detailed analysis of Machiavelli's use of the figure of Cesare Borgia to illustrate the complexity of Machiavelli's arguments. In doing so, he reviews the varying ways students of Machiavelli's thought have proposed that Cesare is or is not the picture of an ideal leader. After all, he had great resources but also came to naught. Orwin suggests that the treatment of Cesare can be the most revealing of Machiavelli's intentions, and that his apparent praise of Cesare is not to be taken at face value. Machiavelli does not raise Cesare to the rank of the great founders Moses, Cyrus, Romulus, Theseus. In the course of Orwin's argument, which involves review of the interpretations of other Machiavelli scholars, he also discusses the role of fortune and the power of the Church to maintain itself against secularizing forces. Machiavelli can praise Cesare faintly given the demand for new modes to restructure the old order (primarily the Church), but show at the same time that the constraining power of the prevailing ("ancient") orders does not permit reform through "new modes" grafted onto the old orders. The revolutionary change would require a founder on the level of Moses, Cyrus, Romulus, and

Theseus; Cesare is not at that level. He exemplifies failed attempts at reform of the past, not the genius to imagine and to bring forth a new political world. Thus, for Orwin, Machiavelli, having worked through the strengths and weaknesses of Cesare, arrives at the conclusion to write of what is needed for another age where fortune shall shine more positively on the prospect of a truly new order. Orwin also agrees with several other contributors to this volume that Machiavelli's aim is not to produce a ruthless order, but neither does he wish to retain the moral teachings of the old (Christian) order. Machiavelli seeks neither a classical nor a Christian model of order. Orwin speculates that the ideal of a "peaceful democratic commercial republic" is one avenue we moderns have explored as a fitting conclusion to Machiavelli's critique of the world he inherited.

In sum, each of these essays presents us with a Machiavelli both familiar and yet strange. Modern idealism conflicts with the lessons of Machiavelli and yet is driven by them. We remain fascinated by Machiavelli in part because he reminds us of what we seek to transcend, but also because we remain uncertain of our capacity to achieve that transcendence. The ravages of the past century deepen this ambivalence, since they called into question any claim to have transcended, or that we know how to transcend, the human condition Machiavelli describes.

His legacy is to have anticipated the dialectic of modern politics wherein we pursue our hopes and aspirations while wondering whether the means employed to achieve such satisfactions ennoble or debase us.

CHAPTER I

Machiavelli's Enterprise

HARVEY C. MANSFIELD

Five hundred years ago, on December 10, 1513, Niccolò Machiavelli wrote a letter to a friend of his in Rome describing one day in his life as an exile from Florence and remarking casually that he had just completed writing *The Prince*.[1] This momentous book, together with its companion, the *Discourses on Livy*, neither published until after his death, announces an enterprise affecting all human beings today: the creation of the modern world.

Machiavelli is famous for his infamy, for being "Machiavellian," but his importance is almost universally underestimated. The extent of his consequence is not appreciated, and the size of his ambition is little known. He makes it possible, even easy, to suppose that his ambition is confined to place hunting with Lorenzo de' Medici and service as drillmaster of the Florentine Republic—as if his thought was bounded by his employment opportunities and he had nothing in mind in the way of self-employment. Of course everyone senses his greatness as a writer, a master of Italian prose with a gift for an acute phrase, often worth citing for effect but almost never actually avowed for use. "I am a Machiavellian" is something one does not hear. But in addition to his maxims, which in truth are deliberately exaggerated, he does not receive much respect as a guide to the future. But a guide with foresight is just what Machiavelli is, if one adds that he made the future to which he guides us.

To see how important Machiavelli was one must first look to see how important he meant to be. His own words are quite expansive. In the dedicatory letter to the *Florentine Histories* he refers to "my enterprise" (*la mia impresa*) without saying what it was; perhaps it was just to write a history of Florence. But in the preface to book 1 of the *Discourses on Livy* he avows a grand purpose that encompasses his whole life: he has a "natural desire" to "work for those things I believe will bring common benefit to everyone" (*Discourses* [hereafter cited as *D*] 1.pref.1).[2] A natural desire is in human nature, not just in the humans of Machiavelli's time, and the beneficiaries will be everyone, all humanity, not just his native country or city. He goes on to say that he has "decided to take a path as yet untrodden by anyone." He will benefit everyone by taking a new path; he is not just imitating the ancients or contributing to the Renaissance, the rebirth of the ancients. Obviously his new path leads back to the ancients, but it does not end there. In the middle of *The Prince* (*Prince* [hereafter cited as *P*] 15.61),[3] a less prominent place, he declares, "I depart from the orders of others," also emphasizing his originality. One soon learns that the "others" include both the Renaissance (a name given authority if not invented by Jacob Burckhardt in the nineteenth century)[4] and the "ancients" he refers to repeatedly. Machiavelli departs from the tradition of thought beginning with the Greek, or Socratic, philosophy that was still powerful in his time in the form of scholasticism and the humanism that revolted against scholasticism. He surely belonged to the broad Socratic tradition in some sense, but he also, mainly, departed from it. And he departs from the Bible while appropriating it to his use. He cannot be interpreted as captured by any tradition or "context." Or if he was, he was a prisoner who tried to escape—not a passive prisoner.

Machiavelli's enterprise is not easy to see even in outline. The pages of his books seem repetitious and confused, and he does not summarize his message to declare in simple terms what he means by departing from the orders of others and taking a new path. A grand division of opinion exists as to what he means. There is an uneducated view of Machiavelli, responsible for his evil reputation as "Machiavellian," held by people who have not read a word of his but would instinctively recoil if they did at the practice of scheming evil that he repeatedly recommends. These nonreaders, who speak of him as the author of Machiavellianism, rest with that judgment and do not try to think out why he might have wanted to present himself as the spitting image of the devil. Then there is an educated view of most Machiavelli scholars, who have read his books, which is primarily devoted to refuting and repudiating the uneducated view. To do this, these scholars latch on to one of Machiavelli's own excuses, such as that the murder of your inconvenient brother may be for the common good (*D* 1.9.2), or they excuse him by taking an objective stance from outside his words. From the standpoint of science it is said that he was only trying to understand, not to judge, or from the outlook of history that he was only reflecting his times, not facing permanent problems.[5] All three excuses diminish his importance and result in a very great underestimation of Machiavelli. In excusing his teaching of evil, they remove him from any sense of the extraordinary, recognized in the uneducated view of nonreaders when they describe conduct as Machiavellian. Either the scholars raise him to a level of protoscientific objectivity above practical concerns, teaching us the "realism" we already have at hand, or they plunge him into a confused context of the Italy of his time—its disunity, its corrupt popes, its scheming princes and ineffectual republics, together with its humanist and other authors, who provided him with intellectual equipment.

The best way to resolve and transcend the difference between educated and uneducated opinion and to give Machiavelli his due is to set aside condescension where it exists and to seize on the common sense that Machiavelli's promotion of scheming evil is something extraordinary and try to see how far it goes. I shall set forth the idea that Machiavelli, with his enterprise, was not caused by his context but was the cause of a context, our context.[6]

To create the modern world Machiavelli initiated a twofold transformation of politics and philosophy that would bring them together: politics with the elevation of philosophy, and philosophy brought down to earth. These two motions come together in the prince, now understood not merely as a ruler but also as a thinker devoted to improving the prospects of princes and incidentally, or not incidentally, their peoples—so that princes become knowers of "the world." It was necessary for Machiavelli to reverse the meaning of *modern* and create a new meaning of *world*. "Modern" would no longer signify the weakness taught by Christianity but would acquire new vigor from obeying human necessities rather than divine commands. "The world" would be *this* world as opposed to the next world of Christianity and to the high-minded morality of classical philosophy. The new meaning of "world" is the context Machiavelli has made for us.

For the transformation of politics, one may start from a few of his best one-line formulations in *The Prince*: "in truth there is no secure method to possess [free cities] other than to ruin them" (*P* 5.20); "spending what is someone else's does not take reputation from you but adds it to you" (*P* 16.64); "it is much safer to be feared than loved" (*P* 17.66); "a prudent lord . . . cannot observe faith, nor should he, when such observance turns against him" (*P* 18.69). These and other such expressions of calculated evil are summed up in the statement of revolt "from the orders of others" quoted above that "it is necessary to a prince, if he wants to maintain himself, to learn to be able not to be good, and to use this and not use it according to necessity" (*P* 15.61). To reach this conclusion Machiavelli opposes the many who rely on "imagined republics and principalities that have never been known to exist in truth." Such writers make a "profession of good in all regards" on which those who do not write or read but merely live by moral principle implicitly rely for support. Machiavelli does not cite names, but one thinks of Plato's *Republic* for an imagined republic or monarchy, Aristotle's imagined monarchy of the good man, and, if God is a prince, *The City of God* of Saint Augustine.

Each of these writers works out what it would mean to be good "in all regards" for an individual and, since men do not live as isolated individuals, for a society as well. The working out has to be imagined because a society that is good in all regards "has never been seen or known to exist in truth." Truth means the "effectual truth" as opposed to what is merely imagined when people profess they are good and philosophers imagine their profession of good in its full extent. The effectual truth of morality comes down to its political effects, when the lofty professions are applied among those who are not good. Machiavelli concentrates the power of this phrase, the "effectual truth" (*verità effettuale*), by using it just this once in all his writings. Indeed, Machiavelli scholars have been unable to find any other use of the phrase in the Italian Renaissance among humanist authors, and I am not aware of any earlier use of it.[7] Its power was intended by Machiavelli to reach his successors, captains in the army of his enterprise, for them to develop—and so it was. He was the pioneer for Bacon, Descartes, and the other founders of modern philosophy who set conditions for knowledge of the world whose necessity he discovered, whose possibility he created. He showed the path for them to follow in a single paragraph in *The Prince*, one could almost say in the flick of this unrepeated single phrase.

We may begin an attempt to understand the phrase that Machiavelli first formulated by contrasting it to the two main alternative notions that he faced of truth made effective. In the Bible the truth of revelation is to be brought to all by God's ministers, as Paul said, "according to the grace of God given unto me by the effectual working [*energeia*] of his power" (Ephesians 3.7, King James Version). Marsilius of Padua (an author known to Machiavelli), quoting Aristotle, speaks of false belief as a hindrance to truth, an obstacle to its becoming effectual. In neither case is the truth itself effectual; rather it is that divine or human aid can make it effectual or not.[8] But effectual truth is truth that can make itself effectual without the aid of outside force; it is truth with its own power to create effects and thus impress itself on those who would otherwise resist truth. This impressive truth is new truth that lacks the advantage of having tradition on its side but that has a power that can overcome the customary resistance to truth of which Machiavelli is acutely aware (*P* 3.8, 6.22–23, 23.94; *D* 3.35.1). New truth is more powerful than settled truth, not despite its newness but because of it; it gains power from its very opposition to whatever is established and inherited. Coming out of the practices and devices of scheming evil, effectual truth signifies the closing of the gap between politics and philosophy and the entrance of Machiavelli himself, the philosopher, as the prince.

Is Machiavelli a philosopher? He does not say that he is. He uses the word very sparingly and does not openly address those he calls "philosophers." He himself reports and seems to approve of Cato's rejection of philosophy for the evil of "honorable idleness" by which it infects and corrupts the virtue of Rome (Florentine Histories [hereafter cited as *FH*] 5.1; *D* 1.pref.2). He rarely speaks of the philosopher, just once in *The Prince*, and three times in the *Discourses* (*P* 19.75; *D* 1.56, 2.5.1, 3.12.1). He seems to confine himself to politics, to the means and conditions for political success. Yet he indicates that he is a philosopher, and repeatedly, insistently, in several ways. If his focus is on politics, it is politics understood expansively as the "world" and "worldly things" (*cose del mondo*). To expand politics to include the world implies that the world governs politics or politics governs the world, or both. In his day the notion of the "world" immediately raised the question of *which* world, this one or the next? Here we find ourselves immediately engaged in the question that defines philosophy and distinguishes it from revealed religion. The question between philosophy and religion can be put in political terms as a dispute over which world governs the other and whether politics can manage or God must provide for human fortunes—*Fortuna* being, as everyone knows, a prominent theme of Machiavelli's.

Machiavelli sets forth the dispute in two separate places that the reader must make the effort to put together. Incidentally, as it seems, to justify not omitting something, he says in a clause in the *Discourses*: "since it is good to reason about everything . . ." (*D* 1.18.1); whereas in *The Prince* he says, again in a clause: "although one should not reason about Moses, as he was a mere executor of things that had been ordered for him by God . . ." (*P* 6.22). He does not expressly argue, for and against, the question whether faith sets limits to reason, as a philosopher who wanted to make himself obvious might do, but leaves a contradiction that is blatant when exposed. Now, why should one not reason about Moses? Moses is a figure in the Bible, the Book of God that commands reverence and is revered. To reason about Moses is to question the reverence in which he is held and to challenge the belief that holds him in reverence. To reason about everything is the work of a philosopher, who as such challenges belief merely by asking questions; to believe is to hold the answers the philosopher questions. Thus we have a distinction between the philosopher, who questions, and the believer, or nonphilosopher, who has answers he does not question. This does not mean that no one who reasons should believe or that the philosopher has no beliefs. Machiavelli himself has beliefs and frequently says he "believes" something, but his beliefs arise from his reasoning and serve it.

It is good, he says, to reason about everything and also good not to reason about everything. The latter must mean that it is good, having reasoned or while reasoning about everything, not to *appear* to reason about everything.

Machiavelli does not call himself a philosopher or say that he is bringing a new mode of philosophy, but leaves these things to be inferred from hints or allusions or incomplete, solitary statements surrounded with innocent, apparently nonphilosophic context. In the famous letter mentioned earlier he left a memorable picture of the life of the philosopher and of himself as philosopher: the one who after noisy, contentious card playing in the inn he frequents, in which he suffers the malignity of his fate, sits down in the evening with his books to the conversation of his mind within itself in the quiet of his study to which he repairs for four hours in the evening, during which he forgets every pain and fears neither poverty nor death. He imagines himself clothed in regal and courtly garments so as to "enter the ancient courts of ancient men, where, received by them lovingly, I feed on the food that alone is mine and that I was born for." Apparently equal to the occasion, he says he is "not ashamed to speak with them and to ask them the reason for their actions, and they in their humanity reply to me."[9] It is hard not to recognize the contrast as the one, dear to the ancients with whom he converses, between the philosophical and the nonphilosophical life. It is a natural difference, one Machiavelli is born for, from which his rowdy "company" of the day, whom he does not hesitate to call "vermin," is excluded.[10] Yet, despite this beautiful description of philosophizing, he still does not call himself "philosopher."

Nor does Machiavelli call himself "prince." He advises princes, an actual prince in *The Prince* and potential princes in the *Discourses*. But in advising them he orders them around and speaks like a prince, as in "I depart from the orders of others," in the critical paragraph we are studying. In *The Prince* he moves from homage or servitude (*servitù*) to Lorenzo de' Medici at the beginning to telling him that "one should not let this opportunity pass" at the end (*P* Dedicatory Letter [hereafter DL]3, 26.105). In a chapter of the *Discourses* devoted to the ordering of Rome, he switches from analyzing Rome to "someone" who might wish "to order a republic anew" (*D* 1.6.4), a someone who might be himself. In our paragraph he considers morality from the standpoint of a prince to explain why it is necessary to do evil. Out of his princely critique of morality he moves quickly to truth, or what is today called epistemology. By following closely what he says in this small space, we shall see how Machiavelli's politics is elevated to truth and his philosophy lowered to what is visible in the world. To begin with, morality is not separable from politics as it was in Aristotle, who wrote two books on ethics and politics, connected but separate, in which morality is first presented for itself and then in political context. For Machiavelli, by contrast, morality must originally and always be judged from what happens if you practice it, which means judged from the standpoint of the prince. Even among friends and relations, to say nothing of fellow citizens or subjects, "a man who wants to make a profession of good in all regards must come to ruin among so many who are not good" (*P* 15.61). A "man" must have the outlook of a prince, a wary prince (see *D* 3.2).

Why is "a profession of good in all regards" supposed necessary to morality? Those who do good rely on others not to take advantage of them, indeed to return that good in gratitude so that do-gooders will not "come to ruin." The many who do not write or read but merely live by moral principle implicitly rely on the argument of philosophy or religion to show convincingly that they can afford to be moral. Good deeds must be accompanied with an explanation, a "profession of good." And because a deed that appears good may be done with evil intent, the doer needs to profess the good he does as well as perform it. But also because evil may appear good, no visible evidence will suffice to prove the intent of the doer, and his profession must appeal to some invisible principle or realm; it must rely on imagination to guarantee its existence. In sum, as Machiavelli sees it, the foundation for morality, what makes it reliable, what justifies taking the risk of coming to ruin by doing a moral deed, is a "profession"—a pretense of philosophy or religion. A profession of good "in all regards" would have to be the good society as a whole, not merely isolated good actions taken by themselves. So Machiavelli says that many rely on "imagined republics and principalities that have never been known to exist in truth."

To understand the pretense of truth in the imaginary republic that Machiavelli rejects, we need to look at Plato, who introduces philosophy in that dialogue as the means to calm down manly anger (or *thumos* in the soul). Plato's case against Homer's poetry offers an ordered universe to remove the reasons for the obstreperous claims of justice (or complaints of injustice) by Homer's heroes and those educated to be inspired by them. In an ordered universe, in the cosmos, the gods are so orderly that they do not involve themselves in human affairs.[11] They live in a philosophical cosmos that is replicated in an orderly human soul, the soul of the philosopher who as such knows the ideas of things. Plato made the honor-lovers among nonphilosophers (the rest were a class of artisans) into guardians of philosophy at first, and then he made philosophers into guardians of the regime. In doing so he elevated human self-importance, shown most vividly in human anger, to justice, and connected human justice to heaven and the eternal cosmos. The result is justice that is both a limitation on the excesses of human anger and a vindication of the just motive behind human anger.

Machiavelli saw, or thought he saw, that Plato's attempt to elevate had led to degradation in Christianity, which came upon the classical world and transformed it into the world of corrupt modernity under which Machiavelli, his Florence, his Italy, and the rest of civilized Europe, lay idle and frustrated. In Christianity Plato's hierarchy of man under heaven (or the super-heaven of the ideas) had been replaced by one of man under God, a personal God who promised salvation to each in heaven. Heaven was no longer the philosophical or intellectual goal that gave meaning to man's life and satisfied while calming his *thumos*, his demand for self-importance; it was now a heavenly world above the earthly world, promising to save the earthly world and to deliver what the earthly world could not. Machiavelli rejected the Christian promise of the heavenly world because heaven was not what it was meant to be in Plato's "profession of good." From a critic of the earthly world, while leaving the honor of that world secure if not intact—as the philosophy of Plato wished— heaven, through its instrument, the Church, became an active meddler and a constant rival of the earthly world, whose honor it held in contempt. The result in Machiavelli's day was the "ambitious idleness" he denounced (*D* 1.pref. 2), the "evil" arising from unemployed honor-seekers. This corruption of virtue was the "effectual truth" of Plato's high-minded philosophy. Thus it was Christianity that invented "effectual truth" by seeking to arm Heaven so as to make it powerful on earth. But since Christianity could punish evil only in Heaven, it could not be effectual on earth, even to restrain its own priests, who "do not fear the punishment that they do not see and do not believe" (*D* 3.1.4). Thus Machiavelli says carefully that "our religion [has shown] the truth and the true way" and refrains from saying that it is the truth (*D* 2.22). On the contrary, the truest truth is that "if where there are men there are no sol-diers, it arises from a defect of the prince and not any other defect" (*D* 1.21.1). Machiavelli appropriates "the true way" of effectual truth from Christianity to use it against Christianity.[12]

Machiavelli was not content with returning to the ancients, for they had been the remote cause of the corruption he saw in his time. They had opened the possibility of an imaginary regime that would not merely offer a goal to actual earthly regimes but would rival and even attempt to displace those regimes. The imaginary republic of Plato's "city in speech" had become the imaginary principality—imagined to be actual—of Saint Augustine's city of God. Imaginary republics and principalities in these professions had been re-placed by the God who could make them come to pass, in this world and in the next. This meant that the cosmos, Plato's intelligible realm of the ideas, which was intended to make sense of the visible world, was now represented by the next world, also invisible, of Christian revelation presiding over this world, still the world of the senses. In both cases, the invisible was used to explain the visible, to make up what it lacked in intelligibility and perfection. Machiavelli's outlook from the standpoint of effectual truth was the reverse; it explained the human aspiration to perfection, which is to the invisible, by the visible effects it produced in this world. He undertook to present and de-fend this world so that we would esteem more than Christianity "the honor of the world" (*D* 2.2.2). He could not present the world without defending it against the imaginary worlds; his reduction of the imaginary requires an inflation and vindication of the visible, the nonimaginary. His notion of the effectual truth is an anticipation of, or a foundation for, the scientific reduc-tionism that was to follow him. Both reductions share the promise of the benefits to be gained from exposing the imposture of our imaginations by which we try to transcend the visible world.

To make his point Machiavelli does not refer in either *The Prince* or the *Discourses* to the next or other world, thus not to the distinction between this world and the next.[13] But he does speak frequently, if never at length, of "the world," in his two main books, leaving to his readers, as always, the task of reasoning out to a suitable length the connections among his references and their sum. It appears, first, that the world is a whole; we find three references to "the whole world" in his two main works (*P* 3.9, 19.81; *D* 3.11.2; cf. *D* 2.2.2). Neither Plato nor the Christians would have admitted that the visible world by itself constitutes a whole, for because of its imperfections it has to be supplemented by supramundane or superhuman intelligence and power. By speaking of characteristics of the world Machiavelli presumes it can be known, but he also speaks of knowing the world (*P* 18.70; *D* 3.31.3). He criticizes the Florentines, the Venetians, and a pope for not knowing the world (*D* 1.38.3, 3.31.3). Above all, he claims for himself that in the *Discourses* he has expressed "as much as I know and have learned through a long practice and a continual reading in worldly things" (*D* DL.3). Both practice and reading are required: the school of hard knocks is needed, but that might not teach you that *this* world, where hard knocks abound, is *the* world. Indeed, once you know this world is the only world, you can infer what practice in necessities (=hard knocks) will tell you.

"Worldly things" have a "limit to their life" (*D* 3.1.1) and are "variable" (*P* 10). Deceit is an aspect of the world; in the "actions of the world" men ordinarily understand little, especially not what is extraordinary (*D* 3.6.8). Yet "in the world there is no one but the vulgar" (*P* 18.71), showing that the truth must eventually come out so as to be appreciated by ordinary men (*D* 1.3.1, 1.8.2, 1.12.2, 2.2.2, 2.21.1, 2.27.4, 3.34.4), though what they appreciate as true may not be true (*D* 1.56; 2.pref.1; 2.19.1). In Machiavelli's "effectual truth" the truth is not forever hidden but shown in its effects. The truth of the world is not shown in the articulation of nature into parts that are intelligible as parts, the parts of a whole. That unintelligibility is the meaning of the unspecific "worldly things" (*cose del mondo*; *P* 10, 25; *D* DL, 1.38.3, 3.1.1, 3.43) that Machiavelli says he studied. Although Machiavelli speaks frequently of nature and natural (e.g., *P* DL), he does not give them definitions except in a provisional way. In the only chapter of the two works whose heading mentions nature, the "same nature" he refers to proves in the body of the chapter to mean "the same customs" for a long time (*D* 3.43). The prince he calls "natural" is nothing but a hereditary prince (*P* 2.7). When commenting on the difference between a cautious and an impetuous nature, he suggests the possibility of changing one's nature according to the times (*P* 25.100; see also *D* 1.41.1, 1.58.1, 2.3.1, 3.39.2). After distinguishing in *The Prince* between the nature of princes and the nature of peoples, saying that to know the prince one must be of the people, and vice versa, he proceeds to discuss them both as if the distinction did not apply to himself (*P* DL.4).

Believe it or not, the whole world can be "excited by indignation," and it can be consumed by love and hate (*P* 19.81); it can be or can conspire against France (*P* 3.9; *D* 3.11.2). It can be characterized as a whole by "weakness" because of Christianity (*D* 1.pref.2) or "corruption" because of French, Spanish, and Italian customs (*D* 1.55.3). Yet it can be "full of peace" and offer "the glory of the world" (*D* 1.10.5–6). Under the good Roman emperors between Nerva and Marcus, when "the world was full of peace and justice," one saw "the world in triumph, the prince full of reverence and glory, the peoples full of love and security" (*D* 1.10.5). These were golden times "when each can hold and defend the opinion he wishes"—a paradise it would seem for John Stuart Mill with freedom for philosophers and glory and security for princes and peoples. These emperors include "the philosopher Marcus," as he is called in *The Prince* in the one instance of the word there (*P* 19.75). But the philosopher emperor is not presented in Mill's paradise; he is plucked out of the "triumph of the world" and paired with the emperor Severus, who is called a criminal in the *Discourses*, to provide a model for a prince, Severus for founding it and Marcus for maintaining it (*P* 19.82; *D* 1.10.4). For Machiavelli, "the world" centers on the necessity to do evil, but it seems not to be bereft of morality, as one might suppose from the adjective "Machiavellian." He wishes to maintain a certain worldly morality of a new kind in which the philosopher, namely, Machiavelli, has a new role. Instead of soothing moral anger and opposing moral contradiction, the philosopher makes friends both with criminality and with moral indignation against criminality. Both are allowed expression or purging because they are natural, not in the sense of intelligible in the light of higher principles, as with the Socratic tradition, but as spontaneous eruptions that can be managed but not suppressed.

In the world are various sects (or religions) and fatherlands, both of them humanly created. Is there one fatherland for all humanity, replacing the heavenly fatherland of Christianity? That might be the earthly fatherland that Machiavelli distinguishes from the heavenly one (*FH* 5.34; cf. *D* 1.2.2, 3.2, 3.25).

The world he defends is grounded in the earth (*terra*) so as to give it resistance to, and leverage against, the attractions of heaven as set forth diversely by the Socratic tradition and by Christianity. The mixed body of a republic or sect is preserved not by aiming at, still less by gaining, an intelligible end. Human institutions become corrupt if they do not return to their beginnings, as opposed to the satisfaction of gaining their ends. At the beginnings of human institutions there is fear; so returning to the beginning requires reproducing original fears. Worldly philosophy abandons ends for beginnings, or finds no end but in its own beginnings.

To preserve either a republic or a principality one must take it back to its beginning, and this means that an appeal to patriotism or to its hereditary line will not suffice. One must revive the original fear that precedes and is the basis for any later patriotism or fealty. Machiavelli was a patriot, to be sure—though for Florence or for Italy? And of course he says in a letter that he loved his *patria* more than his own soul.[14] But as a philosopher he might have said, though he did not volunteer it, that he loves his insight more than his *patria*, and that his undertaking is grander than the defense of his *patria*—unless his *patria* is something even grander than Florence and Italy. His *patria* is the world of which he is a knower, sometimes presented as the earth, sometimes as "Italy."[15] The universal beginning is a first principle but with a home—and the home is defined against what is foreign.

The polemical stance in Machiavelli's thought of "the world" against the other world, whether the imaginary republic of Plato or the imaginary principality of the Christians, might make one think that angry *thumos* has come to prevail in it. He does allow *thumos* in the fear he endorses and in the spiritedness (*animo*) that he wants to release. But far from allowing *animo* to dominate human behavior, Machiavelli replaces the discipline of reason over *thumos* of Plato with that of *necessity* in regard to *animo*. The result is to transform the spiritedness of self-defense into eagerness to acquire. For what is necessity overall? On the one hand, necessity comes easily: "And truly it is a very natural and ordinary thing to acquire" (*P* 3.14). On the other, one needs to think: "In ordering a republic there is need to think of the honorable part and to order it so that if indeed necessity brings it to expand, it can conserve what it has seized" (*D* 1.6.4). "The honorable part" is the "honor of the world" that he criticized the Christians for ignoring, but Machiavelli has transformed it. No longer does the desire for honor come with a claim to justice, as with Plato; in appraising Rome's aggrandizement Machiavelli ignores its injustice and decides in favor of what *he* claims that necessity requires. His instruction calls up both fear and glory, two seeming opposites that when set loose bring drama to the human soul. Still, the combination of necessity and desire that he initiates came later to be called, in a more regular mode of his fundamental notion, the "self-interest" of liberalism and bourgeois society. It represents a transformation of *thumos* resulting from a change of alliance; instead of being allied with anger and the desire for justice, as in Plato, *thumos*, now *animo*, is allied with fear and the necessity of acquisition. Honor can be brought together with necessity if it can be made clear that the honor of the world compels us to insist on recognizing and acting on human necessities over divine commands. In this way, Machiavelli shows, we do as we wish, as we ought, and as honor demands.

If the world is not rational in the way of classical philosophy, according to Machiavelli, how rational is it? Certainly it can be known. It is not chaotic, but it is tumultuous, open to change and discord as to its meaning, for example in the diverse "humors" of princes and peoples (*D* 1.4.1; *P* 9; *FH* 2.12, 3.1). The world has its necessities not in intelligible definitions or essences but in patterns of behavior; in this example princes and peoples are in a rather strange relationship, those few who wish to command in relation to those many who do not wish to be commanded. Here is the classical political division between the few and the many to be found in Plato and Aristotle, but Machiavelli sees it differently. The few and the many are not presented in a manner to bring them together in a whole of quality and quantity.[16] Instead, princes and peoples are set at odds, the former insisting on what the latter insist must not be. Each humor has its necessity, but the two necessities are contrary to each other, and the result is not a harmonious whole but a whole, a world, in which the necessary humor of princes can be accomplished only by deceiving or manipulating the necessary humor of peoples. The one necessity (desiring to command) includes the denial of that necessity by the other necessity (desiring not to be commanded), and princes, if they are to know the world, must understand that peoples as such do not understand the world; princes must see the necessity of deceit. Here we have in sharp focus the kind of analysis of necessities that our social science, unconsciously imitating Machiavelli but very far from matching his acuity, retails with jargon and false precision.

The deceit of the princes is expressed in what Machiavelli, borrowing from the Averroists, calls the "sect" (*D* 2.5.1). All sects obey the necessities of human nature that require the people to be reassured they do not live under the necessity of being commanded, but that their being ruled is justified and that justice is possible. Yet some sects are more in keeping with human necessities than others, and the Christian sect under which Machiavelli lived, with its provisions for the interference of the next world in the honor of this world, denied or overlooked the necessity of the human desire to command, of human ambition. In general, and particularly under Christianity, justice is not possible. But it is necessary to the people to believe that it is. Necessities are not necessarily recognized; in fact they *necessarily* will not be recognized by peoples as opposed to princes. Knowledge of the world's necessities includes the necessary ignorance of most human beings regarding those necessities.

These are the necessities Machiavelli has in mind when he says, to return to the crucial paragraph, that it is "necessary to a prince . . . to learn to be able not to be good, and to use it and not use it according to necessity." One might think that it is unnecessary to give advice to act "according to necessity," as if necessity were a choice one could make or not make. But Machiavelli expands the instinctual necessities that dictate the actions of subhuman animals. When he says that a prince must of necessity use a fox and a lion to defeat a wolf, that is, use both fraud and force, he implies that a human can choose his nature rather than be enslaved by it, but that his choice must still follow what he knows to be his necessity (*P* 18.69). We cannot help noting that human necessity is put to us by Machiavelli in terms of animal necessities, though with their different ways, which is after all a kind of enslavement. Our unique human faculty of choice is set to the task of calculating, not the transcendence, but the greater efficiency of subhuman instincts through human versatility.

Does this not describe the general method of social science today in its various findings of the "determination" of our lives?

To reform contemplative philosophy, Machiavelli moved to assert the necessities of the world against the intelligibility of the heavenly cosmos and the supraheavenly whole. *His* nature, as opposed to that of Plato and Aristotle, lacked the lasting or eternal intelligibles of nature as they conceived it. To assert the claim of nature against theology, Machiavelli changes nature to the world, or, more precisely, because the world is not an intelligible whole, to "worldly things." To understand the world you have to poke your nose into worldly things—and stay there.

The world according to Machiavelli is the world of sense.[17] In replacing the whole of intelligible nature with the world of sense, he discovered the world of fact underneath the reason of things. In doing so he laid the foundation for modern philosophy, which is modern epistemology (as it came to be called) and its two modes, modern empiricism and modern rationalism. Machiavelli's "effectual truth of the thing" means that to understand a thing, you must look at it politically, which means looking at it "in all regards" of human life as a whole. Politics is the human whole, and the human whole is all there is. What is politically effectual in a thing consists both of the effects it produces and the effects it displays, both what it causes and how it is seen. For example, Machiavelli speaks of the dissensions in Rome between the nobles and the plebs, prior to him condemned as having ruined the republic. For Machiavelli, these were the cause not of Rome's ruin but of its strength and freedom. This historical thesis is the beginning of his attack on Plato's imaginary republic, an attack—though he does not use the word—of fact on imagination.

Now, why was Plato's republic imaginary? Why was it a "city in speech," as Socrates called it? Plato knew very well that all actual cities are full of dissension; there is no disagreement with Machiavelli on this point. But he went on to imagine a city of harmonious justice without dissension in order to see what justice required. "Justice" is a word in common use, but by most people ignorantly and incoherently. The real, or strict, meaning of a word is what the thing it describes is in its completion and perfection: real justice as opposed to alleged justice. Plato's dialogues are devoted to developing the truth out of what people commonly and inadvertently assert through reasoning and imagination. In this proceeding reason uses imagination to see (with the eye of the mind) what is the justice one would wish for or pray for. For Socrates, imagination is an aid to reason. The human faculty of imagining permits one to make an image of what one sees and to reason out what is necessary or natural and what is accidental in it. Thus with imagination one can rise above justice as observed to justice as it might be at its best and most complete—from perception to definition or form. Imagination fixes on the visible shape or form of things in order to make an image from which one can make an invisible form or definition. This is how Socrates could think, contrary to Machiavelli and his modern successors, that the invisible is more real than the visible.

For Machiavelli, by contrast, reason does not cooperate with imagination to see the perfection of a thing. The very virtues constituting the perfection of the soul according to Plato and Aristotle must not be understood as perfect or part of perfection. They are "qualities," a neutral term, that bring "either blame or praise" (*P* 15.61), to be appreciated as they appear to others—as effects. Their effectual truth is quite different from the truth one imagines when they are merely thought out without regard to their effect. When looked at from the standpoint of effectual truth, the virtues that Socrates induced from his companions because they were true or real virtue turn out to be apparent virtue quite opposed to effectual virtue, now said to be real. So Machiavelli turns around the upward course of Socratic argumentation and brings it "down to earth." The effect and not the intent, understood as intent toward perfection, is the locus of good, and when judging the intent from the standpoint of the effect, vice, or some combination of vice and virtue, is more powerful than virtue alone, and blame is more effectual than praise.

Machiavelli questions the primacy of the good and dethrones it as the object of human action.[18] Men do not have a natural preference for real or true good as opposed to what is merely apparent, as was the basis of Socratic argumentation; they are satisfied (and stupefied!; *P* 7.30) with the apparent good they see in "good effects," especially if they are impressive or sensational (*D* 1.4.2). Good effects are what they appear to be; they are deeds, faits accomplis. The faits accomplis of Machiavelli are the origin of the modern notion of fact. Fact is what everyone sees, including the vulgar, indeed principally the vulgar, because the vulgar many reveal the effectual truth of the few wise. It is not that the wise disappear or are no longer needed but that their wisdom is effectual, and in that sense is, as it appears to the many of their audience. Wisdom is in its effect on the unwise. Fact is what can gain common consent, typically by being opposed to our intent or wish: facts are stubborn or brute, standing in one's way and demanding acceptance. Sensational fact, such as the fact of Remirro de Orco's death, is especially fact. Behind the prosaic "matter of fact" of Locke and Hume lies Machiavelli's sudden and fearful fact.

Machiavelli's appeal to the worldly prudence of the prince amounts to an appeal to the vulgar, the peoples whom the prince must impress: they set the standard of success. In this sense Machiavelli is fundamentally democratic. The people believe in morality, and in order to believe that morality is possible they believe that some person will make it possible; they personify the abstract notion of good in order to believe in God. Thus Machiavelli shows that Christianity is the effectual truth of Platonism. His own personifications, such as "Italy" or "the French," are spread all over his texts and must be examined for what they personify to be understood.

Imagination or the use of images does not disappear in Machiavelli, but it is demoted from its status in Plato as an aid to reason toward knowledge to a deviation of reason away from "what is done." To illustrate his imagination, I turn to his use of hunting as "an image of a war" in the chapter titled "That a Captain Ought to Be a Knower of Sites," in which can be found the only discussion of "science" in *The Prince* and the *Discourses* (D 3.39.1–2). Machiavelli says that a captain needs "general and particular knowledge of sites" and that "all the sciences" demand practice if one wishes to possess them perfectly, and this one—the knowledge of sites—requires "very great practice." This looks like a humdrum recommendation of the study of geography to princes who are captains of armies, but let us see if there is more. "General and particular knowledge" is equated to science and practice, the practice being part of the science when perfected. This conjoining of theory and practice to make perfect science is quite contrary to the distinction in Plato between the perfect idea and its visible and imperfect approximation, or in Aristotle between the unchangeable essences and the changeable actualizations of a thing. The "perpetual" republic of which Machiavelli speaks (both to deny and affirm; *D* 3.17.1 versus 1.20.1, 1.34.3, 2.30.2, 3.1.3, 3.22.3) is not the one imagined to be what perfect justice would require, as for Plato, but one imagined from reasoning with the necessities that face actual republics and finding remedies for their imperfect prudence. If this Machiavellian republic could exist, it would also be, like Plato's, under a philosopher-king, or prince. The difference is that Plato has in mind not Socrates personally but someone like him—whereas Machiavelli thinks of himself. Basing his republic on the facts of actual republics, he introduces the modern notion that practice follows directly from theory, so that knowledge is perfected with practice: knowledge is power. What Machiavelli knows is effectual; it makes him the prince not just in principle but in fact.

All sites are particular, Machiavelli goes on to say, yet by learning one site very well, as would a hunter, one can easily understand "new countries" with which one is not familiar, since the familiar and the new "have some conformity," making possible a "firm science" (*ferma scienza*). Firm science does not transcend practice, seeking perfection, but unites one practical knowledge with another, achieving perfection by application from familiar to new. Machiavelli cites Xenophon for using "an image of a war" when he shows Cyrus instructing his men to act as if they were on a hunt. In Xenophon's text, however, Cyrus wins a battle against the king of Armenia by pretending to hunt while actually performing a surprise attack (*Cyropaideia* 2.4.22–29). Thus we learn from Machiavelli's hint (for all his quotations and allusions must be examined) that the use of images is necessary to successful fraud. In hunting the hunter not only seeks to appropriate for his own use the object of the hunt but also conceals himself to do so. Then Machiavelli turns to another example, one from what *Livy* shows, of a Roman tribune who spotted a single hill abandoned by, and rising above, the enemy, which he with lightly armed soldiers could climb and then survey what the enemy was doing. This would be "the citadel of our hope and salvation," he says, quoting *Livy*. Is this not rather close to the Psalmist who speaks of God as my rock, my salvation, my fortress?[19] It seems that sites in a war can be analogous to, one might say an image of, sites in different texts. Machiavelli adds that the Roman tribune went about in a soldier's cloak so that the enemy would not notice he was the leader.

Recall that Machiavelli spoke of "an image of a war" (*una guerra*), not of war in general. He is in *a war* with a religion, a particular one, that requires him to recast the nature of philosophy and, hidden in a cloak, to preempt the rock and salvation of that religion, and to substitute for it one of his own.

Machiavelli substitutes the world with its necessities for two rival but related notions. The first is the other world of Christianity, and the second is the cosmos of classical rationalism with its intelligible and intelligent beings. Both notions set the highest virtue in contemplation and hover over this world to criticize it from their very different standpoints, the godliness of Christianity and the nobility of Socratic philosophy. Machiavelli believed that they were related in their high-mindedness, the Christian God being the effectual truth of the good or the idea of the good, as we have seen, for men in their *thumos* would want to personify the good in a being that would guarantee its possession for them. They would want a Providence to take care of them, turning a common noun into a proper noun. Therefore, to defend this world Machiavelli decided that he would have to go beyond the equivocal compromises with Christianity made by the humanists and attack it directly and openly, rather than combine it, and thus compare it, with classical rationalism, as they did. He would have to "depart from the orders of others" and leave the ancients behind, much as he loved them. For the sake of philosophy and "each one" of humanity he would alter the character of philosophy as well as the sort of humanity it recommends. No longer are we to imitate Socrates and Jesus; our models now are Severus and Cesare Borgia, installing the new primacy of evil (*P* 13.55, 19.82). Evil is of course somehow good, but good folk if they want to be reasonable have to admit this.

Attending to this world with Machiavelli, like reflection on the cosmos with Plato and Aristotle, has the effect, and the intent, of calming the *thumos* of human beings. The world as he presents it with its sovereign necessities brings discipline to and redirects the love of drama that lives in *thumos*. In fulfilling this function necessity replaces the soul in classical rationalism, which with its internal harmony discovers and teaches the possibility of an alliance between *thumos* and reason. Machiavelli also proposes this same alliance, but not through the soul; he settles for a lower sort of mindfulness in the use he makes of *animo* as directed by prudent princes. For necessity to have its proper effects on most men it must be conveyed sensationally, as in sensational executions (*D* 3.1.3) that remind restless humans of the fear born of their original necessitous situation. In this way fear comes to transform the classical notion of nobility and its noble fear into excellence in manipulation of the lower, more "effectual" fears of security and survival. There is glory for the prince, but it is shown in the imposition of forms, in dirty tricks such as the manipulation of cruelty, not in shining deeds.

One other phrase from our single paragraph in *The Prince* needs to be examined. Machiavelli says that it appears to him more fitting to "go directly" (*andare direttamente*) to the effectual truth, bypassing the profession of good. To look at the effect or the outcome of an event means to consider it in the light of the necessity, that is, the various necessities, of its participants, and thereby to ignore their opposing intentions regarding its goodness. Goodness is complicated, which is why it requires a "profession of good in all regards." Necessity simplifies by "going directly" to the effect without regard to opposing claims and doubtful or contradictory reasonings. Machiavelli recommends acting first and reasoning—rationalizing—afterward, for "to many things that reason does not bring you, necessity brings you" (*D* 1.6.4).

An example of what he wants to avoid can be seen at the Palazzo Pubblico of Siena, rival of Florence, in the Sala della Pace and its famous frescoes of Good and Bad Government, done by Ambrogio Lorenzetti in 1338–40. These frescoes show the "effects" (as they are called) of good and bad government on opposite walls, the virtues of the one and vices of the other. The effects imply the possibility of choice between virtue and vice. They are connected by a wall, also frescoed, that amounts to a depiction of the sort of profession of good to which Machiavelli refers. It displays both theological virtues and moral virtues, and "justice" appears twice, once under the theological virtues (featuring capital punishment) and once under "wisdom," which leads to "concord," with a cord connecting all citizens to a man who represents the Sienese community. Here is confusion, or let us say complication, arising from the typical problems of classical political philosophy mixed with Christianity: the relationships between intellectual and moral virtue, theology and philosophy, morality and political concord. In this painting the political effects, good and bad, emerge from an articulation of the good; in Machiavelli, the effects result from an imputed necessity that deliberately ignores what people say and thinkers think.[20] Our social science today believes in what it calls the fact/value distinction, meaning that fact is science and value is not. In so behaving, it ignores, as much as it can, the profession of good that accompanies every human action and follows Machiavelli's effectual truth unconsciously and with brusque, unjustified confidence in its own independence.

To sum up this compressed view of Machiavelli's enterprise: It is new and recommends what is new. It shows that the use of dirty tricks is for our good. It reveals the philosopher as prince. It calls for the effectual versus the imagined truth. It finds that truth in the world, which is the world of necessity and the world of sense. It uncovers and explains what would later be called "fact." It solves problems by simplifying them in the manner of modern natural and social science.

A difficulty remains, however, in the notion of effectual truth. Is all truth effectual truth? Is philosophy now to have an agenda for changing the world, rendering it more rational and leaving behind the former philosophy that wished merely to understand, and not to understand for the sake of power to effect change? Machiavelli promises that the effectual truth will work: it will save us from ruin among so many who are not good. But is it true that it works? Have we not seen in the twentieth century that atheist regimes can be as harmful to humanity, indeed far more harmful, than the religious ones that Machiavelli and Hobbes and all the other modern philosophers feared and despised and attempted to replace? The truth of effectual truth has to be judged according to its promises, its professions of good. This truth would be the plain truth, not effectual or tendentious truth. Thus Machiavelli cannot affirm that all truth is effectual and must retain the possibility of appealing to plain truth of the same sort that Plato and Aristotle appealed to without the promise of the modern agenda.

To make this appeal, Machiavelli's promises have to be compared with the promises, or lack of promises, by Plato and Aristotle. Yet here the difficulty stubbornly persists. To make a judgment on the success of Machiavelli's enterprise, one must be aware of the alternative to it in the classical tradition. From Machiavelli's self-description in his famous letter of December 10, 1513, we know that he was aware of the "ancients" to whom he posed questions. He lived in the age known today as the Renaissance, the "rebirth"—and of what? The classical tradition. Yet no achievement of the Renaissance was greater than Machiavelli's enterprise, the founding of a new understanding of philosophy that transformed and superseded the classical tradition. The modern philosophy Machiavelli founded, like the modern science founded by his successors, has the character of progress, each stage going further than the preceding and, if not erasing it, rendering it obsolete. Today it takes a very considerable effort to recall the ancients that Machiavelli summoned up in his study according to the 1513 letter. It is no longer in fashion even among philosophers to ask questions of the ancients and to listen to their answers. This means that it is very difficult to judge whether Machiavelli's enterprise has in fact worked. His great power is there to be appreciated, but his enterprise is covered over by its own success, and he himself, despite his own success, seems simplistic and irrelevant to us today. We are altogether too much impressed by "effectual truth."

CHAPTER 2

The Redeeming Prince

MAURIZIO VIROLI

Every day I discover you to be a greater prophet than the Hebrews
or any other nation ever had.

—Filippo Casavecchia to Niccolò Machiavelli
in Pisa or Florence, June 17, 1509

Even as I am writing these words the bells are ringing far and wide,
unceasingly, telling that the Italians are in Rome: the temporal
power is falling, the people are shouting, "Long live the unity of
Italy!" Let there be glory to Machiavelli!

—Francesco De Sanctis, Rome, September 20, 1870

Niccolò Machiavelli wrote *The Prince* to design and invoke a redeemer of
Italy capable of creating, with God's help, new and good political orders. The
meaning of Machiavelli's most famous or infamous work—the meaning in
the sense of what Machiavelli intended above all to teach—is to be found in
the last chapter, the "Exhortation to Liberate Italy from the Barbarians,"
where he creates, with a stroke of political imagination, the myth of the redeemer. This myth, I contend, sheds light on the entire work, particularly on

the most controversial themes of *The Prince*: political ethics, the virtues of the prince, military matters, and the role of fortune and God in political affairs. An oration on the redeemer: this is what Machiavelli intended *The Prince* to be.

In the "Exhortation," as is well known, Machiavelli compares Italy to the people of Israel enslaved in Egypt, to the Athenians before they were unified by Theseus, and to the Persians under the Medes' yoke: "more enslaved than the Hebrews, more servile than the Persians, more scattered than the Athenians: without a leader, without order, beaten, despoiled, ripped apart, overrun, and having suffered every sort of ruin." He portrays Italy's emancipation as God's compassionate response to its invocation:

> Italy left as if lifeless, awaits the man who may heal her wounds and put an end to the plundering of Lombardy, to the extortions in the Kingdom of Naples and in Tuscany, and who can cure her of those sores that have been festering for so long. Look how she now prays to God to send someone to redeem her from these barbaric cruelties and insults. See how ready and willing she is to follow a banner, provided that someone picks it up.

Then, speaking as if he were a prophet, he promises God's help. Although the great redeemers such as Moses, Cyrus, and Theseus were "rare and marvelous," he writes, "they were nevertheless men," and each of them had poorer opportunities than are offered now: "for their undertakings were no more just, nor easier than this one, nor was God more a friend to them than to you." As in the book of Exodus, God's friendship provides decisive help to the process of emancipation: "extraordinary things without example, brought about by God: the sea has opened up; a cloud has shown you the path; the rock has poured water forth; here manna has rained." A great political leader, Machiavelli stresses, would surely generate sincere love in the hearts of the Italians: "Nor can I express with what love he will be received in all those territories that have suffered through these foreign floods; with what thirst for revenge, with what stubborn loyalty, with what devotion, with what tears! What doors will be closed to him? What people will deny him their obedience? What envy could oppose him? What Italian could deny him homage?"

The first piece of evidence that I believe I can offer to sustain my interpretation that the core of *The Prince* is to be found in the "Exhortation" comes from a survey of all Machiavelli's works. Political redemption from tyranny, corruption, or foreign domination is a recurrent theme in all his political and historical writings. In the preface to book 2 of the *Discourses on Livy*, for instance, Machiavelli writes:

> I will be spirited in saying manifestly that which I may understand of the former and of the latter times [the times of the ancient Romans and modern times], so that the spirits of youths who may read these writings of mine can flee the latter and prepare themselves to imitate the former at whatever time fortune may give them the opportunity [*occasione*] for it. For it is the duty of a good man to teach others the good that you could not work because of the malignity of times and of fortune, so that when many are capable of it, someone of them more loved by heaven [*più amato dal cielo*] may be able to work it.[1]

In the *Discourse on Remodeling the State of Florence* (1520) he writes an eloquent eulogy of a reformer of political orders:

> No man is so much exalted by any act of his as are those men who have with laws and with institutions remodeled republics and kingdoms; these are, after those who have been gods, the first to be praised. And because there have been few who have had opportunity to do it, and very few those who have understood how to do it, small is the number who have done it. And so much has this glory been esteemed by men seeking for nothing other than glory that when unable to form a republic in reality, they have done it in writing, as Aristotle, Plato, and many others, who have wished to show the world that if they have not founded a free government, as did Solon and Lycurgus, they have failed not through their ignorance but through their impotence for putting it into practice.[2]

The Art of War, published in 1521, ends with the evocation of new political leaders capable of offering the kind of political advice that would help Italy to recover from its present condition of corruption and servitude.[3] In the *Florentine Histories* Machiavelli expresses his hope that if in Florence there "rises a wise, good and powerful citizen by whom laws are ordered by which these humors of the nobles and the men of the people are quieted or restrained so that they cannot do evil, then the city can be called free and the state be judged stable and firm."[4]

The ideal of a political redeemer permeates not only his works but also all his life, until his later years, when he devoted his remaining energies to the effort of preventing Italy from falling under the domination of Charles V. On March 15, 1526, he wrote Francesco Guicciardini, who was committed, with much greater political and military responsibilities, to the same task, a dramatic letter in which he reveals that he was hoping that Giovanni de' Medici (Giovanni dalle Bande Nere) could be the redeemer of Italy:

I am going to tell you one thing that you will think absurd; I shall put forward a plan that you will consider either rash or ridiculous: nevertheless, these times of ours demand bold, extraordinary, and unusual decisions. You know—and anyone who knows how to reason about this world knows it, too—that the people are fickle and foolish; nevertheless, as fickle and foolish as they are, what ought to be done is frequently what they say to do. A few days ago it was being said throughout Florence that Giovanni de' Medici was raising a company of mercenaries in order to fight wherever he saw the best opportunity. The rumor alerted me to consider whether the people might not be saying what in fact ought to be done. I believe everyone is agreed that among Italians there is no leader whom the soldiers more willingly follow or whom the Spaniards fear more or respect more than Signor Giovanni. Everyone also agrees that he is brave and impetuous, has great ideas, and is a taker of bold decisions. Therefore we could get him to raise this mercenary company, secretly enlarging his forces, helping him to raise a banner and putting under his command as much infantry and cavalry as possible.[5]

A leader capable of attempting great things, willing to raise a banner and put together a fine army composed of captains and soldiers who love and wholeheartedly follow him: these are the same ideas found in the "Exhortation." In *The Prince*, as we shall see, Machiavelli appeals to the prophetic force of poets; in this letter, he wants to believe in the people's prophetic power. Not without cause, he writes in the *Discourses*: "may the voice of a people be likened to that of God: for one sees a universal opinion produce marvelous effects in its forecast, so that it appears to foresee its ills and its goods by a hidden virtue."[6] A few months later, upon the news that tumults against the Spaniards had broken out in Milan, he launches yet again the idea he had put forth in the "Exhortation," namely, that there is a great occasion to liberate Italy, one not to be missed: "You are aware," he writes Guicciardini, "of how many opportunities have been lost: do not lose this one or, putting yourself in the hands of Fortune and Time, trust in having it again, because Time does not always bring identical circumstances and Fortune is not always the same." Many years had elapsed since he had written the "Exhortation," and many significant events had occurred in Italy. He was now an old man, at the end of his life, but the determination to liberate his country from the barbarians was still on his mind: "Free Italy from long-lasting anxiety: eradicate those savage brutes, which have nothing human about them save their faces and voices." That a man whose dominant passion throughout his life had been love of country and whose overriding concern had been the redemption of Italy composed *The Prince* to inspire and invoke a redeeming prince seems to me to be a rather reasonable interpretation.

A second reason to believe that Machiavelli's fundamental message is the myth of the redeemer is that *The Prince* is not about ordinary princes but about great princes, as Machiavelli clearly asserts in the dedicatory letter to Lorenzo di Piero de' Medici that he had probably initially composed for Giuliano di Lorenzo de' Medici: "Wishing, therefore, to offer myself to your Magnificence with some evidence of my devotion to you . . . I have not found among my belongings anything that I might value more or prize so much as the knowledge of *the deeds of great men* that I have learned from a long experience in modern and a continuous study of antique affairs. Having with great care and for a long time thought about and examined *these deeds* and having now set *them* down in a little book, I am sending them to Your Magnificence" (emphasis added).

To be sure that the reader gets the message that *The Prince* is about political deeds, Machiavelli writes in chapter 6 that:

> no one should wonder if, in speaking of principalities that are completely new as to their ruler and form of government, I cite *the greatest examples [grandissimi esempli]*. Since men almost always follow the paths trod by others, and proceed in their affairs by imitation, although they are not fully able to stay on the path of others, nor to equal the virtue of those they imitate, a wise man should always enter those paths trodden by *great men [uomini grandi]*, and imitate those who have been *the most excellent [quegli che sono stati eccellentissimi imitare]*, so that if one's own virtue does not match theirs, at least they have the smell of it. (emphasis added)

What does Machiavelli actually mean by greatness of spirit? He recognizes greatness of spirit in Cosimo the Elder when Cosimo was regretting his own inability to expand the Florentine dominion. He also acknowledges the greatness of spirit of Lorenzo the Magnificent when the latter had the courage to sail for Naples and meet King Ferrante, who was at the time one of the most determined and dangerous enemies of Florence.[7] Machiavelli also granted greatness of spirit to Cesare Borgia and, although marred by a number of serious vices, to Agathocles of Syracuse,[8] but he speaks of greatness of soul and nobility together only in the chapter of the *Discourses* where he discusses the transition from tyranny to aristocracy in the cycle of governments: "These conspiracies against the prince were not made by weak and timid men, but by those who because of their generosity, greatness of spirit, riches, and nobility above the others, could not endure the dishonest life of that prince."[9] The most eloquent examples of greatness and nobility of spirit are, however, those marvelous and rare men who have founded new and good political orders. Moses distinguished himself for his "virtue," Cyrus for his "greatness of spirit," Theseus for his "excellence." Romulus was "virtuous and prudent." Nothing, Machiavelli remarks, "brings so much honour to a man newly risen up than

the new laws and new institutions discovered by him." True political greatness
is that of redeemers, and *The Prince* extols them as true examples of greatness.

Another piece of evidence from the text of *The Prince* is found in chapter 6, where Machiavelli discusses "new principalities acquired by one's own
troops and virtue," and asserts that Fortune offers founders an opportunity
to show their outstanding virtue by accomplishing grand political deeds:

> In examining their deeds and their lives, one can see that they re-
> ceived nothing from Fortune except opportunity, which gave them
> the material they could mold into whatever form they liked. With-
> out that opportunity [*occasione*] the strength of their spirit would have
> been exhausted, and without that strength, their opportunity would
> have come in vain. It was therefore necessary for Moses to find the
> people of Israel slaves in Egypt and oppressed by the Egyptians, in
> order that they might be disposed to follow him to escape this servi-
> tude. It was necessary for Romulus not to stay in Alba, and that he
> be exposed at birth, so that he be founder of that nation. It was nec-
> essary for Cyrus to find the Persians unhappy about the rule of the
> Medes, and the Medes rendered soft and effeminate after a lengthy
> peace. Theseus could not have demonstrated his ability if he had not
> found the Athenians dispersed. These opportunities, therefore, made
> these men successful, and their outstanding virtue enabled them to
> recognize that opportunity, whereby their nation was ennobled and
> became extremely happy.

It seems to me rather evident that at the outset of his work Machiavelli directs the attention of the reader to the figure of the redeemer that he will develop in the last chapter.

A third indication comes from the structure of the text. Contrary to the
view that *The Prince* inaugurates modern political science, it is in fact an oration written from the first to the last page following the rules of rhetoric. This
does not imply at all that *The Prince* does not contain rigorous distinctions,
empirical considerations, and rational arguments. From Aristotle's *Rhetoric* we
know that one of the means of persuasion, along with *ethos* and *pathos*, is *logos*.

Latin masters of eloquence put the point even more powerfully by stressing that a true orator must know how to combine *ratio* and *oratio*, reason and eloquence. It is a gross misinterpretation of rhetoric to believe that if a text contains rational and empirical considerations or arguments it surely cannot be an oration and must be a scientific or a philosophical tract.

What compels us to regard *The Prince* as a political oration is its structure, the order of the arguments, and the use of examples, metaphors, and images, that is, the whole range of rhetorical ornaments designed to endow the text with persuasive power apt to move the readers to act. Because I have discussed this issue elsewhere, here I only wish to stress that since it is a political oration, *The Prince* must present its most important point—for its author—in the conclusion.[10] And at the end of *The Prince* Machiavelli places the "Exhortation" with the myth of the redeemer.

Against my argument, however, stand a number of powerful objections. The first is that according to some highly respected scholars, Machiavelli composed the "Exhortation" after December 1513, when we know that he had completed at least the main corpus of *The Prince*. Hans Baron, for instance, indicates as the most probable date January to March 1515; Sergio Bertelli suggests 1516; Mario Martelli claims that Machiavelli composed the last chapter much later than the other parts of his work, in 1518, to provide ideological and political support for Lorenzo the Duke of Urbino's project to establish an absolute principality in Florence and central Italy.[11] Martelli argues that Machiavelli saw in that young and ambitious man, who had concentrated in his own hands enormous power, a possible redeemer of Italy; he hastened to compose the "Exhortation," appended it to the rest of the manuscript, and revised chapter 6 accordingly.[12]

If we accept the view that Machiavelli wrote the "Exhortation" in 1515, 1516, or later, it is utterly wrong to claim, as I do, that the overarching meaning of *The Prince* is to be found in the last chapter and that Machiavelli composed his work above all to give life to a redeemer and a founder. Even if these views have been sustained by solid textual and historical considerations, I believe that Machiavelli composed the "Exhortation," or at least its core, along with the rest of *The Prince*, as its own necessary completion and conclusion, not as a later appendage.[13]

To begin with, the "Exhortation" opens with an explicit reference to the considerations that he has discussed in the previous twenty-five chapters ("therefore, considering all the matters discussed above . . ."), and it is conceptually connected with chapter 6, as I have shown. To make his case that circumstances in Italy are favorable for a prince to introduce new political orders and liberate Italy from the barbarians, Machiavelli refers to the position of preeminence reached by the house of the Medici as of March 1513: "Nor is there anyone in sight, at present, in whom she [Italy] can have more hope than in Your Illustrious House, which, with its fortune and virtue, favored by God and by the Church, of which it is now prince, could place itself at the head of this redemption." The words we must focus our attention on are "of which it is *now* prince" (*della quale ora è Principe*). The adverb *ora* in Italian refers to events that are very close in time. It is highly unlikely that a writer like Machiavelli would have used that adverb to denote an event that had occurred two or three or even five years earlier.[14] This suggests that he probably composed the "Exhortation" a few months after Giovanni de' Medici's elevation to the throne of Saint Peter in March 1513. The scholars who maintain that Machiavelli composed the "Exhortation" having in mind an actual political occasion for the liberation of Italy are right, but such an occasion materialized in 1513, when the chief of the Medici family, Giovanni, was at the same time the de facto ruler of Florence and the head of Christendom.

Machiavelli's chief motivation to compose his essay, I must stress at this stage of my argument, was not at all to please the Medici and to get a job from them. Had this been the case, he would have written a quite different text, full of praise for the Medici and for their glorious history, replete with the kind of counsel that men like Giuliano, Giulio, Lorenzo, or Leo X liked to hear. Machiavelli knew better than anyone else that the most important rule of successful flattery is to say what pleases the person from whom one expects to obtain favors. In *The Prince* he does exactly the opposite. Instead of repeating the well-established principles that had allowed the Medici to gain control over the city, Machiavelli gives them advice that they were not in the least able to appreciate and that would surely have irritated them had they read Machiavelli's work. He wanted to believe that one of them could have been moved by his words to try to be the redeemer of Italy: he was not a follower of the Medici; he wanted the Medici to follow him.

Further evidence suggesting that Machiavelli composed the "Exhortation" around December 1513, along with the bulk of *The Prince*, comes from the letter to Francesco Vettori of December 10, 1513. Here Machiavelli cites Dante: "E perché Dante dice che non fa scienza senza lo ritenere lo avere inteso, io ho notato quello che per la loro conversazione ho fatto capitale e composto uno opuscolo *De principatibus*." He refers to *Paradise*, 5.41–42, where Beatrice explains to Dante that the most precious good that God has bestowed on human beings is their free will:

Lo maggior don che Dio per sua larghezza
fesse creando, e a la sua bontate
più conformato, e quel ch'e' più apprezza
fu de la volontà la libertate;
di che le creature intelligenti,
e tutte e sole, fuoro e son dotate.

In the "Exhortation" Machiavelli repeats Dante's concepts and stresses that God does not want to deprive human beings of their free will, not even to redeem them from political oppression: "El rimanente dovete fare voi: Dio non vuole fare ogni cosa per non ci tòrre el libero arbitrio, e parte di quella gloria che tocca a noi" (God does not wish to do everything, in order not to take from us our free will and part of the glory that is ours). We have therefore textual evidence that Machiavelli used a concept that Dante had discussed in a canto of *Paradise* that he had well in mind in December 1513. It is far from being compelling evidence, but it is there, and we know Machiavelli was accustomed to promptly use the same sources and concepts in letters and works.[15]

No less interesting is the clue that comes from Petrarch. We know from the same letter of December 10 that Machiavelli used to carry with him, in his morning walks in the countryside surrounding his property in Sant'Andrea in Percussina, books by Dante, Petrarch, Tibullus, and Ovid. The same letter opens in fact with a line taken from the *Triumpho divinitade* 13: "Ma tarde non furon mai grazie divine."[16] *The Prince* ends with verses taken from the canzone "All'Italia":

Virtù contra a furore
Prenderà l'arme, e fia el combatter corto; ché l'antico valore
Nell'italici cor non è ancor morto.

As in the case of Dante, we have explicit references to Petrarch in the letter of December 10 and in the "Exhortation." The fact that Machiavelli's citations from Petrarch come from different works—the *Triumpho divinitade* in the letter, the canzone All'Italia in *The Prince*—does not weaken the possibility of a temporal coincidence, because Machiavelli could have owned one of the early sixteenth-century editions of Petrarch's works published in Florence that included both the *Canzoniere* and the *Trionfi*, and they were very light books in octavo, easy to carry.[17]

Also, Machiavelli's correspondence with Vettori in the summer of 1513 suggests that the "Exhortation" was composed around that time. One of the dominant themes of their discussion, as has been rightly stressed, was Italy's political and military weakness. In his letter to Vettori of August 10, 1513, in particular, Machiavelli clearly states the point that he expands in the "Exhortation," namely, that Italy's miserable condition was the consequence of the lack of a political and military leader capable of unifying and liberating it. His argument evokes the "Exhortation": "As for the rest of the Italians uniting, you make me laugh: first, there will never be any union in Italy that will do any good; even if all leaders were united, that would be inadequate because the armies here are not worth a red cent—except for the Spaniards', and because there are so few of them, it is insufficient. Second, the tails are cut off from the heads."[18]

The most compelling evidence that should persuade us that Machiavelli must have composed the "Exhortation" before or around January 1514 comes, however, from his life. His letters from March through December 1513 reveal a man deeply wounded in body and spirit but still hopeful of resurrecting himself and fighting back against the malignity of men and fortune. On June 26, for instance, he writes to his nephew Giovanni Vernacci:

My very dear Giovanni, I have received several letters from you, most recently one from last April in which, among other things, you complain that you have not received any letter from me. My answer is that since your departure I have had so much trouble that it is no wonder I have not written to you. In fact, if anything, it is a miracle that I am alive, because my post was taken from me and I was about to lose my life, which God and my innocence have preserved for me. I have had to endure all sorts of other evils, both prison and other kinds. But, by the grace of God, I am well and I manage to live as I can—and so I shall strive to do until the heavens show themselves to be more kind.[19]

On August 4 he confesses that "physically I feel well, but ill in every other respect. And no hope remains for me but that God may help me, and, until now, He has not in fact abandoned me."[20]

As of the summer of 1514, his correspondence shows Niccolò in a completely different spirit. On June 10, 1514, he writes to Francesco Vettori:

So I am going to stay just as I am amid my bedbugs, unable to find any man who recalls my service or believes I might be good for anything. But I cannot possibly go on like this for long, because I am rotting away and I can see that if God does not show a more favourable face to me, one day I shall be forced to leave home and to place myself as tutor or secretary to a governor, if I cannot do otherwise, or to stick myself in some deserted spot to teach reading to children and leave my family here to count me dead; they will do much better without me because I am causing them expenses, since I am used to spending and I cannot do without spending.[21]

Particularly important for my argument is the letter of August 3, 1514, in which Machiavelli informs Vettori that in Sant'Andrea in Percussina he has met a woman "so gracious, so refined, so noble—both in nature and in manners—that never could either my praise or my love for her be as much as she deserves." Faithful to his principle that human beings must follow their nature if they wish to taste some measure of happiness, Machiavelli abandons himself to passion: "I have laid aside all memory of my sorrows," he writes. Even the grand deeds of the great men of antiquity no longer interest him: "I have renounced[,] then, thoughts about matters great and grave. No longer I delight in reading about the deeds of the ancients or in discussing those of the moderns: everything has been transformed into tender thoughts, for which I thank Venus and all Cyprus."[22]

This is a remarkable confession. Machiavelli is telling us that he has abandoned (*lasciato*) his thoughts about matters grave and grand, and that reading, thinking, and writing about the deeds of the ancients no longer delight him as they used to (*non mi diletta più*). He is a man very different from the one who had affirmed on December 10, 1513, that thinking, reading, and writing about grand deeds of politics were his only spiritual nourishment ("il cibo che solum è mio e che io nacqui per lui"), a nourishment that had the power of liberating him from his fears ("for four hours I feel no boredom, forget all troubles, fear not poverty, am not anguished by death: I simply give myself over to them completely").

As time goes by Machiavelli's mood is even more melancholic and depressed. On January 31, 1515, he confesses to Vettori that he is in love again, but he also writes that Donato Del Corno and his lover, Lucrezia, called La Riccia, are "the sole havens and refuges for [his] skiff—bereft of rudder and sail because of the unending tempest."[23] On August 18, 1515, he describes to Giovanni Vernacci his personal condition in the most disconsolate manner: "if I have not written to you earlier, I do not want you to blame either me or anyone else, but only the times; they have been—and still are—of such a sort that they have made me forget even myself."[24] The fall brings no consolation to Niccolò: "I have written to you twice during the last four months, and I am sorry that you have not received them [my letters], because it occurs to me that you will think I do not write because I have forgotten all about you. That is not true at all: Fortune has left me nothing but my family and my friends."[25] On February 15, 1516, Machiavelli speaks of himself as a man "useless" to his family and his friends. All he is left with is his "good health" and that of his family: "I bide my time so that I may be ready to seize good Fortune should she come; should she not come, I am ready to be patient."[26] In

June 1517, Machiavelli's condition is even worse: "since the adversities that I have suffered, and still . . . am suffering, have reduced me to living on my farm, I sometimes go for a month at a time without thinking about myself," he writes to Vernacci.[27] The letters of January 5 and January 25, 1518, show us, once again, a man who feels harshly beaten by malignant luck and utterly disheartened.[28]

It is surely not conclusive evidence, but I cannot imagine a person in such a condition being capable of writing a text as full of strength, determination, and hope as the "Exhortation." I am neither attempting to produce a psychological study nor suggesting some kind of causal connection between Machiavelli's existential condition and the text. More modestly, I claim that the study of Machiavelli's life—in particular the interpretation of his changing passions and beliefs—offers us a useful key to better identify the date of composition of the "Exhortation," and therefore sheds some light on the meaning of the whole text.

Can we believe that an author who openly declares that his intention in writing *The Prince* is to concentrate only on the effectual truth of the matter (chapter 15) could have composed an essay to design an ideal figure and to propose a political myth? My reply is that Machiavelli was a realist sui generis who was not interested solely in describing, interpreting, or explaining political facts but who also liked to imagine political realities very different from the existing one. In the *Discourses on Livy* he envisages a rebirth of ancient Roman political wisdom; in *The Art of War* he fantasizes about the restoration of Roman military orders and virtue. In comparison, the myth of the redeemer in *The Prince* sounds rather sober.

If we really want to see a true realist we must read Francesco Guicciardini, not Machiavelli. And Guicciardini considered Machiavelli a political thinker too keen to generalize and to interpret political events through abstract models and examples taken from antiquity. With subtle irony, in a letter of May 1521, Guicciardini reproaches Machiavelli for his inclination to discuss general forms of government such as monarchy, aristocracy, and republic. In his notes on the *Discourses on Livy*, he remarks that it is a mistake to always cite the example of the ancient Romans, as Machiavelli did so many times, because each situation is unique and contingent. Political decisions should not therefore be taken by looking at abstract models but by using *discrezione* (discretion)—that is, a highly refined form of political prudence that is not based on general rules, that cannot be learned in books, and that very few men have by nature or are able to attain through long practice.[29]

For Guicciardini, Machiavelli was also too keen to suggest highly unusual, perhaps effective, but surely risky courses of political action. In the midst of the dramatic political and military crisis of 1525–27 that led to the sack of Rome, for instance, Machiavelli proposed to Guicciardini and Pope Clement VII that the only way to save Italy and preserve the integrity of the Papal State of Romagna was to arm its people and mobilize them against the invasion of imperial troops. To arm and organize the subjects of Romagna in a militia, Guicciardini replied, would be "one of the most useful and praiseworthy works that His Holiness could undertake," if only it were possible. Given the conditions in Romagna, it was, however, very dangerous. The people were torn by chronic political hostilities, and the Church had neither partisans nor friends there: those who wished to live well and peacefully disliked the Church because they wanted a government that would protect them; troublemakers and evil men disliked the Church because they saw disorder and war as a chance to settle accounts and see to their own interests.[30] Machiavelli's proposal was fascinating, but it did not pass the scrutiny of a genuine political realist. As Roberto Ridolfi, the biographer of Machiavelli and Guicciardini, has stressed, one should always read Machiavelli to find illuminations about the future, and Guicciardini to understand what was really going on in the political life of their times.[31]

Another tenet of Machiavelli's political thought that differentiates him from political realism and helps us to understand *The Prince* is his belief in the power of poetry and myths to inspire grand political action. In the *Florentine Histories* he writes about the failed conspiracy of Stefano Porcari (early 1400–1453) in Rome: "living at that time was a Messer Stefano Porcari, a Roman citizen, noble by blood and by learning, but much more so by the excellence of his spirit. This man desired, according to the custom of men who relish glory, to do or at least to try something worthy of memory; and he judged he could do nothing else than try to see if he could take his fatherland from the hands of prelates and restore it to its ancient way of life, hoping by this, should he succeed, to be called the new founder and second father of that city."[32]

Stefano Porcari, Machiavelli also notes, was inspired by Petrarch: "The dissolute manners of the priesthood, and the discontent of the Roman barons and people, encouraged him to look for a happy termination of his enterprise," but he derived his greatest confidence from those verses of Petrarch in the canzone that begins "Spirto gentil che quelle membra reggi," where he says:

Sopra il monte Tarpeio, canzon, vedrai
Un cavalier che Italia tutta onora,
Pensoso più d'altrui che di se stesso.

Atop Mount Tarpeio, Oh canzone, you will see
A knight whom all Italy honors,
More thoughtful of others than of himself.

Messer Porcari knew, Machiavelli remarks, that "many times poets are filled with divine and prophetic spirit; so he judged that in any mode the thing Petrarch had prophesied in that canzone must come, and that it was he who ought to be the executor of so glorious an undertaking, since it appeared to him that he was superior to every Roman in eloquence, learning, grace, and friends." Machiavelli's *Prince*, as I have already remarked, ends with the words of Petrarch that invoke the rebirth of Italian valor. To my knowledge no realist writer has concluded a political essay with the words of a poet, and with this kind of words.

If my argument that Machiavelli put *The Prince* on paper to design, instruct, and invoke a redeemer of Italy is persuasive, a few implications concerning widely debated interpretive issues are to be drawn. The first touches on the relationship between ethics and politics. As is well known, Machiavelli asserts that "it is necessary for a prince who wants to maintain his state to learn how not to be good, and to use this knowledge or not to use it according to necessity," and that "a prince, and especially a new prince, cannot observe all those things for which men are considered good, because in order to maintain the state, he must often act against his faith, against charity, against humanity, and against religion. And so it is necessary that he should have a mind ready to turn itself according to the way the winds of fortune and the changing circumstances command him. And, as I said above, he should not depart from the good, if it is possible to do so, but he should know how to enter into evil when forced by necessity."[33] In this passage and in others of the same tone, Machiavelli refers to princes in general. But redeemers and founders are more often than ordinary princes forced to be not good and to enter in evil. The founder of a new principality must hurt and damage in various ways the people he is becoming the prince of and the supporters of the previous regime (chapter 3); the prince who wants to emancipate his country from foreign domination must fight a war against a foreign army; the citizen who intends to liberate a city from tyranny must crush the partisans of the tyrant, not to mention the fact that all founders and redeemers will surely have to deal with the envy of their closest followers, and envy, Machiavelli reminds us in *Discorsi* 3.30, can rarely be appeased without resorting to violence.

Because the goal of the redeemer is just, however, he can count on God's friendship: "for their undertakings were no more just, nor easier than this one, nor was God more a friend to them than to you."[34] Machiavelli here explicitly alludes to Moses, the true hero of the "Exhortation" and the whole *Prince*. To have God as friend means not only that the redeemer can count on his help when he has to face almost impossible tasks, but also that God will understand and excuse him if, forced by necessity, he has to enter into evil and be not good. Friends are indulgent. In the Bible, God remains a friend to Moses even after the latter has committed injustices and cruelties. What Machiavelli is telling readers is not that politics is autonomous from ethics but that the redeemer, because of the moral excellence of his task, deserves special consideration.[35] The princes who are merely concerned with preserving their states can have some remedy with God if they perpetrate well-used cruelties ("con Dio e con gli uomini avere allo stato loro qualche remedio"),[36] but the friendship of God is available only to the redeemers.

The second consequence of the interpretation of *The Prince* as an oration on the redeemer concerns the issue of the compatibility of *The Prince*—a text that instructs a prince how to establish and preserve a principality—and the *Discourses*—a text that instructs how to found, preserve, expand, and reform a republic. The answer to this much-debated question is that founders and redeemers are necessary both for republics and for kingdoms. In both cases they must have extraordinary authority, display exactly the same virtues, and face the necessity of entering into evil. The prince of The Prince is the founder not of a reigning dynasty but of an independent state with good armies and good laws that may evolve, and that Machiavelli would like to see evolving, into a republic. There is no hint in the entire work about rules or criteria of succession. This silence is quite resounding, particularly if we compare Machiavelli's *Prince* with other books of advice for princes that do indeed contain indications on the designation of the successor.

The figure of the founder who acts as a monarch but then opens the path for a republic appears also in other works of Machiavelli. The obvious reference is *Discourses on Livy*, 1.9, where Romulus, one of the heroes of *The Prince*, was surely a king, but the political orders he instituted in Rome were more congenial to a free and civil way of living than to a tyranny. When Rome became a republic, very small institutional changes were needed.[37] After all, Machiavelli explicitly tells us, "If princes are superior to peoples in ordering laws, forming civil lives, and ordering new statutes and orders, peoples are much superior in maintaining things ordered [so] that without doubt they attain the glory of those who order them."[38] In the *Discourse on Remodeling the State of Florence*, composed in 1520 at Cardinal Giulio de' Medici's request for Pope Leo X, Machiavelli exalts the figure of the reformer of political orders with words very similar to those he had used in *The Prince*, and openly says that as long as the pope and the cardinal are alive, their power will be a de facto monarchy ("ella è una monarchia"). Afterward, Florence should resume its republican institutions.[39]

Machiavelli's *Prince* is indeed the "book of republicans"—not in the sense that it reveals the horrible vices of the prince and instills in readers a hatred for monarchy, as Rousseau believed, but in the sense that it delineates the image of the founder and redeemer that republican political theory and practice need. Unless we are prepared to believe that good republics come into existence, remain alive, and are reformed only through the wisdom and the active participation of their citizens, we must accept the view that republics need great political leaders, the sort of leaders that *The Prince* extols. Hence, *The*

Prince is not a problematic alternative to the *Discourses* but a fine integration to it. Together they make for a theory of political emancipation.

Finally, interpreting *The Prince* as a text on political redemption also gives us a clue about its impressive longevity and impact. As Antonio Gramsci writes in his *Prison Notebooks*, *The Prince* is not a systematic treatise but a "living work" [*libro vivente*] in which "political ideology and political science are fused in the dramatic form of the 'myth.'"[40] Machiavelli's masterful representation of the new prince sets in motion the artistic imagination of the people the writer wants to convince, and in this way he intends to excite their political passions. The intellectual and political teaching of *The Prince*, Gramsci remarks, is therefore to be identified precisely in the "Exhortation": "having described the ideal *condottiere*, Machiavelli here, in a passage of great artistic effect, invokes the real *condottiere* who is to incarnate him historically. This passionate invocation reflects back on the entire book, and is precisely what gives it its dramatic character."[41] In fact, Machiavelli has composed the entire treatise having in mind the creation of the myth of the redeemer: "the utopian character of *The Prince* lies in the fact that the Prince had no real historical existence; he did not present himself immediately and objectively, but was a pure theoretical abstraction—a symbol of the leader and ideal *condottiere*. However, in a dramatic movement of great effect, the elements of passion and myth which occur throughout the book are drawn together and brought to life in the conclusion, in the invocation of a prince who 'really exists.'"[42]

For Gramsci, in the "Exhortation" Machiavelli speaks in his own voice, or, more precisely, speaks with the voice of a prophet who is capable of representing the deep and historically determined aspirations of his own people and points out to them the road to emancipation by designing before their eyes the new prince and their redeemer. Gramsci's words deserve to be quoted at length because of their interpretive force and their historical relevance:

> Throughout the book, Machiavelli discusses what the Prince must
> be like if he is to lead a people to found a new State; the argument is
> developed with rigorous logic, and with detachment. In the conclu-
> sion Machiavelli merges with the people, becomes the people; not

however, some "generic" people, but the people whom he, Machiavelli, has convinced by the preceding argument—the people whose consciousness and whose expression he becomes and feels himself to be, with whom he feels identified. The entire "logical" argument now appears as nothing other than auto reflection on the part of the people—an inner reasoning worked out in the popular consciousness, whose conclusion is a cry of passionate urgency. The passion, from discussion of itself, becomes once again "emotion," fever, fanatical desire for action. This is why the epilogue of *The Prince* is not something extrinsic, tacked on, rhetorical, but has to be understood as a necessary element of the work—indeed as the element which gives the entire work its true color, and makes it a kind of "political manifesto."[43]

It is just speculation, but I believe that *The Prince* has been able to remain alive for five hundred years, and will probably survive in good health for many years to come, because it is a living work, as Antonio Gramsci nicely put it—a living work in the sense that Niccolò Machiavelli was able to infuse in that text a poignant message about political and moral redemption with the hope of stimulating political action with redemptive goals. In history, political and social redemptions are rare experiences. As hopes and aspirations in the imagination of peoples, however, they are real and long-lasting. Readers perceive that while he was writing about an imagined redeemer of Italy, Niccolò Machiavelli was striving for his own resurrection. As he was composing the pages of *The Prince*, he was no longer a defeated man, deeply wounded in his body and his soul, compelled to live his days as "quondam Secretario," as he writes in a letter of April 9, 1513. He was again himself, the man who found in thinking and writing on the grand politics of founders and redeemers his true spiritual nourishment. What makes *The Prince* unique is that it is a text on political redemption and founding composed by a man who was trying to redeem himself. This is not the only meaning to be found in *The Prince*. Only the theme of redemption, however, casts the right light on all the pages of Machiavelli's oration and permits us to savor its dramatic beauty.

CHAPTER 3

Machiavelli's Revolution in Thought

CATHERINE HEIDT ZUCKERT

This essay was written on the five hundredth anniversary of the announcement of the composition of Machiavelli's remarkable book, *The Prince*. The composition of Machiavelli's book is an event worth remembering, I shall argue, because it changed the way people think about politics; and the way we think about politics obviously affects what we do.

Machiavelli was a sly but not a particularly shy author. In *The Prince* he openly declared that he was doing something new. He wrote: "I fear that . . . I may be held presumptuous, especially since . . . I depart from . . . others. But since my intent is to write something useful to whoever understands it, it has appeared to me more fitting to go directly to the effectual truth of the thing than to the imagination of it. Many have imagined republics and principalities that have never been seen or known to exist in truth; for it is so far from how one lives to how one should live that he who lets go of what is done for what should be done learns his ruin rather than his preservation." To show a prince how he can maintain his state, Machiavelli thus proposed to teach him how "to be able not to be good, and to use this and not use it according to necessity" (61).[1]

Machiavelli's promise to teach rulers how not to be good quickly earned him a reputation as a teacher of tyrants, if not a teacher of evil per se. To British playwrights of the sixteenth century Machiavelli seemed, indeed, to be well named after "Old Nick."[2] His family name has, moreover, subsequently been used to describe a particularly nasty kind of politics, "Machiavellian" politics, in which a practitioner knowingly uses evil means—force and fraud—to obtain his selfish ends. Machiavelli himself explicitly recognized, however, that older writers also recognized the need for princes to use bestial means like force and fraud in order to establish and maintain their rule. It was not his recognition of the need to use immoral means in acquiring and maintaining control of a state that made his teaching novel or original.

Reading more carefully what Machiavelli actually wrote, more perceptive readers have recognized that teaching a prince (or, we might say more generally, a political leader) how not to be good is not the same as teaching him to be entirely bad. Who would need to learn how not to be good? Readers who need to learn to be able not to be good, and to use and not use this knowledge according to necessity, are apt to be those inclined to be good. And if those who are already able to be bad were to read his treatise, they would learn to distinguish "cruelty well-used" all at once against a few particularly problematic individuals from "cruelties badly used" which are repeated against an increasing number of people and so over time add to the numbers of opponents a prince or leader faces. That is, the bad would learn to minimize their use of force in acquiring and maintaining their state.

Among educated people Machiavelli has thus come to be known primarily as a "realist."[3] For example, in February 2013 David Brooks reported in the *New York Times* that reading for a class he had been auditing on "grand strategy" at Yale University had reminded him that Machiavelli teaches his readers some harsh truths about the basis and preservation of political order. There are times, particularly in foreign policy, when leaders or states have to use violence and deceive others in order to preserve themselves—such as, perhaps, the American use of drones in Afghanistan and Pakistan. But, Brooks concluded, these harsh measures are fortunately the exception rather than the rule in our constitutional order.[4] That is a common but, I shall argue, a far too narrow and conventional understanding of Machiavelli's new teaching.

Like other "classical realists," Machiavelli does present a rather dim view of human nature. The reason he proposes to teach political leaders how not to be good is that "a man who wants to make a profession of good in all regards must come to ruin among so many who are not good." He observes further that "one can say this generally of men: that they are ungrateful, fickle, pretenders and dissemblers, evaders of danger, eager for gain. While you do them good, they are yours, offering you their blood, property, lives, and children . . . when the need for them is far away; but, when it is close to you, they revolt" (66). He admits that "if all men were good, his teaching would not be good; but," he urges, "because they are wicked and do not observe faith with you, you also do not have to observe it with them" (69). Among Christians who accept the doctrine of original sin, however, the notion that most human beings are fundamentally wicked would not be particularly novel or original. (And Machiavelli's contemporaries were at least Christians in name and by education.) There were, moreover, "realists" like Thucydides among the ancient historians Machiavelli urged his readers to study. Machiavelli's new teaching does not consist, therefore, in his generally negative view of human nature and the need to impose government with force if human beings are to be made orderly, safe, and prosperous.

To see what is truly novel about Machiavelli's teaching, we need to look a bit more closely at the "imaginary republics and principalities" with which he contrasts his "effectual truth." Plato's *Republic* is the first work that usually comes to mind, because Socrates admits that the "city in speech" he and his interlocutors construct is not apt ever actually to come into existence. Evils in cities will not cease, Socrates famously proclaims, until philosophers become kings, or kings philosophers. The guiding purpose of his city in speech thus becomes the education of philosophers, who are said to possess all the virtues, because they (and only they) can rule justly. Aristotle seems more moderate and practical when in his *Politics* he does not write about anything so fanciful as philosopher kings. He argues simply that because the virtuous ought to rule, the best city should be designed to educate some citizens to become virtuous so that they can rule the others.[5] Cicero tried to bring philosophy and practical politics even closer together in his notion of magnanimity, but in *The City of God* (19.23) Augustine argued against Cicero that it is not possible for a just city to exist on earth. Justice is to be found only in heaven with God; but, Augustine nevertheless insisted, human rulers, judges, and heads of household still needed to be educated to do their duty in the "city of man" on earth. Aquinas famously embraced a more Aristotelian understanding of virtue and the requirements of political rule, although he added the theological virtues of hope, faith, and charity to the cardinal virtues of courage, moderation, justice, and wisdom praised by the ancients. In sum, the tradition to which Machiavelli places himself in opposition agreed that a few virtuous men ought to be educated so that they could rule all the rest. There was, in other words, an aristocratic bias, that is, a bias toward the rule of the few truly morally good and rational human beings, in traditional discussions of not merely how rulers should be educated but also what the best form of government is. Machiavelli's "effectual truth," on the other hand, has a decidedly democratic bias and is skeptical of the "goody-goody" character of previous thought. And that combination of a democratic bias with skepticism about the political effectiveness of moral virtue is, I shall argue, where the true novelty, even revolutionary character, of Machiavelli's political thought lies.[6]

The core of Machiavelli's teaching a prince "how not to be good and to use or not use that knowledge according to necessity" is to be found in his redefinition of the traditional virtues of liberality, mercy, and faith. The basis of the arguments he presents about these "virtues" is to be found, however, in a general observation he makes—both in his discussion of "civil principalities" in *The Prince* and in his praise of the Roman republic in his *Discourses on Livy* (1.4–5)—about the existence of two "humors" in every city. There are "the people [who] desire neither to be commanded nor oppressed by the great, and the great [who] desire to command and oppress the people" (39). These two humors (*umori*) are obviously opposed, so that neither can be satisfied except at the expense of the other. Divided into these two humors, Machiavelli thus claims, every city is characterized by a fundamental conflict between those who want to rule and those who do not want to be ruled. (I will simply note in passing that Machiavelli obviously does not think that Aristotle is correct when he maintains in his *Politics* (1.1252a25–1253a3) that political associations develop naturally out of families and tribes. On the contrary, Machiavelli suggests, most people do not want to be commanded, much less oppressed, by anyone else. Political order does not arise or exist by nature; it is man-made (*Discourses* 1.1).

Depending on the relative strength of these two "appetites" (*appetitti*), as Machiavelli also calls the humors, there are three possible results: principality, liberty, and license. In a book purportedly devoted to the education of a prince, Machiavelli does not explain how liberty can be achieved through a balancing of the two humors; that is the subject of book 1 of his *Discourses on Livy*. In *The Prince* Machiavelli confines himself to urging the prince, whether he comes to power with the aid of the great or of the people, once in power to seek the support of the people. The reasons he gives are telling.

First, Machiavelli points out, the great will always see themselves as the prince's equals and demand ever more offices and goods as the price of their support. Attempts to satisfy them will necessarily fail and, in failing, add to the prince's enemies. It is possible, however, for a prince to satisfy the people, because "the end of the people is more decent [*onesto*] than that of the great, since the great want to oppress and the people want not to be oppressed" (39).

The second reason Machiavelli gives why it is better to seek the support of the people than of the great is even more fundamental. A prince will never be able to secure a hostile people, because they are many, whereas the great are few. As Machiavelli reminds his readers with the examples of "lovely" fellows like Cesare Borgia, Agathocles, and Liverotto, the great in any particular city can be brought together under false pretenses and slaughtered; but a prince will have no one to rule if he murders all or most of his people. To be sure, Machiavelli acknowledges, a prince needs subordinates to help him rule; but he observes that a prince can do perfectly well without any given set of "great" persons, since the prince "can make and unmake them every day" (40). He makes some great by giving them lands and offices or, conversely, unmakes them by taking away their lands and offices along with their lives. Machiavelli thus shows his reader that the great are not different from the many by nature. "Greatness" is a product of a person's position. As he states in the *Discourses* (1.58), human nature is the same in all. Because those granted high offices have more power and goods, however, they no longer feel as liable to oppression as those subject to the government. Rather than desiring merely not to be oppressed, they come as a result of their great positions to wish to acquire more by oppressing others.

Like Aristotle in his *Nicomachean Ethics*, Machiavelli suggests that the great come to think of themselves as virtuous and thus deserving of rule as a result of their education and experience. Like Aristotle, Machiavelli also suggests that the primary means through which human beings come to their understanding of what is good and bad, virtuous or vicious behavior, is praise or blame. But where Aristotle seeks true virtue in a "golden mean" between two extremes, Machiavelli lists the qualities reputed to be virtuous or vicious in terms of opposites: liberal or mean, generous or rapacious, cruel or merciful, a breaker of faith or faithful, and so on. And when virtues are thought to be simply in opposition to vices, there can be no middle position or way. Machiavelli contends, moreover, that it is impossible for a prince to possess all the qualities thought to be good. The *virtù* he recommends thus appears to be a mixture of what has traditionally been thought to be good and bad. The good qualities in his list of opposites include ancient virtues like liberality and Christian virtues like charity and faith; but neither the difficulty of making a good choice nor Machiavelli's originality consists in the mix.[7] The difficulty appears initially to be that a prince who does what is necessary to maintain his state will necessarily incur the infamy associated with some vices. Insofar as virtue and vice are merely matters of praise and blame or reputation, Machiavelli thus observes, a "prudent" prince will "avoid the infamy of those vices that would take his state from him," but not "care about incurring the infamy of those vices without which it is difficult to save one's state." Machiavelli concludes, however, that "if one considers everything well, one will find something appears to be virtue, which if pursued would be one's ruin, and something else appears to be vice, which if pursued results in one's security and well-being" (62). In other words, *virtù* is not merely a matter of opinion or reputation; it can be apparent or real. The problem, as Machiavelli somewhat circuitously presents it here, is that people have not understood what is truly virtuous and vicious. He thus presents a new substantive understanding of what is truly good and bad in a ruler.

He begins by specifying which of the opposed characteristics traditionally thought to be good should be avoided by a truly virtuous prince and which reputed "vices" he should accept if he wants to maintain his state. The first supposed virtue Machiavelli treats is liberality.

Generosity had traditionally been praised as a virtue. But, Machiavelli objects, a prince who attempts to acquire a name for his liberality by generously rewarding his friends and putting on lavish displays will necessarily deplete his own resources; and once he has depleted his own resources, he will have to burden his subjects with new taxes and so arouse their hatred. As a result, he will lose the support of many and, having become poor, be contemned by all. It is better, therefore, for a prince to accept a reputation for being stingy or mean in the short run, so that he can conserve his own resources to defend himself from whoever makes war on him without burdening his people. In the long run, Machiavelli concludes, such a prince is truly liberal to "all those from whom he does not take, who are infinite," and mean "with all those to whom he does not give, who are few" (63).

Machiavelli acknowledges that three of the historical figures he urges a prince to imitate—Alexander, Caesar, and Cyrus—were not liberal in his sense. In seeking to acquire power, Machiavelli admits, princes like these ancient generals could be liberal in the traditional sense, because they gave their supporters goods seized from others. However, he warns, once these princes came to power, they would not be able to continue giving away the goods of peoples who had become their subjects without arousing their hatred. He is not recommending that the princes of modern states become conquering generals like the most famous ancient statesmen. He is promoting a new conception of leadership.

Machiavelli's discussion of whether a prince should be merciful or cruel, loved or feared, follows the same pattern as his analysis of liberality. Not only does he reverse traditional notions of good and bad; he also advises the prince to secure the advantages of many rather than favoring an aristocratic few. Cesare Borgia provides a notable example. Earlier in *The Prince* Machiavelli had observed that Cesare brought "good government" to the Romagna by appointing a cruel man named Ramirro de Orca to prosecute the former lords of that province who sought to enrich themselves by murdering and robbing their subjects. But after Ramirro had imprisoned or killed the most notable malefactors, and terrorized everyone else into submission, Cesare saw that such cruel means of keeping order were no longer necessary and that they might, indeed, make him hated. So, to show that it was not he, but the harsh nature of his minister, that was to blame for the cruelty, he first established a civil court in the center of the province, with a most excellent president, and advocates for all the cities. Then he had Ramirro killed and his minister's body, split in two, put on display in the public square with a wooden block and a bloody knife to show that such cruelty would no longer be tolerated.[8] Cesare was reputed to be cruel, but, Machiavelli suggests, in using cruelty to punish a few criminals and so bringing peace and faith to the Romagna, "he was much more merciful than the Florentine people, who so as to escape a name for cruelty, allowed Pistoia to be destroyed" (65). Because a new prince has to use force to establish order, Machiavelli insists, he cannot avoid acquiring a reputation for cruelty. Admitting that it would be best for a prince to be both feared and loved, as a new prince might be if he succeeded in establishing and maintaining order where there had been none, Machiavelli nevertheless observes that, since it is difficult to be both loved and feared, it is safer for a prince to be feared. Human beings will promise much out of "love" so long as they are not asked actually to do it; but when pressed to do what they have promised, they refuse and revolt. A prince who founds himself entirely on their words will be lost, because "love is held by a chain of obligation, which, because men are wicked, is broken at every opportunity for their own utility, but fear is held by a dread of punishment that never forsakes you" (66–67). In other words, people will not fulfill their promises to you if you do not have means of forcing them to do so.

Machiavelli brings his arguments concerning the true or effective virtues of "liberality" and "mercy" together by warning the prince that, although he should make sure that he continues to be feared, he should not make himself hated. And he will not be hated if he abstains from taking the property or the women of his citizens and subjects. Indeed, Machiavelli shockingly observes, a man will more quickly forget the death of his father (who would have had to die sometime) than the loss of his patrimony. Machiavelli thus urges the prince to exercise what had traditionally been called self-control, if not moderation, lest he be perceived to be rapacious and thus become hated. In making this recommendation, however, Machiavelli does not appeal to a prince's desire to be reputed to be good or virtuous. He appeals to the self-interest of the prince qua prince by arguing that a prince will maintain his power if and only if he leaves the property of his subjects alone. He seeks to persuade the prince who, as one of the great, wants to command and rule that he will be able to satisfy his desire best by satisfying the desire of his people not to be oppressed by making them feel safe in their persons, families, and property.

As in the case of liberality, so in the case of cruelty and mercy, Machiavelli admits that famous ancient generals constitute exceptions. He observes that Hannibal could not have controlled his large army, composed of men with different customs, loyalties, and languages, who were fighting, moreover, in a strange land, unless he had used "inhuman cruelty." Likewise, Machiavelli observes that the Roman general Scipio, who ultimately defeated Hannibal, would have undermined the discipline and success of the Roman army if the bad effect of his "mercy" had not been undone by the Senate. Machiavelli does not relate the details of the incident in which Scipio displayed his mercy, but if readers look it up in Livy (29.8–9), they will find that Scipio failed to punish an officer, that is, another aristocrat, who had destroyed a conquered people. By failing not only to discipline a disobedient officer but also to avenge the people he had oppressed, Scipio fostered potential rebellions both in the Roman army and among their subjects. If the Senate had not stepped in to enforce the law and restore discipline, the Roman army would not have been able to save the republic by defeating the cruel Carthaginian.[9]

Machiavelli's virtuous prince will avoid arousing the hatred of his people, but he is not simply their friend. On the contrary, Machiavelli argues, a prince has to deceive both his allies and his people.

Turning to the question of how a prince should keep faith, since he cannot expect others to keep their promises to him, Machiavelli insists that princes cannot rely solely on force (or the fear its use can arouse). "There are two kinds of combat," he observes, "one with laws, the other with force. The first is proper to man, the second to beasts; but because the first is often not enough, one must have recourse to the second." This lesson was taught "covertly to princes by ancient writers, who wrote that Achilles, and many other ancient princes, were given to Chiron the centaur to be raised." For "to have as teacher a half-beast, half-man means nothing other than that a prince needs to know how to use both natures" (69). The failure to recognize and deal with the bestial parts of human beings thus appears to be particularly modern or, in Machiavelli's context, Christian.

Of the methods of fighting characteristic of the beast, Machiavelli recommends that a prince imitate those of the fox and the lion, "because the lion does not defend itself from snares and the fox does not defend itself from wolves." But, he further observes, "those who stay with the lion [that is, who rely solely on brute force] do not understand this." In *De officiis* Cicero had urged his son to avoid the bestial ways of fighting characteristic of both the lion and the fox unless it was absolutely necessary to employ them. And he warned his son that deceptive, cowardly measures were especially unworthy of a noble gentleman who should, perhaps above all, be true to his word. Machiavelli reverses Cicero's advice by insisting that a prince must use both force and fraud in order to acquire and maintain a state. Indeed, he argues that "a prudent lord . . . cannot observe faith, nor should he, when such observance turns against him, and the causes that made him promise have been eliminated" (69). Precisely because circumstances are always changing, an astute prince will always be able find a reason not to keep his word.

In insisting on the need to use fraud as well as force, Machiavelli might appear to be equating keeping faith with honesty or abiding by one's promises. He builds on the association of faith with religion, however, first, by justifying his advice with an ironical inversion of the Golden Rule. "If all men were good," Machiavelli concedes, "this teaching would not be good; but because they are wicked and do not observe faith with you, you also do not have to observe it with them" (69). Although Machiavelli first observes that ancient writers recognized the need to fight both like men and like beasts, and so suggests that moderns might not, the connection he draws between faith and religion should remind his reader that it would be strange for Christians, who presumably believe in the doctrine of original sin, not to recognize the need to deal with the bestial aspects of human nature. And, in fact, he observes that one of the most Christian of all princes knew very well not only "how to use the fox," but also "how to color this nature, and to be a great pretender and dissembler." Pope Alexander VI provides Machiavelli with an example par excellence of a prince who "never did anything, nor ever thought of anything, but how to deceive men, and he always found a subject to whom he could do it." Other princes and people tended to believe the pope, especially when he swore by the God he was supposed to represent on earth. So Machiavelli observes that "there never was a man with greater efficacy in asserting a thing, and in affirming it with greater oaths, who observed it less" (70).

Ancient princes may have been better generals, but, Machiavelli suggests, modern princes are better dissemblers. Having urged modern readers to study the art of war as it was practiced by the ancients in the first half of *The Prince*, in the second part of his treatise Machiavelli advises them to combine the art of war with the modern art of dissimulation, which he associates particularly with Christianity. Unlike the Roman emperors Machiavelli discusses, Christian princes could not hope to be declared to be state divinities and worshipped along with the other gods of the city if their service to the people, the Senate, and the city was deemed worthy of such an honor after they had died. Purporting to seek their reward after death only in heaven, Christian princes claimed more modesty and merely to be serving God and his people. Unlike pagan princes, Christian leaders did not rely on augurs or oracles to let them know God's will (cf. *Discourses* I.11–14). So when things did not go as desired, these Christians could attribute the misfortune to the will of an unfathomable God. Rather than accepting blame for the suffering of their people, they would try to succor and comfort the people in their misery. The most astute of these modern princes knew not only that it is necessary "to appear merciful, faithful, humane, honest, and religious," but also that "a prince, and especially a new prince, cannot observe all those things for which men are held good, since he is often under a necessity, to maintain his state, of acting against faith, against charity, against humanity, against religion" (70).

Machiavelli emphasizes that a prince should take great care not to say anything that is not "merciful, faithful, humane, honest, and religious," especially religious. Most people judge by appearances; so when the effects of the prince's actions correspond to his explanations of his purposes and motives, they will believe that he has done what he has done for the reasons he gives. "In the actions of all men, and especially of princes," Machiavelli concludes, "where there is no court to appeal to, one looks to the end. So, let a prince win and maintain his state: the means will always be judged honorable, and will be praised by everyone" (71). This famous observation has often been inaccurately abbreviated as simply saying that the end justifies the means. In fact, Machiavelli points to one specific end, acquiring and maintaining the state. This end justifies the means, moreover, particularly in the eyes of the people. If a state is led by a prince who secures the lives, family, and property of his subjects, his people will believe that the prince is doing what he says he is doing—mercifully, faithfully, humanely, and honestly—for the sake of God and his people. As Machiavelli repeatedly reminds his readers, however, in fact princes act for the sake of acquiring and maintaining their own power and fame.[10]

Machiavelli's redefinition of the true "virtues" of a ruler obviously constitutes a severe debunking of both "virtue" and "rule." Rather than a noble endeavor undertaken from a sense of duty in order to achieve a common good, Machiavelli argues that effective rule will be undertaken and conducted solely on the basis of a clever calculation of the best means an ambitious man can use to satisfy his desire to command and oppress. The "effective truth" Machiavelli teaches is that a would-be ruler will best and most reliably satisfy his desire to command by acting so as to secure the lives, families, and properties of his subjects. The art of government, as he presents it, does not consist in the education of noblemen to become virtuous rulers. It consists, rather, in persuading those who wish to command to satisfy their people's desire not to be oppressed by appealing to their own desire to rule rather than any illusory dedication to a common or higher good.

There is or can be a certain conjunction of the prince's desire to command and the people's desire to be secure, but these desires remain essentially opposed; it requires great ingenuity, in fact, to conceive of the means by which they may both be satisfied.[11] Machiavelli points to one way they can both be satisfied by reminding his reader that there are two ways of fighting—the human way, with laws, as well as the force and fraud used by beasts. He indicates what he means by the human way of fighting with laws when he observes that France is an example of a well-ordered and well-governed kingdom, and that the first of the "infinite good institutions on which the liberty and security of the [French] king depend . . . is parlement" (74). Machiavelli then explains:

> The one who ordered that kingdom, *knowing the ambition of the powerful and their insolence, and judging it necessary for them to have a bit in their mouths to correct them*, and on the other side, *knowing the hatred of the generality of the people against the great, which is founded in its fear, and wanting to secure them, intended this not to be the particular concern of the king*, so as to take from him the blame he would have from the great when he favored the popular side, and from the popular side when he favored the great; and so *he constituted a third judge to be the one who would beat down the great and favor the lesser side without blame for the king.* (74–75, emphasis added)

By enabling the people to resist the ambition and insolence of the nobles by accusing and trying them of crimes against the king, the French parlement contributed not only to the security of the people, but also to the security of the king. In a monarchy the laws are the laws of the king. And those who have the power to threaten his rule are the nobles or "great" who see themselves as equals to the king and wish to acquire more wealth and power for themselves, if not simply to replace him. By giving the people the power to check the arrogance and ambition of the nobles, the institution of such a court enabled the king to use the people as a means of securing his rule without his having to act directly or with force against the nobility.[12]

Just as Cesare Borgia brought good government to the Romagna by using Ramirro to frighten everyone into submission and then avoided responsibility himself for the use of such cruel means by replacing his assistant with a civil court, so, Machiavelli suggests, the king of France has acted both to secure his own rule and to escape blame for the means by setting up a court in which the people judge the nobles.[13] Machiavelli acknowledges that a general like Agathocles or Severus can use force and fraud effectively to keep himself in power for the duration of his life; indeed, Machiavelli concedes, so long as they depend on a professional army to keep them in place, these "tough guys" will need not only to persist in using such bestial means, but also to allow the soldiers to oppress the people. But, he suggests, a prince would be better advised, like Hiero, to replace the mercenary soldiers he uses to acquire power with trained subjects or citizens to maintain it (*The Prince* 6, 13, 25, 55–56).

In *The Prince* Machiavelli thus seeks to persuade his princely readers to institute what we have come to know as a constitutional monarchy, based on an army composed of their own people, and characterized by a balance of powers that secures the rule of law. In other words, he foresees the development of the modern nation-state. Because such a nation-state could be established only in a relatively large territory, he concluded *The Prince* with his famous call to the Medici to muster and train an army "to seize Italy and to free her from the barbarians."[14]

What Machiavelli does not mention in *The Prince*, which is at least purportedly addressed to a Medici prince, but what he states quite explicitly in his *Discourses* (1.46, 52; 3.22, 28) is that a young, virtuous political leader at the head of a citizen army who seeks and acquires popular support the way Machiavelli argues that a prince should in order to acquire and maintain power for himself constitutes the greatest threat to the preservation of a republic.[15] Ordinary people do not perceive the seeds of tyranny that are concealed by the favors a popular leader does for them. Happy to see such a popular leader put down the great who have lorded over them in the past (1.16), the people are often willing to see him abolish the constitutional checks or restraints that prevent any single individual from becoming a tyrant (1.40–45). Whereas Machiavelli advocates a kind of alliance between the prince and the people in *The Prince* to keep the great in check, in the *Discourses* he seeks to create a kind of alliance between the other "great" men and the people against any emerging prince or tyrant. The remedies Machiavelli proposes for the threat to a republic posed by a potential prince are, first, to make both the people and other ambitious citizens suspicious of the motives and ambition of seemingly virtuous young leaders (1.28–30). In other words, he urges them not to be taken in by the appearance of religion, mercy, and humanity he advised a prince to project, but to suspect that their "captains" have more dangerous hidden aims. Second, Machiavelli counsels other ambitious or "great" citizens to compete with emerging young heroes for popular favor (1.52). Such competition among individuals ambitious for high office will almost necessarily produce public policies aimed at satisfying the desires of the people. To ensure that there is rotation in office and that term limits are respected, he points out, ambitious citizens must be willing not only to cede offices they have held to their competitors, but also to serve under them. To expose attempts on the part of ambitious individuals to overthrow the republic, it is also necessary to institute procedures whereby such individuals can be accused and tried before large popular juries. These trials will not necessarily produce just results for the individuals in question, but the danger of facing such a trial will serve as a check, if not a deterrent on individual ambition. And the trials themselves allow the people to "vent . . . those humors that grow up in cities" (1.7, 24). Unorganized popular resistance to the oppressive desires of the great is not sufficient to check them, Machiavelli emphasizes. The blind fury of a mob can be immensely destructive, but it soon subsides and thus has no lasting positive effect (1.46; 3.11). It takes a single mind to design institutions, and a single leader to arm and organize an effective force capable of defending a city from external aggression and maintaining order inside it. The great advantage of republics over principalities is not that they do not require princes or leaders; it is that they are not stuck with one, because they can elect a succession of different individuals able to act in a variety of circumstances (1.20; 3.9).[16]

Because all effective political action requires organization and thus leadership, Machiavelli addresses all of his political writings to individuals in positions of power or ambitious to hold them. But in urging them to institute and maintain "good government" by securing the lives, families, and properties of their subjects or fellow citizens, he does not appeal to their sense of justice, mercy, or public-spiritedness. On the contrary, he appeals to their ambition—their desire for status and wealth. His debunking of traditional notions of virtue and vice was a necessary part of his broader contention that government should not serve the interests of the best, but that it should, instead, serve the interests of most. So long as people believed that it was possible to educate truly good, just, courageous, and wise human beings to take care of the rest, they would seek to find and produce such exceptional leaders. Machiavelli does not claim that there are no such human beings; he maintains simply that they cannot rule effectively, and that both they and their people will suffer when they try to govern on the basis of traditional notions of virtue. He does not expect ordinary people to understand the intricacies of military strategy or institutional design, that is, the means by which their basic desires can be satisfied. He is certain, however, that they are the best judges of the outcomes or effects.

Machiavelli's shocking advocacy of the use of force and fraud, along with his debunking of traditional notions of virtue and vice, has led readers to ignore the democratic or popular ends he consistently seeks to achieve by proclaiming his "effective" truth. As Machiavelli redefines the virtue or excellence of rulers, it consists in discovering and implementing ways of satisfying their people's desire not to be oppressed. By making the effective end or object of government the satisfaction of popular desires, and the people the judge of their satisfaction, Machiavelli changed our understanding of both the end of government and the standard by which it is and should be judged. He also very much diminished our appreciation of the nobility of public service.[17] Perhaps the pendulum has swung too far in his direction.

CHAPTER 4

Machiavelli's Women

ARLENE W. SAXONHOUSE

Machiavelli has suffered the fate of many of the political theorists from the past: to be known more by the adjectival forms that derive from their names than by what they actually wrote. Plato suffers from being considered "Platonic," abstract, metaphysical, asexual, when in fact the dialogues he writes are very much grounded in our everyday experiences and filled with sexual innuendo and earthiness. Hobbes suffers from the adjective "Hobbesian," describing men as egotistical, seeking power after power, and living a life that is solitary, poor, nasty, brutish, and short. The Hobbes who played tennis well into his eighties, sang bawdy sons, and relaxed by translating Homer is largely unknown. As a consequence, perhaps, the message of his *Leviathan*, explaining what he viewed as necessary so that others could play tennis into their eighties, is often ignored. And Machiavelli, too, is recognized as being, well, Machiavellian, expounding a theory of ends justifying means, presenting to the world the political leader ready to pursue political power at any cost, to shed all concern with moral constraints, to be manipulative. The pictures we have of Machiavelli, thin-lipped, with a sardonic smile and beady eyes, do little to undermine the vision of the "Machiavellian" Machiavelli.

With all three authors just mentioned, it is easy to extract passages that support the adjectives that come from their names. In Machiavelli's case, for instance, he famously writes: "Many have imagined republics and principalities that have never been known to exist in truth; for it is so far from how one lives to how one should live that he who lets go of what is done for what should be done learns his ruin rather than his preservation. For a man who wants to make a profession of good in all regards must come to ruin among so many who are not good. Hence it is necessary to a prince, if he wants to maintain himself, to learn to be able not to be good, and to use this and not use this according to necessity" (*The Prince*, chap. 15).[1] Or in his *Discourses on Livy* when he comments on the fratricide of Remus by Romulus, he remarks, "So a prudent orderer of a republic, who intends to help not himself but the common good, should contrive to have authority alone; nor will a wise and understanding man ever reprove anyone for any extraordinary action that he uses to order a kingdom or constitute a republic. It is very suitable that when the deed accuses him, the effect excuses him; and when the effect is good, as was that of Romulus, it will always excuse the deed" (1.9.2).

Or he presents as one of his models of a political leader Cesare Borgia, who had put one of his ministers in charge of an unruly town. The minister was able to subdue the town and put it back in order only with considerable cruelty, and then, "because he [Borgia] knew that past rigors [had] generated some hatred for Remirro, to purge the spirits of that people and to gain them entirely to himself, he wished to show that if any cruelty had been committed, this had not come from him but from the harsh nature of his minister. And having seized this opportunity, he had him placed one morning in the piazza . . . in two pieces, with a piece of wood and a bloody knife beside him. The ferocity of this spectacle left the people at once satisfied and stupefied" (*The Prince*, chap. 7). This Machiavellian Machiavelli, though, is no more adequate than the Platonic Plato who does indeed write about bodiless love or the Hobbesian Hobbes who does describe men as seeking power after power. By looking at the women in Machiavelli's life and in his writings, I want to argue that we get a richer Machiavelli, but also one who becomes a far more radical and dangerous Machiavelli than his comments on the spectacle of the bisected Remirro, for example, might suggest. Just as by looking beyond the familiar in Plato and in Hobbes we get a richer sense of the depth and power of their thought, I find in Machiavelli's portrayal of women a deeper challenge to traditional thought and a far more radical legacy than even the radical legacy usually associated with him—namely, a legacy that I call the ambiguity of form or the shattering of the chain of being. It is this legacy, captured by his women, that I believe opens up the world in which we find ourselves today.

Let us begin by recalling perhaps the most famous passage using the female image from his writings, the final paragraph of his chapter on Fortuna in *The Prince*. There he writes: "It is better to be impetuous than cautious, because Fortune is a woman; and it is necessary if one wants to hold her down, to beat her and strike her down. And one sees that she lets herself be won more by the impetuous than by those who proceed coldly. And so always, like a woman, she is the friend of the young, because they are less cautious, more ferocious, and command her with more audacity." One need not be a rabid feminist to bristle at this image. Here is the theorist announcing the necessity for a masculine *virtù* of force and audacity, a manly energy asserting itself against the feminine force of disorder.

I want, though, to set this Machiavellian image of the prince as the manly conqueror of Fortuna against the very human Machiavelli we find in the collection of letters exchanged between him and his friends, and then turn to some of the women who appear in his other writings in order to suggest that the sexual opposition we find in that famous paragraph from chapter 25 of *The Prince* dissolves; we get instead a far more disturbing portrait of sexual ambiguity—one that leads to a breaking down of boundaries between the sexes and supports the broader movement that violates the hierarchical world of defined status. This violation depends on the capacity for imagination, a capacity to transcend the limits that the natural world seems to impose, revealing Machiavelli's advocacy of the imagination as a way to transcend the limits of nature. This boundary effacing, abetted by the imagination, is far more powerful than the brawn implied in the beating and holding down of the woman Fortuna or the killing of Remus by Romulus.

But first to the Machiavelli and the women who appear in his letters. In our own day of abbreviated e-mail exchanges, where style and personality are encoded in the relative placement of a colon, semicolon, and parentheses, we must return to a period when communication via frequent letters was the norm. The collection of the letters exchanged between Machiavelli and his friends, often straddling a line between literary narratives and informal thoughts on events both public and private, is a treasury of descriptions of his own life, his reflections on the private lives of those around him, and a commentary on the political events of his time. The letters reveal the demons in Machiavelli's life, but also his delights, and especially his everyday engagement in "the affairs of the heart" (if I may express myself euphemistically without the full force of Machiavelli's and his friends' much cruder but admittedly more vivid language). Machiavelli's letters do much more than report events, make requests, offer opinions, reveal anxieties or disappointments. They become arenas for the imagination, for the creation of stories, dramas, and fables. In the process of telling his stories, friends metamorphosize into bulls and swans, wrens and vultures.

We must be wary about taking the letters as accurate reports of Machiavelli's life—just as we must be careful about taking every phrase in his treatises as a clear expression of his views. In a letter to his friend Francesco Guicciardini, he writes, "For some time now I have never said what I believe or never believed what I said; and if I do sometimes tell the truth, I hide it behind so many lies that it is hard to find" (May 17, 1521, L 270).[2] Truth fades into lies, lies into truth, and we the readers of Machiavelli's letters and works know not what to believe. He is always playing with us, both enchanting us and mocking us.

The Machiavelli we find in his letters is rather at odds with the image evoked when he writes of the audacity required to conquer a feminine Fortuna. The letters reveal a Machiavelli subject to Cupid and a variety of women; they show a Machiavelli eagerly submitting to feminine charms and gladly letting himself be mocked by the women he encounters. Within a year or so after he penned his chapter on Fortuna for *The Prince*, he writes to his epistolary companion Francesco Vettori about a "creature" whom he describes as "so gracious, so refined, so noble—both in nature and circumstance—that never could my praise or my love for her be as much as she deserves." About his relationship with this perhaps fictional "creature," as he regularly refers to her, he reports to his friend:

> And do not think Love employed ordinary means to capture me, be-
> cause aware that they would be inadequate, he resorted to extraordi-
> nary ones about which I was ignorant and against which I declined
> to protect myself. Suffice it to say that although I am approaching
> my fiftieth year, neither does the heat of the sun distress me, nor do
> rough roads wear me out, nor do the dark hours of the night terrify
> me. . . . I have laid aside all memory of my sorrows, that not for any-
> thing in the world would I desire my freedom—even if I could have
> it. (August 3, 1514, L 238)

Because of her, Machiavelli continues, "I have renounced thoughts about matters great and grave. No longer do I delight in reading about the deeds of the
ancients or in discussing those of the moderns; everything has been transformed into tender thoughts. [This is Machiavelli!] Consequently if you need
to write anything about the lady, write, and discuss the other matters with
those who appreciate them more and understand them better; I have discovered nothing but harm in these matters, but in the matters of love there are
always good things and pleasures" (August 3, 1514, L 238). Whether his "creature" existed or was simply the figment of Machiavelli's very powerful imagination, we simply do not know. And we cannot be sure whether he creates
this creature to express his anguish about his own political impotence in 1514;
but note how he willingly presents himself in this letter as in thrall to a female creature from whom he seeks no release. Unabashedly, he gladly yields
to the feminine force.

In another letter whose veracity we must question, Machiavelli describes
a visit to a prostitute in 1509. It is certainly one of the most unpleasant and
coarsest letters in a collection of frequently coarse letters, and the details are
highly offensive. My references will be abbreviated and sanitized. After expressing envy of his correspondent's sexual conquests, Machiavelli goes on
to describe how he was seduced by a vile old hag who washed his shirts.
"The house she lives in is more than half underground—the only light you
see enters through the door." When Machiavelli chances on her one evening,
she invites him in to offer for sale some "shirts," whereupon he "made out in
the gloom a woman . . . affecting modesty." The "old slut" asked him to try

on the "shirt" and pay for it later. Afterward, "feeling like taking a look at the merchandise," as he puts it, he lit a lamp and discovered how physically grotesque she was. The letter lingers, detailing the ugliness of the woman, and concludes by assuring his friend that he will never get "horny"—his language—in Lombardy again (December 8, 1509, L 178). The letter is revolting, and Machiavelli spares no effort in making it so. Though we do not know whether the encounter happened or not, Machiavelli again portrays himself as a slave to the power of female sexuality, submitting to rather than conquering Fortuna. In part, the letter shows a self-mocking Machiavelli who reveals himself as a subject rather than a prince, controlled by others rather than controlling, and brought to this condition by sexual famine.[3]

Let us consider just one more letter for the moment, this time from January 1515. Responding to a friend's description of a love affair born of idleness, Machiavelli analogizes the submission to love of political power. About himself, he writes that love "binds me with his fetters," and he describes himself as being "in absolute despair of my liberty." This letter began with a sonnet about "the youthful archer" who

with such great force . . . let one [arrow] fly
That I feel its painful wound still; thus I
Confess and recognize his power.

He continues in prose to admit that the fetters with which Cupid—"that little thief"—has bound him are so strong that he is unable to "conceive of any means of unfettering" himself, and then adds that if "fate or other human stratagem would open some path for me to get out of them, perhaps I should not wish to go down it; so do I find these fetters—now sweet, now light, now heavy,—and they make such a tangle that I believe I cannot live happily without this kind of life" (January 31, 1515, L 247). This warm embrace of the fetters with which love has bound him hardly matches the virile prince who beats and strikes the female in the effort to control Fortuna.

In addition to the letters with their nameless women, there are also those that mention the well-known women who appear in his life. For many years there was the Florentine courtesan La Riccia, known as the curly-haired woman. In a letter to his friend Vettori, he wonders how long she will endure him, noting that she now calls him "House Pest." He adds that despite this she "sometimes lets me kiss her on the sly," but he also notes that "just today La Riccia said to me in a certain conversation she feigned to be having with her maid, 'Wise men, oh these wise men, I don't know what they have upstairs; it seems to me they turn everything topsy-turvy'" (February 4, 1514, L 229). Vettori, in an unusually reassuring letter, responds: "I am not surprised if La Riccia in anger has blamed the advice of wise men. But I do not think for this reason that she does not bear love toward you and that she will not open her door to you when you want. I have judged her to be humane and kind" (February 9, 1514, L 230).

In 1525 there was Mariscotta, a courtesan in Faenza. Machiavelli's friend Guicciardini dashes off a brief note to him in which he writes: "I do not want to leave out that I understand that after your departure Mariscotta spoke of you very flatteringly and generally praised your manners and conversation. That warms my heart because I desire everything that makes you happy and I assure you that if you come back here you will be most welcome and perhaps even more caressed" (July 29, 1525, L 291). Machiavelli responds: "This morning I received your letter in which you tell me what good grace I am [in] with Mariscotta; I glory more in this than anything I have in this world. I shall be pleased if you would give her my regards" (August 3, 1525, L 292). We may doubt whether this really gives Machiavelli more "glory" than anything in this world, but the submission factor is there again. There was as well the actress Barbera, with whom he began an extended affair after 1525, for whom he wrote his comedy *Clizia*, and with whom he collaborated to produce the comedy.

In addition to all these mistresses and courtesans, there was also a wife: he married in August 1501 at the age of thirty-two a certain Marietta Corsini. They had seven children, two of whom died in infancy. One letter from Machiavelli to his nephew notes simply in the midst of reporting family business: "Marietta gave birth to a baby girl who died after three days. Marietta is well" (August 4, 1513, L 217). We do not have any letters from him to Marietta, but there are letters from his friends to Machiavelli while he is away from Florence reporting on Marietta, often detailing how irritated she is at him for being away for extended periods. One friend writes: "Madonna Marietta is angry and does not want to write to you. I cannot do anything else" (November 26, 1502, L 58). Eight weeks earlier Machiavelli had told her he would be gone only one week. Three weeks after the first letter this friend writes, "Madonna Marietta is cursing God and she feels she has thrown away her body and her possessions" (December 21, 1502, L 65). Later, it is their son who writes, "Madonna Marietta reminds you to come back soon and to bring her something" (July 30, 1520, L 261).

Despite her reported annoyance at Machiavelli's frequent extended absences, there is an affectionate letter from Marietta to Machiavelli early in their marriage in which she writes about one of their newborn children; he has pale skin and a dark head of hair and looks just like Machiavelli, and to her, he is handsome (November 24, 1503, L 83). About this same child who looks like Machiavelli, a friend assures the absent Machiavelli: "Truly Madonna Marietta did not deceive you, for he is your spitting image. Leonardo da Vinci would not have done a better portrait" (November 11, 1503, L 75). Cuckoldry was not beyond the scope of friendly mocking by Machiavelli's correspondents.

The letters, then, are filled with Machiavelli the sentimental sop, wounded by the arrows of Cupid, Machiavelli the prisoner of love, Machiavelli the potential cuckold. This is hardly a Machiavellian Machiavelli, the aggressive, active man of virile strength willing to employ treachery and force to conquer those around him, ready to control others through treachery. He is the passive subject bound by his own desires to submit himself to love. Machiavelli reinforces this self-mockery in *Clizia*, written for his mistress Barbera. Appropriating the plot of a comedy from ancient Rome, he gives the characters Italian names but otherwise changes little. One of the characters, an old man, is besotted by a young girl who has grown up in his household. At the beginning of the comedy he is in competition with his son for this girl. He plots to have the girl married to one of his servants so that he can keep her from his son as well as have sexual access to her. His wise and aptly named wife, Sofronia, devises a still more cunning plot to foil her husband's plan. The husband is so embarrassed by his behavior that he submits himself to her, saying at the end of the comedy: "My dear Sofronia, do as you wish. I'm prepared not to go outside your arrangements."[4] Barbera was to play Sofronia. The name of her finally submissive husband, all of whose efforts at trickery and treachery fail miserably, is Nicomaco, that is, a brief version of Niccolò Machiavelli. The foolish man out-tricked by his wife is the alter ego of the author of the comedy. Machiavelli—so familiar, let us say, as the ancestor of contemporary theories of political realism, regularly quoted along with the Athenians of the Melian Dialogue as the exponent of power politics—seems a long way off as the female conquers the not so virile Nicomaco.

Let me turn from the women who inhabit Machiavelli's actual or imaginary life to some of those we find in the pages of his most famous writings. In contrast to the women of the letters, these women do not bind men with the fetters of Cupid. These are women who, despite their sex, deserve the adjective "Machiavellian," women who themselves conquer Fortuna through their manly boldness and daring. As models for princes, these women raise questions about divisions, about the traditional boundaries between what is male and what is female and the resources we have to conquer Fortuna.

Perhaps the most shocking and infamous—even for Machiavelli—of the women who inhabit his texts is Madonna Caterina from the town of Forli. Some conspirators in the town killed her husband, who was their lord, and took Madonna Caterina and her children hostage—but they could not capture the fortress of the city. Madonna Caterina persuaded the conspirators to allow her to enter the fortress, saying that she would deliver it to them. The conspirators, she said, might keep her children as hostages. And here let me quote Machiavelli's dramatic telling of this story: "Under this faith they let her enter it. As soon as she was inside, she reproved them from the walls for the death of her husband and threatened them with every kind of revenge. And to show that she did not care for her children, she showed them her genital parts, saying that she still had the mode for many more of them. So, short of counsel and late to perceive their error, they suffered the penalty of their lack of prudence with a perpetual exile" (*Discourses* 3.6.18).

Machiavelli makes sure to include "Madonna" before Caterina's name whenever he refers to her.

In the same chapter on conspiracies in which he records the tale of Madonna Caterina, Machiavelli writes of Epicharis, a former mistress of Nero's. Though she was complicit in a conspiracy against him, she managed to deny it effectively, causing Nero to become so confused that he did not condemn her (*Discourses* 3.6.9). Machiavelli also reports on Marcia, the mistress of the emperor Commodus, who, constrained by necessity when she discovered her name on a list of those the emperor planned to execute, fomented the conspiracy that led to Commodus's assassination (*Discourses* 3.6.10). Taking circumstances into her own hands, Marcia did not let Fortuna determine her fate.

In chapter 17 of *The Prince* Machiavelli addresses the questions of whether the prince should practice cruelty or mercy, whether it is better to be feared or to be loved. After affirming that "it is impossible for the new prince to escape a name for cruelty because new states are full of dangers," he turns to his first example in this chapter: the Carthaginian queen Dido, who, Machiavelli suggests, gives voice to Virgil when she says, "The harshness of new things and the newness of the kingdom force me to contrive such things." We all know the sad story of Dido and her ill-fated love for Aeneas, throwing herself onto the funeral pyre while he, without a backward glance, sets off to found Rome. Machiavelli, though, treats her not as the spurned and suicidal lover but as one who is a model for his assertions about the necessity for a ruler to willingly act with apparent cruelty. She is the educator not about the sweet virtues of family life—a role that might befit a woman. No, she is the resource to teach about the harsh realities of political rule, that a new prince (that is, all princes) must not care about the infamy of cruelty. We learn this first through the speech of a woman, before moving on to the "inhuman cruelty" of Hannibal (*The Prince*, chap. 17). Machiavelli does not remark on her sex; she is simply there as a model, like Moses, Cyrus, or Agathocles, to teach about the virtues of political leadership and the founding of political regimes.

In the *Discourses* Dido appears in a list that includes Aeneas as an exemplar of those constrained to abandon their fatherland, "who are not many." "They cannot use so much violence but must seize some place with art" (*Discourses* 2.8.3). Dido is learned not only in cruelty; she is learned in the art of making and maintaining confederacies. In all these cases women show daring and stamina and become models of those who could conquer Fortuna. Machiavelli's women with *virtù* escape gendered expectations and transcend gendered boundaries.

In the middle of chapter 25 of *The Prince*, on Fortuna, Machiavelli proposes an alternative mode of behavior that does not match the virile model of the *virtù* of the prince who controls the last paragraph of the chapter. Rather, the model he proposes in the middle of the chapter is a much more feminine one, or rather, let me be clear, what was for the time at which he wrote the feminine. Here he writes in a far less frequently cited passage that to conquer Fortuna the prince must learn to be fickle and know how to change with the changing times. In fact, this feminine fickleness, the ability to adapt our natures to changing times, becomes the preferred mode for the political actor, and the real problem for us—as Machiavelli sees it—is that we find it difficult to be fickle, to so easily adapt our natures to the times. Because learning this feminine fickleness is so difficult, his princes must turn as a last resort to the masculine violence of the final paragraph of the chapter. That is what they know best, or, to state it as bluntly as Machiavelli might, men do not know how to become women. They lose their states because they ignore the lessons women, who are able to transform themselves and are not imprisoned by their natures, might teach them. As Machiavelli writes of the prince, also in chapter 25: "if the times and affairs change, he is ruined because he does not change his mode of proceeding. Nor may a man be found so prudent as to know how to accommodate himself to this, whether because he cannot deviate from what nature inclines him to or also because, when one has always flourished by walking on one path, he cannot be persuaded to depart from it." And so we tend to be stuck, either as men or as women, falling prey to a Fortuna that demands flexibility, or even more than flexibility—what I shall call fluidity. The second way to conquer Fortuna requires beating and holding her down. The first way is to change our natures, to ignore the givens of nature—or to deny that there is a nature. The women of Machiavelli's work know how to be men—and how to be women. Potential princes too often know only how to be men. They must learn also to be fickle women. They must have the capacity to imagine themselves as free from the limits nature may have placed on them.

Machiavelli's women, then, by becoming like men (or by serving as models for the necessary practices of princes) capture for me the true radicalness of Machiavelli's writings. This radical quality lies not in the advice to be cruel or to break faith, not in the practical invocations about how to rule, to let the ends justify the means, but in what I from now on shall refer to as the shattering of the chain of being and fostering the permeability of the boundaries that many perceived (and still perceive) to be established by nature—or by God.

A. O. Lovejoy perhaps introduced the explicit language of a chain of being in his 1933 William James Lectures in Philosophy at Harvard in order to summarize a complex confluence of ideas, what he called "endemic assumptions" and "intellectual habits" around the central notion of a hierarchical world emanating from the divine being and descending hierarchically to the lowly levels of inanimate nature.[5] He described this metaphor as "the strict but seldom rigorously applied logic of the principle of continuity—of an infinite number of links ranging in hierarchical order from the meagerest kinds of existents, which barely escape non-existence, through 'every possible' grade up to [the most perfect being (*ens prefectissimum*)] . . . every one of them differing from that immediately above and that immediately below it by the 'least possible' degree of difference" (Lovejoy 1936, 59).

While deriving its theoretical heft from the Platonic divisions of worlds of being and becoming, the divided line of the *Republic*, and the ladder of love in the *Symposium*, this heavily laden metaphor achieves its most powerful and influential expression in the writings of a fifth-century A.D. author who has come to be known as Pseudo-Dionysisus the Areopagite, the inventor of the very word "hierarchy" (Lovejoy 1936, 3, 19). Though he applied this conception of almost infinite gradations with a clear hierarchical order assigned to the entire structure of the Church, the model spread to apply to all facets of existence. The grand hierarchical vision set each individual or natural being, from angels to the stones, on a plane above or below another. With the caveat that for the purposes of exposition I must simplify, and simplify terribly, this is a world of status that emphasizes one's place on the hierarchical chain determined by one's proximity to God. It is also a static world: one does not move within the hierarchical framework without upsetting the whole order, a finely articulated world of careful differentiation. The desire to ascend is the vice of pride. Underlying this hierarchical imagery also resides the analogical thinking of the medieval period, so that God's rule over the universe was like the king's rule over his empire, which in turn was like the father's rule in the family and like the rule of the soul over the body. This hierarchical vision was part of what Lovejoy termed the "endemic assumptions" that emerged during the Middle Ages and finds its resonance in the poetry and literature of later centuries. Each individual type had his or her place in the universe, the particular rung on the ladder or link in the chain on which one was to stand in the descent from or ascent to divine being.

How well this metaphor accorded with the practice of the time one can well question, but the literature of medieval writers resounds with it as the language of order, hierarchy, differentiation, species. It is this world—or perhaps this imagined world—that Machiavelli smashes as he brutally dismantles its structure, questions its premises, and builds a worldview that ignores just those principles at the heart of the chain of being. Machiavelli takes us in his writings—his letters and treatises, his histories and his comedies—on a journey from hierarchy to equality. This is not a gentle journey, a kind of Tocquevillian gradual spreading of equality. It is not a journey that takes us to the equal rights that dominate the political discourse of the twentieth and twenty-first centuries. It is a dismantling of an edifice built on certainty, order, and clarity of place—an edifice that was not subject to changes over time, but stood as a reflection of God's rule over the universe. Many of Machiavelli's most powerful images highlight his dismissal of the verities of the chain of being and his opening up of the world in which we live to change, movement, absence of place—and especially the disorder that arises from this dismissal.

In chapter 6 of *The Prince* Machiavelli writes of those who acquired principalities by virtue and their own arms. Their success required the "opportunity" to found their new principalities, opportunity here defined not in terms of parentage or wealth but in terms of a condition of disarray waiting for someone to appear in order to restructure it. If disorder does not exist, the prince needs to create it if he—or she—is to create the new regime that is his or hers. Machiavelli's women, I would argue, are part of his efforts to create that disarray, that shattering of the hierarchical order, that undermining the old world of a particular link on the chain. By letting women exhibit the qualities of a virile prince and urging men to imitate women in their fickleness, Machiavelli is blurring the boundaries that distinguish male from female and set each in hierarchical relation to the other.

The blurring of the boundaries between male and female is emblematic of Machiavelli's thought. We wander too between human and animal. In the letters that Machiavelli shared with his friends, filled as they are with fantastical stories, the characters he places in these stories often become, as mentioned before, a variety of animals—bulls, swans, wrens, vultures. The distinctions between human and animal dissolve, just as do those between male and female. Fluidity captures the world we live in. In a famous passage from chapter 18 of *The Prince*, Machiavelli urges us to be like—or rather be—the lion and the fox. Notice the slippage in language in the following quotation: "A prince being thus obliged to know well how to act as a beast must imitate the fox and the lion, for the lion cannot protect himself from traps, and the fox cannot defend himself from wolves. So one needs to *be* a fox to recognize snares and a lion to frighten wolves" (emphasis added). Machiavelli's point is that we can do this. We can become the fox and the lion just as in his letters his friends become bulls and swans; women can become men, and men can become women, something his friends do in his letters as well. The male does not have to be—indeed ought not to be—only virile, and the female must take on the qualities of what traditionally had been seen as masculine. He must change form as the times require, and times change as the static world of the chain of being is left far behind.

But how do we accomplish this transformation? Obviously even Machiavelli does not imagine the medical advances of the twentieth and twenty-first centuries. Rather, let me here return to chapter 15, with which I began. There Machiavelli warned, "Many have imagined republics and principalities that have never been seen or known to exist in truth." Dismissing such republics, Machiavelli appears to criticize the imagination for removing us from the experiences of our world, from what he calls the effectual truth. But if we return to his letters, whether the one in which he describes his encounter with the prostitute or his submission to an unnamed "creature" or the fanciful stories he narrates about his friends, we see a Machiavelli enmeshed in a world of the imagination, of creative restructuring of the "effectual truth" for his and his friends' amusement and education.

This homage to the imagination appears perhaps most vividly in the justly famous letter from 1513, written after his exile, in which he reports that he is writing a little work concerning principalities—how they are acquired, how they are retained, and how they are lost. He writes that after he returns home from the local inn and barroom games with their "thousand squabbles and endless abuses and vituperations," "when evening comes," he takes off his "workday clothes[,] covered as they are with mud and dirt[,] and puts on the garments of court and palace"; he then retreats into his study and crosses a threshold to converse with the ancients (December 10, 1513, L 224).

Machiavelli moves across that "threshold" in the evening from his present sorrows and the "malice of [his] fate" into an imaginary world where he converses with men long dead. He creates in this world an imaginary republic of letters where he is received solicitously by the inhabitants of that court. Leaving behind a life "cooped up among these lice," he creates in his mind a world where discourse is the only nourishment he needs, the food "for which I was born." No stomach grumbling here to remind us of the effectual truth. Engaging with the ancients in this fashion is an activity of metamorphosis: "I transfer myself into them completely." Transformed, he slips into this world of the imagination, transcending boundaries between past and present, self and other, even life and death. Machiavelli becomes both ancient and modern, "two souls," as he says, "in one body" (December 10, 1513, L 224).

In this letter, Machiavelli turns himself into other than what he is, a man caught by contemporary circumstances, confined to selling wood, eating with his household "what food this poor farm and my miserable patrimony yield," and drinking and playing games at the local inn. But after he crosses the threshold of the imagination, he inhabits the courts of the ancients, dressed in "clothes of court and palace." Only in this world of imagination can he write *The Prince*. His princes of the world, like himself in his literary works, must be able to transform themselves creatively, to imagine what is not and to expand beyond the apparent limits of the natural world. It is here that Machiavelli's women enter, for women must imagine themselves as men, and men must be able to imagine themselves as women. This is the real rebellion against nature, against hierarchy, against form that Machiavelli urges on us.

In a letter written in 1506, seven years before he wrote *The Prince*, Machiavelli told Soderini:

> The reason why different actions are sometimes equally useful and sometimes equally detrimental I do not know . . . [but] I shall be presumptuous enough to give you my view . . . just as nature has created men with different faces, so she has created them with different intellects and imaginations. As a result, each man behaves according to his own pattern of intellect and imagination. . . . The man who matches his way of doing things with the conditions of the times is successful . . . because times and affairs often change—both in general and in particular—and because men change neither their imaginations nor their ways of doing things accordingly, it turns out that a man has good fortune at one time and bad fortune at another. And truly, anyone wise enough to adapt to and understand the times and pattern of events would always have good fortune or would always keep himself from bad fortune; and it would come to be that the wise man could control the stars and fates. But such wise men do not exist: in the first place men are shortsighted; in the second place, they are unable to master their own natures. (September 13–21, 1506, L 121)

Years before he writes his letter of December 10, 1513, describing his imaginary discourses with the ancients, and years before his chapter on Fortuna in *The Prince*, Machiavelli recognized the need for a fluid human nature to master our natures, though he feared that humans were incapable of such transformations. *The Prince* urges us to go beyond the confines of traditional forms, to see the self as a part of, rather than in opposition to, this fluidity on which depends the re-creation of our world. Machiavelli's women become guides to this fluidity of nature. The art of politics entails imagining what we are not, and in the modern world that Machiavelli envisions for us, that means transcending the boundaries that any natural order may impose, initially by shattering the chain of being. Attending to the women in Machiavelli's writings helps us see a Machiavelli, I suggest, far more radical than one who claims that we must look to ends rather than to means, who advocates realism in the political world. It is a man who, by suggesting that men become women and women men, confronts us with a world in which we must make our own boundaries, define our own natures, and accept the never-ending challenge of constant self-transformation—an imagination that takes us beyond the effectual truth of what we see with our eyes.

Machiavelli ends his long letter of December 10, 1513, with this curious suggestion: "Whoever has been honest and faithful for forty-three years, as I have, is unable to change his nature; my poverty is a witness to my loyalty and honesty." Does this mean that Machiavelli is urging on others what he doubts he himself can accomplish? Or is this his ultimate deceptive stance as the man who never said what he believed or believed what he said? I prefer the latter reading and find myself—along with Machiavelli's other readers—always caught in a world of ambiguity and uncertainty about Machiavelli and about not only the status, but even the existence, of his women. It is that ambiguous world that enables us to dismiss the chains of the chain of being and opens up the frightening prospect of an unlimited imagination unbound by any natural hierarchy or order that Machiavelli bequeaths to us in the modern world.

CHAPTER 5

Machiavelli and the Business of Politics

DAVID WOOTTON

There have long been debates about whether Machiavelli represents something entirely new in political thinking. His own position on this question was profoundly ambiguous: he opens the *Discourses* with a reference to the discovery of new worlds, but then turns to talk only of the imitation of the ancients.[1] We cannot, of course, answer the question of Machiavelli's originality just by reading Machiavelli; we have to compare him to his predecessors, his contemporaries, and his successors. What makes that enterprise a little more difficult than it might be is that later authors, convinced that Machiavelli was responsible for everything that was new and important, tended to take it for granted that the ideas that mattered to *them* were already to be found in *him*. Sometimes they were right about this; but often they were wrong, and we have tended to go wrong with them.

What I want to do in this chapter is make an effort to separate out Machiavelli from Machiavellism by exploring a number of key concepts—the state, interest, reason of state—and asking how far they are Machiavelli's concepts and how far they are, rather, Machiavellian concepts, developments of his way of thinking. Part of my purpose is to get a better sense of the historical Machiavelli; but I am also interested in how the key concepts with which political thinking was conducted in the seventeenth century, by Hobbes and by Locke, and to a large degree is still conducted, came into existence. For where Machiavelli was not responsible for the key innovations, it becomes important to know who was. Thus I hope to place Machiavelli's achievement in a new perspective. And I plan to show that it is in Machiavellism, rather than in Machiavelli himself, that we find the beginning of what we think of as a characteristically modern problem (it is sometimes called "the Adam Smith problem"), the problem of how to reconcile rational, interested behavior with morality, virtue, and justice, which only becomes a problem when the two have already been rendered irreconcilable.

Unresolved Definitions of State

Shakespeare's play *The Tempest* was first performed in 1611. It opens with a shipwreck; in the second scene Prospero, the deposed duke of Milan, explains to his daughter Miranda how they came, twelve years before, to be expelled from their homeland and to be cast ashore on an island. Prospero explains that he had put his brother Antonio in charge of the management of "my state." As a result, Prospero, caught up in his occult researches, grew a stranger to "my state." So Antonio, as he became expert in the techniques of government,

> set all hearts i' the state
> To what tune pleased his ear; that now he was
> The ivy which had hid my princely trunk,
> And suck'd my verdure out on't. (184–87)

Eventually, inevitably, Antonio seized power and made himself "Absolute Milan." The word "state" occurs three times in this passage, in which Prospero, and Shakespeare through him, sketch a picture of the functioning of a Renaissance princedom: the state is something the prince manages; it is something separate from the person of the prince, for the prince can become a stranger to it; and the state consists of people whose hearts can be alienated. As Prospero's brother Antonio himself says later in the play, when plotting another usurpation, such people

take suggestion as a cat laps milk;
They'll tell the clock to any business that
We say befits the hour. (288–90)

What is "the state" here? In Shakespeare the term slides between at least three different meanings. It can mean the territory and subjects ruled over by a prince or government; it can mean the authority exercised by the ruler, "th' outward face of royalty"; it can mean—indeed, it generally means—the political system or regime through which power is exercised and the people who make up that system. Thus at one moment it is Antonio, who has become the state, who manipulates the people; at another it is Antonio who manipulates the people, who are the state. We can find exactly the same sorts of slippage in a contemporary work, Sir Walter Raleigh's *Maxims of State* (published posthumously in 1642). And we find the same slippages between these three senses in Machiavelli and in all the authors who discuss the state before Hobbes.[2]

But in Raleigh there is a fourth usage, which goes back fifty years or so: the word "state" is used to refer to the different types of constitution, for the word "constitution" in this sense had not yet come into existence, and there were problems with the two traditional sets of alternatives: *polis*, *urbs*, or *città*, terms that referred to city-states, and *respublica* or commonwealth, terms that were beginning to be used, in the wake of Machiavelli, to exclude monarchies rather than to include them (for monarchies had once been a type of republic, since the word "republic" originally referred to any legitimate political system). Thus we find authors in the 1560s and 1570s writing about "a princely state" and "an absolute state," and even before that of "a mixed state."[3] Machiavelli, and indeed Dante before him, had written about free states, but now the word "state" was being used more generally in place of the Aristotelian concept of a polity.

Because of these shifting meanings it is often wrong to translate Machiavelli's word *stato* as "state"—while it is often right to translate his terms "cities" and "republics" as "states." Sometimes by *stato* Machiavelli and his contemporaries mean something like politics in general, as when Machiavelli says that the French have not understood *lo stato*; sometimes they mean those things which the state controls—the territory, the subjects—as when Francesco Vettori says that the pope wants to ensure that the Church does not lose *stato* unless what is lost is given to the members of his family; but generally they mean the agent that does the controlling, the regime. In an earlier usage, people had been "in the state." Thus Agnolo Pandolfini asked, "What is it to be in the regime [in *istato*]? What use will you gain from it: . . . to be able to be overbearing, to crush, to rob with impunity?" "O mad, arrogant, haughty, avaricious tyrants! They cannot bear for others to be their equals; they do not want to live without crushing and stomping on the weakest . . . that's why they want power [*lo stato*]."[4] In other words, to be in the regime is like being a member of the nomenclatura, or what Orwell called "the inner party." Politics is about getting into the state and staying there.

In Machiavelli's eyes the state exists to serve the purposes of the political leaders. The state belongs to them, they acquire it, and they benefit from it. This view of the state is, however, somewhat at odds with Machiavelli's conception of the rationality of political action. Machiavelli assumes that rulers can act rationally, and to act rationally is to act in the interests of *lo stato*. Thus Machiavelli's friend Vettori, in their famous correspondence, insists that we will never be able to understand what politicians are really up to. "I know that this king [Ferdinand] and these princes are men like you and me, and I know that we do many things carelessly, and even some things that are very important to us; and we must think that they do likewise." The whole point of Machiavelli's idealized prince, however, is that he *will not* act carelessly, and consequently everything he does will be intended to strengthen *lo stato*. When Machiavelli, against Vettori, insists that politics is a rational activity which can be interpreted by getting at the underlying thinking of the participants, he is assuming that politicians do not just cash in their chips after a win; unlike merchants, they do not retire to a country estate: they keep playing. The interests they serve, as a consequence, are not their own but those of the state. Like the king, the state never dies and never retires. The prince, when he is acting as a prince, should not be a man like you or me, but a rational actor.[5]

There is a literature that tries to identify the moment at which the modern conception of the state is born, but this seems a somewhat futile exercise, particularly when it concentrates on the state as an abstract idea, for the abstract idea of the state is, like Shakespeare's "outward face of royalty," simply a reworking of the very old idea of the king's two bodies—his natural body, which grew old, sick, and died, and his mystical body, of which it could be said that it could never die.[6] Thus in the traditional cry "The king is dead, long live the king!" the first half refers to the natural body of the old king, the second to the mystical body inherited by the new king.

What is more important is to see that the word "state" functions as a synonym or substitute for a number of other words: thus in Machiavelli the alternative terms are city, republic, government, and prince, whereas in Shakespeare they are royalty, government, power, and people. The importance of the idea of the state before Hobbes, I would suggest, is not what it means, but rather the very slipperiness of its meaning. It enables the speaker to slip back and forth between the ruler and the ruled, the common good, the constitution, and the government, between legitimate authority and power politics, including within it all those mechanisms that make it possible for the ruler to rule. In other words, the term "the state" encapsulates the whole field of politics in both the classical, or normative, and the modern, or Machiavellian, senses of that word, but that field is seen from the point of view of the ruler. *L'arte dello stato*, the enterprise of ruling, is important to Machiavelli precisely because he has no word that corresponds to the noun "politics."[7] "The state" stands for the politics of ruling, or power politics, and for the institutions and resources that make that politics possible. It is because the word needs to slip and slide in its meaning that contemporaries never pause to define it, never choose to concentrate on one meaning at the expense of the others. We might take "gender" as an example of a word whose importance for our own intellectual culture derives precisely from the slipperiness of its meaning. Thus we might say that Machiavelli was engaged in "state studies" in the same slightly puzzling and ambiguous way that we now engage in "gender studies."

Machiavelli did not invent the language of the state, but it is not going too far, I think, to say that he invented "state studies." Just as gender studies is engaged in a questioning of the traditional concepts of masculinity and femininity, so Machiavelli's state studies was engaged in a questioning of the traditional concepts of justice and virtue, the normative framework within which politics was supposed to be conducted.

Defining "Reason of State"

Machiavelli's term for "state studies" was *l'arte dello stato*. In later writers this became *ragione di stato* or reason of state, and the term was particularly associated with Giovanni Botero's *Ragione di stato*, first published in 1589. In Botero as in Machiavelli the state is conceived as something you make or build, as a shoemaker makes shoes. Politicians build states; and to have a state is to have a resource that only other rulers have. Politics is thus about creating, acquiring, and retaining states, just as warfare is about creating, acquiring, and retaining armies. Of course once you have an army or a state there is a range of things you can do with it—you can use it to acquire personal wealth, or glory, or you can reinvest in a bigger state or a more powerful army. States and armies are, like money, means to an end; and the end is determined by those who control them.

Botero, unlike Machiavelli, does have the word "politics"; this is a crucial difference between them—indeed, Botero refers to what he calls "modern politics," meaning the unscrupulous politics of Machiavelli.[8] (It is precisely because Botero presumes that Machiavelli is the founder of modern politics that he is blind to his own significant contribution.) In *The Prince* Machiavelli avoids even the adjective "political" because for him it necessarily refers to ancient politics, good government, the politics grounded in distributive justice advocated by Aristotle. In the *Discourses* he does write about *il vivere politico* (bk. 1, chap. 55), which is precisely the best form of political life.

There is another word missing, or almost missing, from Machiavelli's vocabulary, one that we tend to assume he uses, just as we tend to assume he uses the word "politics." Machiavelli is familiar with the word "interest"—he uses it in his diplomatic correspondence, and it is used by those issuing him his instructions—but he never uses it in *The Prince* or the *Discourses*.[9] Why not? Because the term is of no use to him. On the one hand, it is an obvious truism that politicians have an interest in acquiring and holding power. On the other, different politicians set out, and different political systems are set up, to use power for very different purposes. Venice seeks stability, whereas Rome sought expansion. In Rome conflict was tolerated, even encouraged, while other states seek harmony. Some rulers want power at any price; others want glory, and are even prepared to transfer their own power to a republic in order to acquire it. Thus Machiavelli writes not about interests but about the good and the useful—always with the implication that one could specify "good for what" and "useful for whom." Of course all rulers and political systems have an interest in survival, which is why warfare must be their primary preoccupation. But again and again Machiavelli insists that glory is the true goal of the politician, and glory can be irretrievably lost if power becomes one's sole preoccupation, whereas it is entirely possible to win glory in defeat, as Hannibal did.[10] It is this recognition that individuals always have more than one goal, and that different states have different goals, that makes Machiavelli something other than a Machiavellian, and his politics different from what Botero calls "modern politics."

The situation is quite different for Botero. He assumes that the only states that count are princely, and thus they all have similar interests. And he wants to argue that honesty, piety, and prosperity are the foundations of a sound policy: the interests of the ruler, the state, and the subjects coincide in the pursuit of common goals. Thus politics can be guided by interest because rulers are mistaken if they think they have to choose between conflicting values, and states are mistaken if they think there are different paths to success. It is a puzzling feature of Botero's attempt to tame what he thinks of as Machiavellian politics that he ends up more Machiavellian than Machiavelli himself—that is to say, everything he says can be presented as a policy for the pursuit of enlightened self-interest. "Virtue" and "glory," so important to Machiavelli, become irrelevant, because they coincide with, are indistinguishable from, cold calculation. Botero arguing with his opponents is like a rule utilitarian arguing with an act utilitarian. The act utilitarian says, "Do what works best here and now." The rule utilitarian says, "Think of the long-term benefits of having rules." They are both utilitarians, just as Botero is every bit as much a theorist of reason of state as are his cynical and irreligious opponents. Indeed, we may say that the central paradox of Botero's book is that it is an attack on reason of state, written within the logic of reason of state.

Because the only goal of the state, according to reason of state theorists, is survival, everything that concerns it can be reduced to a question of interest. As the duc de Rohan put it in the 1630s, "Princes rule the people, and interest rules princes."[11] Interest is, for reason of state theorists, what the state is about, full stop. And this is true because for them the state has become an impersonal entity; individuals want glory, salvation, wealth, pleasure, but states want one thing and one thing only—power, which makes possible survival. The state, by pursuing its one and only interest, survival, acquires power, in the same way that the businessman, by pursuing profit, acquires wealth. Botero insists that he is reintroducing normative questions into politics, against the followers of Machiavelli and Tacitus, who have excluded all such questions from political discussion. But by insisting that interests and values coincide he is actually legitimizing the exclusion of normative questions from politics, while for Machiavelli "virtue" and "glory" had always been something quite different from, and superior to, mere success.

Of course not everyone accepted either cynical Machiavellism or Botero's superficially respectable reworking of Machiavellian themes. Boccalini claimed that free citizens produce the most effective states because they identify with the state they are called on to defend. Boccalini thus presented the Dutch as embodying a new type of politics, one directly opposed to the reason of state advocated by princes; his politics represented an updated version of Machiavelli's.[12]

Reason of State After Machiavelli

Thus the language of reason of state is fundamentally different from Machiavelli's in that it is a language of politics and of interests—and the two are paired because politics is the pursuit of interests, and interests are rational objectives—as the duc de Rohan put it, "interest never lies," which is to say that one should always do what it says. The term "interest," which originated in Italy, moved more slowly northward across Europe than the terms "state" and "politics." "Interest" seems to have been new in French in 1588, and in English it became established only after 1640; its spread marks a preoccupation with power politics instead of good government, a preoccupation that was still alien to Machiavelli, and even to Raleigh.

With Botero, the language of modern politics, the language of "states," "politics," and "interests," begins to take shape. And with this new language comes a new view of rational action; understanding this places us in a position where we can begin to consider the history of the term "reason of state." My contention is simple: we have lost sight of the origins of reason of state, and we have forgotten the original meaning of the word "reason" in the context of the state.

Machiavelli's friend Francesco Guicciardini is conventionally said to be the first to have written about reason of state.[13] His actual phrase, or rather the phrase of his spokesperson in a dialogue, is "ragione ed usu degli stati."[14] What he is discussing is the tactics Florence should employ in any war with Pisa: all Pisan soldiers should be killed or else held prisoner until the war had been successfully concluded with the capture of the city of Pisa itself. Such behavior would be contrary to the "usu delle guerre di Italia," according to which prisoners were constantly being exchanged and ransomed. Guicciardini's phrase is surely a reworking of a phrase of Caesar's, "ratio atque usus belli" (*De bello gallico* 4.1), and Guicciardini writes elsewhere of the "ragione di guerra." Let us not worry for a moment about what "ratio" means here; what matters is that reason of state is an extension of reason of war.[15]

The second key usage of the phrase is in Giovanni della Casa.[16] He was delivering a speech to Charles V soon after 1547, calling on him to return Piacenza, which the emperor had seized in the course of a war. Della Casa insisted that *ragion civile* required the return of the territory, even if the false reason of state often advocated by cynical politicians might tempt the emperor to hang on to it. Again, we are dealing with an extension of wartime behavior into a peacetime situation, but it is clear that by *ragion civile* Casa means "civil law," just as *ragione canonica* means Church law, and just as references in Latin texts to the *ius belli*, the law of war, are translated as *ragion di guerra*. So *ragion* can mean law, and *ragion di stato* means here something like "international law"—although that is not what it means in later texts.

Translation is a difficult business because words in one language do not have a one-to-one correspondence with words in another language; one word often has several meanings; and words change their meaning over time. We come across *ragione di stato, ratio status, raison d'état,* reason of state, and it is easy to assume that there is some sort of common meaning that stretches across these four languages, and that the four terms are effectively interchangeable. But in their understanding of "reason" Italian and Latin are different from French and English. In Italian, *ragionare* can just mean to talk; sometimes it means to reason or debate; sometimes to bargain or negotiate. In one letter Machiavelli describes how, acting on behalf of Guicciardini, he has cautiously entered into negotiations about a betrothal and a dowry. The word is *ragionare* (August 17, 1525). Talking (*ragionare*) sometimes ends with a deal being done. And in an often-quoted letter to Vettori (April 9, 1513), Machiavelli says that because he is no good at talking about the wool business, or the silk business, or about profit and loss, he sticks to talking about politics (*ragionare dello stato*)—the implication is that talking politics is a form of talking shop. This helps us, I think, get a feel for the way in which *ragionare* implies something more than mere reasoning.

In Renaissance Italian, *una ragione* is also the term for both an account book and a business enterprise.[17] You can invest in *una ragione*, in which case you own part of the business. *Ragionare* carries with it the suggestion of bargaining and talking shop because *ragione* simply means "business." It is thus perfectly reasonable to translate the phrase *ragione di stato* as "the business of politics." And of course a business is an impersonal entity which has interests; its overriding interest lies in making profits and avoiding losses. If you can have a silk business or a wool business, you can also have a politics business, and the rulers of Florence, the Medici, being bankers, would have found it straightforward to apply business metaphors to politics.

Let us go back to Caesar's phrase, *ratio atque usus belli*. According to the standard Latin dictionary, Lewis and Short, *ratio* can mean a business matter, a transaction, a business; it can also mean a reckoning, an account, a computation, as well as a reason, law, or proof. The dictionary proposes to translate *ratio atque usus belli* as "the art and practice of war," but here too *ratio* may carry the implication that war is a business or an enterprise. Once you have embarked on the enterprise of war, certain things follow: you may have to lay waste to the countryside, for example, in order to deny food to the enemy, even if it means the peasants will starve. That is how armies go about their business.

So I want to suggest that we have now distinguished three distinct but often overlapping meanings of the word *ragione*—it can mean "reason," it can mean "law," and it can mean "business." The logic of war, the law of war, and the tradecraft of war all tell you that you can massacre the inhabitants of a town that has held out against a siege; but the law tells you what you may do, while the logic and the tradecraft tell you what you would be sensible to do. Reason of state, from Botero on, does not tell you what you may do; it tells you what you must do if you can think straight. "Reason of state" means the logic of power politics.

Reading Machiavelli during the wars of religion, what politicians and political commentators found was an advocate of reason of state. Is it better for a ruler to be feared or loved? Should a ruler rely on fortresses or on the loyalty of his people? Is it all right to lie and even murder to achieve one's political goals? These were questions that seemed to arise out of a systematic instrumentalism concerned solely with political survival. But reading Machiavelli this way was a form of misreading. The questions Machiavelli asked were designed to establish what you could do and still win glory, honor, reputation.

We might say that Machiavelli, like Tacitus, understood the business of politics, but he refused to think of politics as just a business. Consequently Machiavelli does not write about *ragione di stato* or *ragione di guerra*, any more than he uses the language of interest except when writing diplomatic reports. Politics for him, and war for him, are not mere businesses: they are opportunities to win glory and renown. If you begin to think of them as mere businesses, then you will never be capable of glorious actions. My suggestion, then, is that Machiavelli is playing, quite deliberately, with a profound ambiguity when he says he cannot talk (*ragionare*) about profit and loss, he can only talk (*ragionare*) about the state—for he is both suggesting that talking about the state is very like talking about profit and loss and maintaining that when he talks about the state, he is not talking only about profit and loss, even if other people may be.

So far we have learned that the model for reason of state is *ragione di guerra*—the law of war, the logic of war, the enterprise of war. The ambiguities we find in early references to reason of state simply reflect the ambiguities that already exist in the concept of *ragione di guerra*. As reason of state moved from city-state to monarchy, from Italy to France, those ambiguities dropped away. Reason of state became about making rational choices under conditions of uncertainty.[18] But this simply reinforced the way in which political behavior was comparable to economic behavior—one maximized profit, the other power, but both could be conceptualized in terms of interests.

Machiavelli's Influence on Hobbes

Machiavelli's central claim to fame as a political philosopher—a claim he makes for himself, as well as one we make for him—is that he turned away from idealistic discussions of how politics ought to be conducted to concentrate on a realistic study of what works.[19] Politics, for Machiavelli, is about gaining and keeping power, and power is something the politician must pursue relentlessly, just as the Hobbesian individual pursues pleasure. As far as Machiavelli is concerned, both states and individuals are endlessly acquisitive: states seek power, but individuals seek wealth, pleasure, and status. I think one could reasonably say that Machiavelli's vision of the state provides the model for Hobbes's conception of the individual in the state of nature, for states are always in a state of nature with regard to each other, and indeed with regard to their subjects.[20] Thus Hobbes remakes the individual in the image of the Machiavellian state—in this respect he goes beyond Machiavelli. The individual in Hobbes has only one goal, pleasure, while in Machiavelli he still had several, and one of these was still virtue (even though Machiavelli's understanding of virtue was entirely Roman, and not at all Christian).

So in Hobbes, following the example of Machiavelli but going beyond him, we have two visions of the endless pursuit of something that can be seized moment by moment but never securely grasped—the individual pursuing pleasure and the state pursuing power. In both cases rational calculation should help one achieve the best possible outcome, although in both cases decision making has to be carried out under conditions of pervasive uncertainty. The politician is haunted by what Machiavelli calls *fortuna*, the knowledge that power never endures indefinitely; and the Hobbesian individual is haunted by the prospect of death. There is, in short, a fundamental symmetry between the logic of power and the logic of pleasure; both logics are indifferent to questions of value; and both logics can lead to short-term rewards but no enduring security (which is why happiness can only be pursued, never secured).

But it would obviously be wrong to say that Machiavelli and Hobbes stand for the same things. After all, it was with the ancients that Machiavelli conversed when he removed his workaday clothes and sat down at his desk; while as far as Hobbes was concerned it was this reading of classical texts which had undermined political authority and prepared the ground for the English Civil War.[21] And when Hobbes looked back it was Galileo, not Machiavelli, whom he hailed as the greatest philosopher of all time; Machiavelli and Galileo may have had in common their admiration for Lucretius, but Machiavelli could have no sense of what Galileo would accomplish.[22] Hobbes wanted political science to be deductive, not, as it was for Machiavelli, an extrapolation from experience; and he wanted it to demonstrate the emptiness of the classical conception of liberty, not, as it still did for Machiavelli, its profound significance.

Moreover, one of the central purposes of *Leviathan* was to address the claims asserted by Christians to have a right, or indeed an obligation, to interfere in politics, claims that had been intensified by the Protestant and Catholic Reformations. Machiavelli had watched Savonarola in action, but he knew nothing of Luther and Loyola. He had lived through invasions and civil conflicts, but he could not imagine the wars of religion which, over the course of a century, were to engulf France, Germany, the Netherlands, and the British Isles, and which would eventually result in the decline of both Spain and the Italian states. Nor could he imagine how these conflicts would give rise to the prototypical modern states, the states of Richelieu and of Cromwell.

If we want to understand the gulf that separates Hobbes from Machiavelli, a good starting point is, once again, *The Tempest*. Shakespeare was inspired to write *The Tempest* by the story of the wreck of the *Sea Venture* off the island of Bermuda in 1609.[23] The *Sea Venture* was carrying a new governor, Sir Thomas Gates, to Virginia. After the wreck Gates faced a mutiny: Why, many of the crew wanted to know should they continue to obey their governor? Had not his authority gone down with the ship? Might they not now choose their own commanders? Why should they sail on to Virginia, when Bermuda itself was so delightful, especially as the whole island could be theirs? (Andrew Marvell, in his painfully beautiful poem "Bermudas," which was based, as loosely as Shakespeare's *Tempest*, on the same event, was later to describe the island as an earthly paradise.) Gates managed to regain control, have two ships built from scratch, and sail on to Jamestown, but the story of the wreck presented in a new form two questions that were far from new: Why do we obey authority? And what makes for a good life? It was, in miniature, a foreshadowing of the English Civil War and the American Revolution; and Shakespeare's Prospero, who rules over his island by the unscrupulous use of an irresistible magic power, is, in his unchecked supremacy, more than a Thomas Gates, rather a precursor of Hobbes's Leviathan.

In *The Tempest* the question of what makes for a good life is put by Gonzalo, in a speech derived from Montaigne's essay "Of Cannibals":

> Had I plantation of this isle, my lord,—
> . . . .
> And were the king on't, what would I do?
> . . . .
> I' the commonwealth I would by contraries
> Execute all things; for no kind of traffic
> Would I admit; no name of magistrate;
> Letters should not be known; riches, poverty,
> And use of service, none; contract, succession,
> Bourn, bound of land, tilth, vineyard, none;
> No use of metal, corn, or wine, or oil;

No occupation; all men idle, all;
And women too, but innocent and pure;
No sovereignty;—
. . . .
All things in common nature should produce
Without sweat or endeavour: treason, felony,
Sword, pike, knife, gun, or need of any engine,
Would I not have; but nature should bring forth,
Of its own kind, all foison, all abundance,
To feed my innocent people.
. . . .
I would with such perfection govern, sir,
To excel the golden age. (851–78)

Thus Gonzalo would be a king without sovereignty, governing a people who would be prosperous without labor or private property. The Machiavellian problems that we have been discussing—the problems of politics and self-interest—would cease to exist. But of course this solution is no solution; Gonzalo contradicts himself as he speaks, and after the tempest all the temporary inhabitants of Prospero's island return to normal life, just as the crew of the *Sea Venture* eventually reached Virginia. The good life lies outside their and our grasp.

In *Leviathan* Hobbes explained why we should obey authority, but he insisted that there was no answer to the question of what makes for a good life. "For there is no such *finis ultimus* nor *summum bonum* as is spoken of in the books of the old moral philosophers" (chap. 11). Virtue, the life lived according to nature (as recommended by the Stoics), the *ataraxia* or freedom from perturbation of the Epicureans, the intellectual contemplation of the Aristotelian philosopher—all these are dismissed. We engage, of necessity, in the endless pursuit of those experiences we desire, a pursuit interrupted only by death. It is possible to make some prudential calculations while engaging in this pursuit, but no one can say that mountaineering is better than stock car racing, or that philosophy is better than savoring fine wine. Hobbes himself desired philosophical knowledge; but he did not conclude that philosophers have some special insight into the purpose of life or that the philosophical life is the best life.

There is something odd, for us now, about Hobbes's vision of the world: it seems simultaneously right and wrong, true and false, perceptive and deceptive. On the one hand, Hobbes's fundamental subjectivism seems incontestable: each individual must choose for himself or herself what pleasures to pursue. And on the other, many of us want to believe that John Stuart Mill was right to insist that poetry is better than pushpin. In other words, the Hobbesian emphasis on pleasure throws into question our ability to make qualitative judgments, but we cannot dispense with them. We all talk a language of values and morals, but since Hobbes it has been difficult to see how to ground that language outside pleasure and pain, suffering and happiness. Locke, for example, for all his emphasis on rights, acknowledges that in the end right and wrong must be reducible to questions of pleasure and pain. And if, like Hume, we set out to restate moral questions as questions of expediency, then it is hard to escape the feeling that something important has slipped through the net as a result of redefining virtues as interests.

So too, it has come to seem self-evident that the pursuit of happiness is the purpose of life, but what is happiness, beyond a mere succession of pleasures? The difficulty of answering these questions, which define the culture we live in, was brilliantly analyzed by Alasdair MacIntyre in *After Virtue*, which appeared in 1981.[24]

MacIntyre's claim was simple: we can no longer *do* moral philosophy because we have no sense of an independent realm of value, aside from pleasure and pain. We are all, whether we like it or not, infected with Hobbism. The ship of virtue has been wrecked on the rocks of pleasure, and we have no idea how to make her seaworthy again. MacIntyre's own solution to this problem was to convert to Catholicism; Peter, not pleasure, was to be his rock.

MacIntyre begins *After Virtue* by defining what he calls "the Enlightenment project," a project which, it turns out, begins with Machiavelli. There are some obvious ways in which we can make sense of the idea that Machiavelli invents the Enlightenment project. We have, for example, his manuscript copy of Lucretius, written throughout in his own hand, and there seems no reason to doubt that he found in Lucretius his personal philosophy, a philosophy grounded in the rejection of all religious explanations for the human condition.[25] The Enlightenment project, we might say, is the project to construct a modern Epicureanism, one in which *ataraxia* is replaced by happiness. But it would be wrong to concentrate solely on the moral dimension of the Enlightenment project; for the answers to our two questions—why obey authority, and what is the good life?—are inevitably interlinked. It is in political philosophy, MacIntyre implies, that the Enlightenment project had its origins.

The Business of Politics and the Pursuit of Glory

In this chapter I have been looking at the pursuit of power and pleasure in the Renaissance and beyond, into the Enlightenment. We have seen that Machiavelli is in one sense both the architect of reason of state and the founder of the Enlightenment project; but in another sense he is opposed to what Botero calls modern politics, in that he still hankers after virtue and glory. My reading of Machiavelli is encapsulated in the suggestion that we must understand his remark that he can only reason about the state, not about profit and loss, in two conflicting ways—he means to say both that politics is a business, his business, and at the same time that it is something more than a mere business.

As the term *ragione* moved north, to the Savoy of Botero, the France of Richelieu, the England of Hobbes, the word "reason" lost its original connotation, its link to the world of account books and business investments. As a result, nobody quite knew what sort of reason "reason of state" was meant to be. Guicciardini, right at the beginning, understood that it was a way of saying, in the words of Michael Corleone in *The Godfather*, "It's not personal, Sonny, it's strictly business." But for Machiavelli, I have tried to suggest, politics really was personal; it was never strictly business. As he sees it, politicians do not exist to serve the state; rather, the state exists to serve politicians.

Machiavelli knew that these two options do not exhaust the possibilities. It often seems as though, to adapt Rohan's dictum, the state rules over the people, politicians rule the state, and interest rules the politicians; but in the best states it must be the people who control the politicians, and their interests which direct the state. Machiavelli's true legacy, his most signal achievement, was to combine two seemingly irreconcilable ways of thinking about politics, to be both the supreme realist and always, even when writing a handbook for princes, an idealist. This double understanding is always difficult to sustain; it is all too easy to slide into the contradictions that undermine Gonzalo's speech even as he utters it. Machiavelli remains the best person to read to understand the difficulties of combining realism and idealism when thinking about politics, and to find out how one might overcome them.

It is precisely this tension that his Machiavellian successors sought to eliminate from political discourse, and which Locke sought to restore by insisting on "this Fundamental, Sacred, and unalterable Law of *Self-Preservation*" (*Second Treatise* §149). In doing so he was reintroducing into normative politics the principles of *ragione di guerra* and turning them against those of *ragione di stato*, which had sought to render the people passive, submissive, and obedient. Locke's theory of the law of nature is an account of how easily the people can find themselves in a state of war with their rulers; for Locke the state has become an entity whose powers must be limited and restrained, and rebellion is the last resort by which the people regain control over the state when its powers are used against them. In his famous essay "The Liberty of the Ancients Compared with That of the Moderns" (1819), Benjamin Constant insisted that the ancients had no conception of citizens having rights that could be exercised *against* the state. Nor did Machiavelli, Bodin, Botero, and Hobbes (except insofar as he acknowledged an inalienable right of self-defense). In that crucial respect, they are all premodern, not modern. Thus in order to understand Machiavelli we need to keep in mind at all times that he is both the last of the ancients and the first of the moderns, which is to say that we can never understand him if we read him in isolation, without comparing him to his predecessors and successors.[26]

CHAPTER 6

Machiavelli and Machiavellianism

DAVID C. HENDRICKSON

Niccolò Machiavelli is best known to the world not as a person but as a concept. "Machiavellian" is an adjective we are all familiar with. It may today be used far from its place of origin to apply to business or personal relationships, but it was in the sausage factory of politics that it received its birth.

In politics, it meant a doctrine of political success, by means however foul. It embraced oath breaking, dissimulation, assassination, and other such methods as were au courant in the fetid atmosphere of the Italian state system circa 1500. Machiavellism was, according to one of its most important chroniclers, "the infamous doctrine that, in national behaviour, even unclean methods are justified, when it is a question of winning or of keeping the power which is necessary for the State. It is the picture of Man, stripped of all transcendent good qualities, left alone on the battlefield to face the daemonic forces of Nature, who now feels himself possessed too of a daemonic natural strength and returns blow for blow."[1]

In the shadings of political demonology, Machiavellism falls well short of Nazism or Bolshevism in its connotations of utter wrongdoing. Providence has evidently desired to show that the doctrine of progress is an illusion, and has introduced these recent examples to confuse the hopeful and test their faith. Machiavellism used to be first among equals in the literature of political abuse; with these more recent examples in mind, it might even have some pretensions to respectability.

In fact, it always did so, at least among the great, though they were not, as Machiavelli recommended, keen to advertise that fact. Machiavellism prefigured the doctrine of reason of state, allowing for a code of morality for statesmen much less exacting than that required for ordinary mortals. That underhanded means might be necessary to preserve the great human communities we call states was not as terrible a doctrine as that an individual man might do anything he pleased; there was a greater force to the state's discretion than to any individual's (though also, it is necessary to add, greater opportunity for abuse). Still, if excuses must be sought for acts that pass beyond the law, the state could make a claim for latitude that no individual could make for himself; even those who rejected the further reaches of Machiavellism could see the sense in that.

By common reputation, Machiavelli taught the doctrine that the end justifies the means. That his ends were sacred, embracing the glory of a *patria* for which he was willing to forfeit his soul, can be entered in his defense, but the users of the term "Machiavellism" are not really interested in the fine biographical details of Niccolò Machiavelli, a diplomat in the service of the Florentine Republic from 1498 to 1512, the author whose most famous books were published after his death, there to await their enrollment on the *Index Librorum Prohibitorum*. Whoever and whatever he was, the term "Machiavellian" means something that soars far beyond the details of his life and is even semidetached from the message of his books: it connotes not only an underhanded approach, a willingness to countenance any means, but also the idea that the purposes of the Machiavellian actor are to be condemned as malign as well.

It would, however, be impossible to say for sure whether the foul breath of Machiavellism puts the wind in the sails of our statesmen, because it is of the essence of Machiavellism, if you are a Machiavellian, to denounce the doctrine yourself as an infamous reproach against decency. Frederick the Great did that, right about the time he swallowed Silesia.[2] That world in which men and women speak of religion and duty and morality is the world of appearances; deep down, you are supposed to think what you really think and do what you must do. In this conception, the world of appearances is a thing to be manipulated in accordance with the pieties of a given day, and no sort of guide to action.

Probably Machiavelli's most startling contribution to political thought was this discovery of the gap between profession and practice, how there existed a broad canvas of political calculation behind the glossy paint supplied by conventional morality. To understand politics, you had to see this; if you were in politics, you needed especially to see it, for it was the key to your survival. If you lived only in the world of profession, you were done for in practice.

Of course, the ancients knew that: there was a long tradition of reason of state in antiquity, but it had been buried and forgotten when civilization fell into a deep coma after Rome was sacked and its inheritance was scattered. Machiavelli played a leading role in the recovery of that inheritance. History knows this grand awakening as the Renaissance, the glasnost of the fifteenth and sixteenth centuries. No one in that era more intrepidly explored the implications of Roman history than Machiavelli. Here was a newly discovered civilization from a buried past that appeared to Machiavelli and his contemporaries to have done "whatever there was to do, in philosophical speculation, political action or cultural achievement." When the range of ancient works was discovered and digested, writes the historian John Hale, Renaissance thinkers wanted to live in the past rather than in their own time. The newly awakened spectacle of antiquity was all the more enthralling because it presented "the wholeness of a completed cycle, from obscurity through world empire to barbarian chaos."[3]

Machiavelli's understanding of Rome is key to his significance—so I will be arguing. I take as my point of departure an exploration of the view that the Scottish Enlightenment took of Machiavelli, as this holds important clues for Machiavelli's relationship to both antiquity and modernity. We want to then examine his discussion of Roman foreign policy in his *Discourses*, wherein he sets forth a range of options that have not only philosophical but also practical significance: they bear some similarity to the American predicament in the world today. Finally, we need to assess Machiavelli's relationship with the doctrine of political realism, of which he is often considered a founder. His view of Rome is worlds apart from that of Thomas Hobbes, another realist; that fundamental difference must be registered in our understanding of what political realism teaches.

I will declare my conflicted views on Machiavelli at the outset, so readers will not have to guess as they wind their way through the labyrinth to follow. I love it that Machiavelli sought to tell the truth about politics, that he made a heroic attempt to see the political world as it really was. Machiavelli did not necessarily see clearly on that point—as a friendly but critical Francesco Guicciardini said, it was not true that all men are bad, and if you treat good men as such you are ruling unwisely.[4] But that Machiavelli sought to see clearly, that he tried to go to the effectual truth of things and thus administered an electric shock to intellectual life, is just fabulous and exhilarating. Who cannot admire that?

Machiavelli is usually known as the political theorist who justified official lying—and yes, he did do that—but he also was the first modern to tell the truth as if nothing else mattered, and at a time when so many, inhabiting a fictional world, had created a shroud of untruth in both church and state. "He taught modern Christian Europe politics, as if Christianity or a Divinity or divine justice did not exist."[5]

Much as I think that we should dress up just like Machiavelli did and converse with ancient writers in the wee hours—yes, it is my solemn advice that college students should do so regularly—it is also highly advisable not to be carried along too far in our reverence for certain aspects of Machiavelli's life and thought. He pierced the veil of power, took off its mask for all to see. That was a fundamental revelation that cracked the European mind wide open. But we are also supposed to feel some shock at his doctrines, supposed to understand that they are offensive to basic propositions of morality and justice. I think some of those doctrines should be regarded as such. Insofar as Machiavelli really was a Machiavellian—that is a question to be held in suspense—we are indeed obliged to condemn him as a teacher of evil.

A View from the Enlightenment

Adam Smith knew something about the moral sentiments, and his were offended when he read Machiavelli's depiction of Cesare Borgia's doings in the Romagna.

> In Italy, during the greater part of the sixteenth century, assassinations, murders, and even murders under trust, seem to have been almost familiar among the superior ranks of people. Caesar Borgia invited four of the little princes in his neighbourhood, who all possessed little sovereignties, and commanded little armies of their own, to a friendly conference at Senigaglia, where, as soon as they arrived, he put them all to death. This infamous action, though certainly not approved of even in that age of crimes, seems to have contributed very little to the discredit, and not in the least to the ruin, of the perpetrator. That ruin happened a few years after from causes altogether disconnected with this crime. Machiavel, not indeed a man of the nicest morality even for his own times, was resident, as minister from the republic of Florence, at the court of Caesar Borgia when this crime was committed. He gives a very particular account of it, and in that pure, elegant, and simple language which distinguishes all his writings. He talks of it very coolly; is pleased with the address with which Caesar Borgia conducted it; has much contempt for the dupery and weakness of the sufferers; but no compassion for their miserable and untimely death, and no sort of indignation at the cruelty and falsehood of their murderer.

Smith went on to contrast the "foolish wonder and admiration" bestowed on great conquerors with the opprobrium dished out to ordinary thieves and murderers, noting that the former were "a hundred times more mischievous and destructive" than the latter.[6]

Smith's world was evidently not that of Machiavelli. In the interim, a revolution in consciousness had taken place, summed up by the word "politeness." Sentimentality—and the novel—were in; cruel and unusual punishments, even those conducted with an economy of violence, were out. An eighteenth-century observer of Borgia's scheming would not treat it coolly, would not be pleased with the execution of the plot, and would be indignant with the cruelty and falsehood of the murderer. It had become fashionable to denounce such things, and most thinkers noted the great improvements that had taken place in the monarchies of Europe since the sixteenth century. It was not just a European conceit: Jefferson attested to it, as did John Adams. The dark days of two hundred years before, when murders and assassinations set the tone for statecraft, were no more after the Treaty of Utrecht in 1713; among the beliefs of the eighteenth century was that their own enlightened age had transcended that mode of existence. We often hear today of the European Union representing an attempt to transcend the older ways of a nefarious statecraft that had previously done in its individual nations; the age of Utrecht felt the same way about the ruthless statecraft unmoored from legal or ethical ideals that dominated the sixteenth century, riven to and fro by papal monarchy and religious intolerance. Enlightenment developed, notes John Pocock, as "a critique of Calvinist Protestantism (and enthusiasm) as well as of Nicene Catholicism (and superstition)."[7] In transcending that terrible stalemate, the Enlightenment did not look back to Machiavelli.

Smith's great friend David Hume had a similar reaction to Machiavelli. The following passage, from his essay "Of Civil Liberty," discloses a profound gap between Renaissance and Enlightenment:

MACHIAVEL was certainly a great genius; but having confined his study to the furious and tyrannical governments of ancient times, or to the little disorderly principalities of ITALY, his reasonings especially upon monarchical government, have been found extremely defective; and there scarcely is any maxim in his *Prince*, which subsequent experience has not entirely refuted. *A weak prince, says he, is incapable of receiving good counsel; for if he consult with several, he will not be able to choose among their different counsels. If he abandon himself to one, that minister may, perhaps, have capacity; but he will not long be a minister: He will be sure to dispossess his master, and place himself and his family upon the throne.* I mention this, among many instances of the errors of that politician, proceeding, in a great measure, from his having lived in too early an age of the world, to be a good judge of political truth. Almost all the princes of EUROPE are at present governed by their ministers; and have been so for near two centuries; and yet no such event has ever happened, or can possibly happen. SEJANUS [of the praetorian guard] might project dethroning the CAESARS; but

FLEURY [a French minister of the eighteenth century], though ever so vicious, could not, while in his senses, entertain the least hopes of dispossessing the BOURBONS.[8]

Hume went on to note that Machiavelli and other Italian thinkers were basically clueless with regard to the significance of commerce; that was a gaping omission that made Machiavelli's thought seem archaic to Hume. That limitation also suggests that Machiavelli is not best seen as a representative of modernity but as "the last of the ancients," one who provided a distillation of Roman statecraft "unshrouded by natural law idealism."[9] From the standpoint of international relations theory, Hume's correction of Machiavelli is constructivist in tenor, the message of which is that you cannot be a good judge of political truth without knowing the norms and customs of a particular age. These change: what might be a brilliant success in one era would be a disaster in another. Montesquieu made the same judgment in noting that the world had "begun to be cured of Machiavellianism. . . . What were formerly called *coups d'état* would at present, apart from their horror, be only imprudences." Because of commerce, Montesquieu believed, "men are in a situation such that, though their passions inspire in them the thought of being wicked, they nevertheless have an interest in not being so."[10] Hume and Smith followed the same line of reasoning as Montesquieu, putting their enterprise on a sounder footing than Machiavelli's in figuring out the meaning of modernity. They understood, as Machiavelli did not, that it was constituted by the transition from glory to interest.[11]

Three Methods of Expansion

The *Discourses on the First Ten Books of Titus Livius* contains Machiavelli's most extended reflections on foreign policy, featuring especially a discussion of the three modes of expansion for republics. After treating in the first book of his *Discourses* of Rome's internal conduct, he took up in the second book "what the Roman people did in relation to the aggrandizement of their empire." Machiavelli marveled at this aggrandizement and hoped (though was not quite sure) it could be emulated by the Italians of his day. In detail he describes the methods of association, successfully disguising an imperial ambition, by which Rome gained the mastery of the known world.[12]

In describing the Roman ascent, Machiavelli stresses the fact that Rome never fought two wars simultaneously. They "did not engage in war with the Latins until they had beaten the Samnites so completely that the Romans themselves had to protect them with their arms; nor did they combat the Tuscans until after they had subjugated the Latins, and had by repeated defeats completely enervated the Samnites. Doubtless if these two powerful nations had united against Rome whilst their strength was yet unbroken, it may readily be supposed that they could have destroyed the Roman republic." But such was not the case. Machiavelli provides a brief sketch of the series of wars that successively subdued Rome's enemies in Italy and abroad and notes that "when these had been victoriously terminated, there remained in the whole world neither prince nor republic that could, alone or unitedly, have resisted the Roman power."

The reason for Rome's success was not good fortune but extremely clever and deceptive technique. Once Rome achieved sufficient power to make others fearful of attacking it, it became its option to "make war upon such neighboring powers as may seem advantageous, whilst adroitly keeping the others quiet." The "salami tactics" that were employed in the twentieth century are here clearly anticipated by Machiavelli's Romans. Anticipating that states will bandwagon with a strong power rather than balance against it, Machiavelli relates how the Romans made their conquests piecemeal, and how none of the powers who would ultimately succumb to the Romans had the wit to see the future danger to themselves.[13]

Despite Machiavelli's praise of Rome's courage and sagacity in conducting this expansion, he emphasized the lost liberty of the peoples the Romans conquered and seemed genuinely to mourn over it:

Nothing required so much effort on the part of the Romans to subdue the nations around them, as well as those of more distant countries, as the love of liberty which these people cherished in those days; and which they defended with so much obstinacy, that nothing but the exceeding valor of the Romans could ever have subjugated them. For we know from many instances to what danger they exposed themselves to preserve or recover their liberty, and what vengeance they practised upon those who had deprived them of it. The lessons of history teach us also, on the other hand, the injuries people suffer from servitude.

Machiavelli's republican sympathies burn brightly as he contemplates whence arose the love of liberty among the independent nations, such as the Tuscans, the Romans, and the Samnites, who inhabited Italy before Roman expansion overwhelmed its rivals.

And it is easy to understand whence that affection for liberty arose in the people, for they had seen that cities never increased in dominion or wealth unless they were free. And certainly it is wonderful to think of the greatness which Athens attained within the space of a hundred years after having freed herself from the tyranny of Pisistratus; and still more wonderful is it to reflect upon the greatness which Rome achieved after she was rid of her kings. The cause of this is manifest, for it is not individual prosperity, but the general good, that makes cities great; and certainly the general good is regarded nowhere but in republics.

Reflecting on the causes of the great transformation such that "in ancient times the people were more devoted to liberty than in the present," Machiavelli attributes this to a Christian religion that made men feeble—here we find his famous judgment that a religion that teaches humility and a contempt for worldly objects is not the stuff of which empires are made, though he immediately adds that Christianity rightly understood encourages men to love their country and that they ought therefore to be willing to defend it. But it was not only this (allegedly false) interpretation of Christianity that was to blame. He also insists that the loss of attachment to liberty between ancient and modern times was due to the Roman conquest itself, which destroyed all the ancient republics by force of arms and kicked the life out of those who were subdued. "Only those cities and countries that are free can achieve greatness," for only they allow citizens to compete in emulation for the highest honors of the state and to enjoy tranquilly the fruits of their labors.

The beautiful lessons that Machiavelli gives here on the superiority of free government—resting on a popular foundation and securing rights to private property—are attenuated when we come to his discussion of the best manner of expansion for republics. Republics, Machiavelli insists, are undoubtedly best for their own citizens, but ruinous for other free peoples. Contrary to what our age might identify as the common sense of the matter, Machiavelli insists that "hardest of all servitudes is to be subject to a republic." Republics "aim to enervate and weaken all other states so as to increase their own power," and they have the longevity to make their strictures stick. Machiavelli contrasts this harsh republican regimen with the light treatment that foreign subjects might expect of a prince. If such a prince has only an ordinary dose of humanity, he "will treat all cities that are subject to him equally well, and will leave them in the enjoyment of their arts and industries, and measurably all their ancient institutions." To act otherwise would show the prince to be "a barbarous devastator of countries and a destroyer of all human civilization, such as the princes of the Orient."

Two centuries after Machiavelli, Montesquieu wrote that the "spirit of monarchy is war and expansion; the spirit of republics is peace and moderation."[14] Machiavelli, by contrast, identifies war and expansion with republicanism, whether ancient or modern, and he seems to think that a prince, unless he was a monster, would treat a population he subjected much better than would a republic, whose rule was to weaken its neighbors while increasing its own power.

There was, however, a crucial difference among the ancient republics in how they sought the increase of their power. For Machiavelli, that made all the difference. Whereas Athens and Sparta were hostile to strangers and refused to admit them to citizenship, Rome both broke its enemies and welcomed them. It tried by all possible means to increase its population, both by "making it easy and secure for strangers to come and establish themselves there" and, after destroying the neighboring cities, by compelling "their inhabitants to come and dwell" among them. Rome, following this policy, was able to put two hundred thousand men into military service, whereas "Sparta and Athens could not raise more than twenty thousand each."

This difference in policy is one of Machiavelli's most trenchant examples showing the effect of different policies, as opposed to better material circumstances or good fortune, in explaining Rome's success. Lycurgus, the founder of the Spartan republic, "did everything possible to prevent strangers from coming into the city," prohibiting foreigners from becoming citizens through marriage and "all other intercourse and commerce that bring men together." Nothing could compensate for the relative weakness that this comparative lack of population imposed on Sparta. Its material base was too weak to hold its conquests. The same was true of Athens. Only Rome, by its superior policies, escaped the evident disutility of military force that Athens and Sparta suffered by their cloistered policies toward those whom they subjugated.

All this is prefatory to Machiavelli's crucial discussion of which is the best among "the three methods of aggrandizement" employed by republics. The first is the method of confederation, employed by the ancient Tuscans and Greeks and by the Swiss of Machiavelli's day. It entails the equal association of several republics, none of which have "any eminence over the other in rank or authority."

The second method, employed by the Romans, is "to make associates of other states; reserving to themselves, however, the rights of sovereignty, the seat of empire, and the glory of their enterprises." We might call this method one of "imperial association," emphasizing both the imperial primacy of the center and the equitable treatment of protectorates.

The third method, followed by the Spartans and the Athenians (and his own city of Florence), was "to make the conquered people immediately subjects, and not associates." Machiavelli's discussion of the best mode of aggrandizement—he hates the third, greatly admires the second, and has a grudging admiration for the first—is of key importance in understanding his approach to foreign policy.

Machiavelli's rejection of the despotic empires that Athens and Sparta maintained over their conquests is not based on the immorality of the practice but on its evident disutility. Because these cities did not know how to exploit their victory, by making protectorates of the conquered and treating them to a share of the spoils, their successes proved more costly than their defeats, as their holdings were plagued by revolts and had no adhesion to the center beyond domination. All this Machiavelli deemed extremely pertinent to his own city of Florence, for the Florentines had stupidly pursued the same counterproductive policy. "If this system of making subjects is disadvantageous to warlike republics, how much more pernicious must it be for such as have no armies?"

It is significant that Machiavelli pours scorn on a method showing the disutility of force, as the folly of war is usually considered a liberal or anti-Machiavellian theme. But this, it turns out, is a very limited concession, as can be seen by the manner in which Machiavelli decides between the two remaining options. Of these, Machiavelli declares heartily for the Roman method, though not without some ambivalence as to its practicality in his own day. Rome both made associates and increased its population, bestowing on it a greater scale of power than anything hitherto achieved.

> Having created for herself many associates throughout Italy, she granted to them in many respects an almost entire equality, always, however, reserving to herself the seat of empire and the right of command; so that these associates (without being themselves aware of it) devoted their own efforts and blood to their own subjugation. For so soon as the Romans began to lead their armies beyond the limits of Italy, they reduced other kingdoms to provinces, and made subjects of those who, having been accustomed to live under kings, were indifferent to becoming subjects of another; and from having Roman governors, and having been conquered by Roman arms, they recognized no superior to the Romans. Thus the associates of Rome in Italy found themselves all at once surrounded by Roman subjects, and at the same time pressed by a powerful city like Rome; and when they became aware of the trap into which they had been led, it was too late to remedy the evil, for Rome had become too powerful by the acquisition of foreign provinces, as also within herself by the increased population which she had armed. And although these associates

conspired together to revenge the wrongs inflicted upon them by Rome, yet they were quickly subdued, and their condition made even worse; for from associates they were degraded to subjects. This mode of proceeding (as has been said) was practised only by the Romans; and a republic desirous of aggrandizement should adopt no other plan, for experience has proved that there is none better or more sure.

There are some dubious logical leaps in Machiavelli's argument. The trap into which Rome led its associates would seem not to be easily replicable. After all, the promise of nearly equal association was a false one, and meant, in the end, that Rome's allies were "degraded to subjects." Would not others given such assurances by a rising power, having absorbed Machiavelli's history lesson, learn to distrust them? For what seems to distinguish the Roman from the Spartan and Athenian methods, apart from the crucial difference in population base, is that the latter openly proclaimed their ambition of ruling by violence, whereas the Romans hid their objective of subjugation and indeed covered it in the language of association and equality. Despite this evident duplicity, Machiavelli seems in no doubt that the Roman method is the best.

Next best is the method of forming confederations. Machiavelli acknowledged that the method of confederation did not allow for extensive conquests—a failing—but it had two other big advantages:

the one, not to become easily involved in war, and the other, that whatever conquests are made are easily preserved. The reason why a confederation of republics cannot well make extensive conquests is, that they are not a compact body, and do not have a central seat of power, which embarrasses consultation and concentrated action. It also makes them less desirous of dominion, for, being composed of numerous communities that are to share in this dominion, they do not value conquests as much as a single republic that expects to enjoy the exclusive benefit of them herself. Furthermore, they are governed by a council, which naturally causes their resolutions to be more tardy than those that emanate from a single centre.

This is a remarkable discussion of what might be termed the modalities of multilateralism, suggesting why multilateral alliances have difficulty reaching consensus and are hobbled from undertaking energetic action by the difficulty of getting the parties to agree on the sharing of costs and benefits. He goes on to argue that twelve to fourteen is the maximum number of such confederate states, a postulate with keen implications in the early days of the American union, with its thirteen united states, and not without relevance today in considering the dynamics of multilateral organizations. In modern experience, the move beyond twelve to fourteen states often forces, sooner or later, a fundamental choice between hegemony and breakup, a sort of primordial showdown between centralizing and decentralizing forces. Machiavelli was on to this peculiar dynamic between widening and deepening, one which hovers round all the grand confederal experiments in world history.

Machiavelli allows that the method of confederation does have certain real advantages—it ensures security, allows some share of military glory, and offers Italy a better option than its customary disunity—but it is the Roman method by which he is enthralled. He is amazed that this rich experience has not "even been taken into account by anyone," with the result that "Italy has become the prey of whoever has chosen to attack her." He sees history as a redeemer of the present, its lessons once known to shed a powerful light on what must now be done.[15] But he also seems to ascribe the neglect of ancient precedents not simply to ignorance but also to the belief that such precedents were inapplicable to contemporary Italian affairs and therefore useless. That was, in fact, a very cogent criticism. On the face of it, however, Machiavelli does not accept this conclusion; he will only allow that if imitating the Romans seems too difficult, it should not be too difficult to imitate the confederate method of the Tuscans, "especially the Tuscans of the present day."

Francesco Guicciardini read the *Discourses on Livy* after Machiavelli's death and wrote a short treatise on Machiavelli's work. He was sharply critical of many of Machiavelli's passages. Given particular attention by Guicciardini was Machiavelli's account of the Roman conquest, which emphasized the deceit the Romans practiced. Guicciardini showed that Machiavelli's account was deeply implausible. He pointed out the obvious limitations, in life and in statecraft, to a policy of fraud:

> I do not call it fraud if the Romans made pacts with the Latini such that they might endure their rule with patience. This was not because the Latini did not notice from the first that under the colour of equal confederation there lay servitude; but being helpless and not treated in such a way as to make them desperate, persuaded them to wait, not until they recognized the objectives of the Romans, which they would have had to be very stupid not to realize from the first, but until such time as with increased numbers of men and being really expert in military discipline they might hope to be able to meet the Romans as equals. It was therefore prudence, not fraud, on the part of the Romans, to treat the Latini fairly; and I think it very true that without such arrangements and prudent ways of going about things not only may one seldom rise from a lowly condition to great fortune, but one would even be hardly likely to preserve one's power. But as for fraud, it may be questionable whether that is always a good means of attaining power, for while by deception one may bring off some fine things, too often a reputation for deceit spoils one's chances of attaining one's ends.[16]

A good many of Guicciardini's criticisms of Machiavelli anticipate themes of the eighteenth-century Enlightenment. He was saying here, as George Washington would later more emphatically say, that honesty is the best policy. Guicciardini objected, as Adam Smith would later do, and as we all should do today, to Machiavelli's partiality for "extraordinary and violent methods." Discussing Machiavelli's observation that "a new prince in a city or province taken by him, must make everything new," Guicciardini insisted on the weakness invariably incurred by force: "Violent remedies, though they make one safe from one aspect, yet from another . . . involve all kinds of weaknesses. Hence the prince must take courage to use these extraordinary means when necessary, and should yet take care not to miss any chance which offers of establishing his cause with humanity, kindness, and rewards, not taking as an absolute rule what [Machiavelli] says, who was always extremely partial to extraordinary and violent methods."[17]

Perhaps the most interesting feature of Machiavelli's discussion in the *Discourses* is that one might from his premises reject his conclusion. Let us first take the horrific costs of the Roman conquest for subjugated peoples into full view, which Machiavelli seems perfectly willing to do. Consider, secondly, the sheer unlikelihood of making commercial Florence, with its unarmed populace and dependence on mercenaries, the leader of a project to revive Roman glory, duly noting that, even acting in near-unison, the states of Italy were weaker than Spain, France, and Germany, and not much superior to the Ottomans. Let us accept, finally, that any prince who had the benefit of reading Machiavelli's Roman history would see at once that the assurances of a rising power that modeled itself on Rome could not be believed. This meant that such a prince was more likely to ally with the weak than to succor the strong, to balance rather than bandwagon. The Roman experience, rather than paving the way for a similar attempt by a modern prince, rather showed Europeans to be on their guard against that very thing. The whole system of the balance of power, which arose from the laboratory of Renaissance Italy, was justified as preserving the freedom and independence of states as against a renewal of the Roman tyranny.[18]

Given these considerations, it would seem to follow that the method of confederation offered a more eligible means to Italian security and freedom than the Roman method. That is the conclusion that Americans like Jefferson and Washington drew for their own union; they had no intention of emulating the dead-end cynicism of the Italian states and were determined to avoid the dose of poison that Machiavelli had recommended. They built their union on consent, not on force. That too measures the gap between Renaissance and Enlightenment.

That Machiavelli would not pronounce himself for the confederal solution is not easily understandable. It suggests that his thought remained wedded to ideals of glory and conquest, in preference to the coming idea of the free association of republican equals. It also suggests a myopic failure to grant to others the rights it claims for itself. That myopia made him a poor guide—in profession, at least, if not in practice—in resolving Italy's predicament and in speaking to our own.[19]

The dilemmas identified by Machiavelli suggest a remarkable parallel with the contemporary international order, so often defined in terms of U.S. hegemony. The "liberal Leviathan" that now presides—very shakily, it is true—over the international system is the central plank in a configuration of power that is a sort of halfway house between confederation and empire.[20] It is usually described as a hegemony (a word derived from the Greek *hegemon* and denoting leadership in a coalition of allies). It partakes, however, of both confederal and imperial tendencies. Its leaders seem conscious of the fact that neither ideal type by itself can offer a solution to the problem of international order, so it cleaves to both of these contradictory notions. Machiavelli's ambivalence on the question—confederation or empire?—is suggestive of America's own.

Machiavelli's advice can be read as making citizens, not subjects, in the course of republican expansion, a prescription bearing some comparison with the early American practice of making new states equal to the old as the federal union expanded across the continent. But even more remarkable is the manner in which former enemies are seduced into the lap of the empire and become extensions of it. The Romans, notes Richard Tuck, often saw their interests as in alignment with those of oppressed citizens elsewhere and made appeal to that solidarity:

> Rome's mission, in the famous words of Vergil, could be thought of as "parcere subjectis and debellare superbos" ("to spare the oppressed and bring down the proud," Aeneid 6.852). Rome's status during its expansion into the Eastern Mediterranean as the only republic left in a world of military despotisms undoubtedly contributed to its self-image as a liberator, freeing the subject peoples of Greece and Asia from the despotic descendants of Alexander's generals (though, as the ruthless destruction of Corinth in 146 B.C. testifies, Rome could in practice be even more tyrannical to the Greeks than the Kings of Macedon or Pontus had ever been). Rome certainly felt free to respond to appeals for help from populations engaged in struggles

against their rulers or in war with their neighbors, and to some extent its entire imperial expansion was driven by a succession of such responses. The Jugurthine War of 112 is a good example: Rome's initial involvement in the affairs of Numidia was as an international arbitrator to resolve a civil war there and to enforce the settlement, but—in an entirely familiar way—the war escalated, Rome was drawn in and eventually a Roman protectorate was established, which in turn became a Roman province.[21]

There are remarkable similarities between Roman expansion of the second century B.C. and U.S. expansion of the past seventy years. Unlike Rome, America does not make provinces, but both histories feature the incorporation of former enemies as protectorates and the cultivation of insurgents against despotic enemies. Neoconservatives and liberal hawks may fairly be seen as defining the mission of the United States as that of liberating the oppressed and detonating despotic rule, and they have driven U.S. expansion (or tried to) on the old Roman road. They are doing it now (circa 2014–15) in Ukraine; they tried to do it in Iraq in 2003 (in what seems an obvious failure until one appreciates that Iraq still has need of U.S. airpower, advisors, and military equipment). It is a notable fact, disturbing in its significance, that this pattern of conduct—simultaneously looking for enemies to fight and protectorates to create—is very similar to the road marked out by Machiavelli.

Our leaders would do better to try the old Tuscan method. The Roman road, it may be recalled, does not end well for the republic.

Machiavelli and Political Realism

Machiavelli's attitude toward Rome was far from uncritical but was certainly more adulatory than that of his successors in Western political thought. Hobbes announces his philosophic enterprise, in the preface to *De Cive*, by excoriating those whom Machiavelli had celebrated: "what sort of animal was the Roman People? By the agency of citizens who took the names Africanus, Asiaticus, Macedonicus, Achaicus, and so on from the nations they had robbed, that people plundered nearly all the world."[22] Whereas Machiavelli glorified early republican Rome for perfecting the ways of military expansion, Hobbes made the people of Rome the villain of the piece. Whereas Machiavelli foresaw humanity gripped by endless war, Hobbes forecasts the possibility of universal peace. Machiavelli and Hobbes are alike in insisting on the right of states to self-protection, but there are significant contrasts in their understanding of this right. It makes a great deal of difference whether vast dominion (as with Machiavelli) or safety (as with Hobbes) is your watchword.[23] A century after Hobbes, William Robertson also lamented the awful consequences following from the Roman conquest, which left the conquered peoples losing "not only the habit but even the capacity" to think for themselves: "the dominion of the Romans, like that of all great Empires, degraded and debased the human species."[24]

Machiavelli himself does not conform to the cardboard portrait of realism one finds in international relations textbooks (states aggrandize their power without reference to norms and ought to do so). He understood that there were certain limits. He descants eloquently on the difference between the good and the bad Roman emperors, and sees that it was their fidelity to justice that made the good ones good and earned them the love of the people and the senate. He burns with understandable indignation at the incapacity of Italy to fend off the barbarians, in the shape of French, Spanish, German, and Swiss armies. His purposes in resisting this grim servitude were exemplary, and his life was one of sacrifice in the service of his country. He would have given more if they would have let him. He even offered up his soul, only to be expelled from office and tortured when the republic came to an end.

Machiavelli occasionally bows to conventional notions of the good, the true, and the beautiful. But he also inverts them, makes a sort of ethical irrationality of human experience, with good producing evil and evil producing good. Without any certain landmarks, it is easy to get lost, morally speaking. Many others, reading Machiavelli, did get lost. Machiavelli invited the prince down that path with a sort of breezy abandon and with invocations of necessity—you are screwed if you do not, so get with the program—but it is not in my opinion the path of true policy. Even at the time, Erasmus counseled more wisely.[25]

As Mark Hulliung observes, Machiavelli "deliberately inverted the master symbols of Latin literature, and each of his inversions was an intentional subversion of the humanist creed: by turning the Stoicism of Cicero upside down, Machiavelli forced the *studia humanitatis* to give birth to Machiavellism." Everything done in the name of those inversions cannot be attributed to Machiavelli, nor even most of it—just some of it, and that is quite enough. Hulliung comments that, for Cicero, "Roman foreign policy was the most just ever known"; for Machiavelli, "it was the most Machiavellian."[26] Which is preferable: hypocrisy or villainy? I prefer a world in which vice is made to pay some kind of tribute to virtue.

Such was Machiavelli's brilliance, such the ambiguity of some of his passages, that he can be claimed on more than one side of our political debates. From almost the first moments interpreters differed over whether Machiavelli's discussion of the *arcana imperii*, the secret arts practiced by princes behind closed doors, was "a way of alerting the people to the tricks of their rulers or . . . a way of teaching rulers how to trick the people more expertly."[27] These "red" and "black" schools of thought have hovered about the interpretation of Machiavellian (and Tacitist) ideas from the very beginning, and the truth is surely that Machiavelli gives some ammunition to both camps. Very intelligent critics, like Rousseau and Diderot, were of the red republican school. Wrote Diderot: "It's as if he had told his fellow-citizens: 'Read this work well. If you ever accept a master, he will be as I describe him to you: there's the wild beast to which you will abandon yourselves.' So it was the fault of his contemporaries if they misunderstood his purpose: they mistook satire for encomium."[28]

Others took Machiavelli as the farthest thing from a satirist, one who had taught avowedly the black arts. "It is seriously incongruous and dangerous," warned Jean Bodin, "to teach princes the rules of injustice in order to assure their power." Invoking Cicero, Innocent Gentillet observed, "Friendship is the true bond of all human society and whosoever wishes to do away with good will among men (as Machiavelli did among princes) will succeed in eliminating all the pleasure, consolation, contentment, and security that exists among men."[29] Making more concessions to Machiavelli's view, but still drawing back, was Justus Lipsius (1547–1606), a Flemish writer on reason of state much lauded for his mastery of the classical sources. Lipsius, notes Noel Malcolm, exerted a huge influence. While subscribing to some Machiavellian assumptions and accepting that "the art of ruling must make some compromises with vice," Lipsius also distinguished among "three levels of fraudulent behaviour: 'light' (involving dissimulation, the concealment of intentions), 'medium' (involving the active deception, or corruption by bribery, of enemies), and 'great' (involving such actions as breach of treaty). The first, he wrote, was advisable, the second tolerable, and the third unacceptable." Lipsius believed that a moral politics was possible even with such dissimulation: "Wine does not cease to be wine if it is lightly diluted with water; nor does prudence cease to be prudence, if you add some little drops of fraud." As Malcolm notes, however, Lipsius also insisted "that the permitted frauds were tolerable only when done for the common good; any deception not aimed at that end was a great sin."[30]

Machiavelli also believed in the subordination of reason to state to the common good, but in other respects he went too far. He crossed the line. He took his examples, as Hume wrote, from too many furious and disorderly governments. He too much relished dominion and glory, as against the interests that would make men and women tractable. He minimized the degree to which justice must remain the great standing policy of civil and international society. To his credit, he saw that a prince must give justice to the people; to his discredit, he was unwilling to do justice to the nations. In the still relevant benediction of Henry Wheaton:

> Unfortunately for his own fame, and for the permanent interests of mankind, this masterly writer, in his patriotic anxiety to secure his country against the dangers with which it was menaced from the Barbarians, did not hesitate to resort to those atrocious means already too familiar to the domestic tyrants of Italy. The violent remedies he sought to apply for her restoration to pristine greatness were poisons, and his book became the manual of despotism, in which Philip II. of Spain, and Catherine de Medici, found their detestable maxims of policy. But policy can never be separated from justice with impunity. Sound policy can never authorize a resort to such measures as

are prohibited by the law of nations, founded on the principles of eternal justice; and, on the other hand, the law of nations ought not to prohibit that which sound policy dictates as necessary to the security of any State. "Justice," says Burke, "is the great standing policy of civil society, and any eminent departure from it, under any circumstances, lies under the suspicion of being no policy at all."[31]

CHAPTER 7

Machiavelli's *Prince*

An Americanist's Perspective

THOMAS E. CRONIN

Machiavelli's *The Prince*, written in 1513 and published in 1532, is the most famous and provocative essay on political leadership ever written. Half a millennium later, we debate it, condemn it, and still learn from it. Inventive and disturbing, *The Prince* is rife with luminous and paradoxical propositions about governance.

Our destiny is determined not only by chance (*fortuna*), Machiavelli instructs, but also by prudent, disciplined leadership. Fortune may determine about half of what happens to a country or state, but it is the choices that leaders make—especially how they adapt to changing times and take advantage of opportunities—that are critical to the survival and success of a state.

Machiavelli dared to take on Plato and Cicero. With icy realism, he challenged long-held classical idealism and Christian beliefs. He mocked the Church and its unarmed prophets. And he shocked readers by suggesting what many considered to be immoral and unconstitutional strategies of leadership. But Machiavelli understood not only what we want to be but how we actually behave. His essay is a blunt dissection of contradictions inherent in political life.

Leadership is full of mystery and paradox. People everywhere despair when their leaders are ineffective. Yet we are also inherently suspicious of strong leadership. Thus the paradox—power can corrupt, yet the absence of power can paralyze and lead to a different kind of corruption.

This chapter looks at *The Prince* for what it can teach us about leadership, power, and governance.

For most people, most of the time, leadership is an evocative word, rich in positive meaning, often connoting empowerment and liberation. But at other times, and for many people, the word connotes manipulation, deception, and coercion. Both views are right.

The terms "leadership" and "power" are often used interchangeably by those discussing Machiavelli, but a word of caution is in order. Leadership nowadays suggests persuasion, influence, and mutual engagement. Power, on the other hand, suggests command, orders, and the use of force. Leaders, we want to believe, earn followers. Power wielders force compliance or submission.

Machiavelli's imagined prince is a composite power wielder and leader: part nation builder, part homeland security architect, part commander in chief, part Greek tyrant. Assuming that his prince will have the best interests of the state in mind (a debatable assumption), Machiavelli analyzes the various ways a prince can maximize his power and reputation. An effective prince is the means to a stable and well-functioning principality. The ultimate goal of the prince, Machiavelli suggests, is for the principality to flourish, for its people to be secure and prosper. This, says Machiavelli, will enable the prince to accomplish great things and bring glory to the community as well as to the prince.

It is easy to misread *The Prince* as simply a handbook for the education of a prince. Originally titled *The Principality*, the treatise, however, is his blueprint for how city-states or principalities can survive and thrive in a world of predators. The ultimate goal is the well-being of the state rather than just the well-being of the prince. This celebrated work may appear as a textbook for princeship, but it is primarily an enlightened and pragmatic way of thinking about the preservation of an energetic, successful state.

Machiavelli believed his writing would help Florence defend itself against invading forces as well as local thugs who might succeed in destroying the city-state. Where chaos and instability reign, he suggested, freedom and prosperity, property rights, and ideals of truth and beauty can only be a dream. The first responsibility for an effective prince is security, order, and stability in the state—the prerequisites for prosperity. Outside of this, the state should interfere as little as possible with the rights of individual citizens.

The premise of *The Prince* is that appropriate leadership can defeat disorder, corruption, and other forces that lead to a state's demise. But the challenge for those of us who read *The Prince* today is that we have witnessed too many examples of power being terribly misused. Still, we also have before us examples of what happens in a leadership vacuum.

Machiavelli's prince, even if autocratic by today's standards, was explicitly imagined as preferable to the misery and suffering of a defenseless and subjugated people. The state must be created and sustained, and a powerful, pragmatic leader is the necessary first ingredient before there can be prosperity or community. Having a powerful prince, even with the possibility of corruption, is better than the chaos, pillage, and servitude that come from losing a war.

The Prince is often misunderstood as a call for a permanent national security state, a ruthless, dogmatic military junta needed for a constant state of war, and all for the benefit of a ruling prince. This was not Machiavelli's intent. Yet people invariably read into this text notions of "might makes right," or "necessity knows no laws," and the image of an imperial, militarily belligerent demagogue endures.

Machiavelli focused with laser-like single-mindedness on the here and now of the time in which he was writing—what was necessary for founding and sustaining a state. The effective prince may have to choose between saving his soul and governing effectively. Machiavelli delegates the salvation of souls to others. *His* goal—and the goal of his proposed prince—is the salvation of the city-state of Florence. Statecraft, for the prince, must supersede soulcraft. The sociologist Max Weber would later reframe this as the leader's ethical obligation to governing responsibilities, as opposed to a preoccupation with ultimate ends.[1]

The Man and the Writer

Friends and biographers describe Machiavelli (1469–1527) as witty, garrulous, and sometimes acerbic, prickly, and abrasive. Average in height, slight of build, hollow-cheeked, even "bird-like," he was also a bit of a randy rogue, well known in local taverns and brothels.

Machiavelli was born on May 3, 1469, and raised in the heart of Florence (population around sixty thousand). His family, variously described as impoverished gentry or middle class, were citizens of Florence. His father was a notary with some legal training. The senior Machiavelli owned a house in Florence and a country place seven miles south of the city but apparently was an unreliable provider.

While we do not know much about Machiavelli's youth or young adult years, we know he received a classical education. He was tutored in Latin, rhetoric, and Roman and Greek history, and attended lectures at the local university. He had little or no experience with commerce, and, unlike some of his famous contemporaries, such as Michelangelo, Da Vinci, or Botticelli, did not develop a talent for art or architecture. He did, however, write poetry and a few plays. For Machiavelli, as for some notable Greek and Roman authors who preceded him, the well-ordered, well-led state *was* a work of art, indeed the highest form of human endeavor.

Florence was a comparatively wealthy banking, manufacturing, and commercial center at the time. It was also a hub of Renaissance art and philosophy. As Machiavelli was growing up, the city had more than its share of turmoil and political turnover. By the time he was a young man, however, Florence was a republic, governed (at least ostensibly) by a Great Council, which consisted of roughly three thousand ruling-class nobles and business elites. This Great Council delegated most matters to a more select council of about eighty people. Small committees presided over military affairs and other matters of state.

One of Machiavelli's intellectual mentors apparently arranged for him to become a civil servant in the city government. He became a top administrative and diplomatic aide for foreign affairs and was soon also asked to oversee military preparedness for the city-state of Florence.

His civil service job in the old Chancellery at the Palazzo Vecchio consisted of assisting Florence's emissaries as they conducted diplomatic missions. His responsibilities included extensive correspondence and briefings for his superiors on a range of matters such as how to deal with Rome and other neighboring city-states, and with France and Spain. He often journeyed to other capitals, sometimes staying for a few months. He regularly tried to forge alliances or helped, with checkbook diplomacy, to buy protection for Florence. His responsibilities grew to include military affairs—a purview for which he was ill prepared, yet which he apparently enjoyed.

During the years 1498 to 1512, Machiavelli learned both how Florentine politics worked and why other governments were effective or not. An acute observer as well as participant, he essentially became a practicing political scientist, focusing much of his attention on the interplay of competing state interests and the exercise of statecraft.

He developed the view that leaders' "success or failure depends on whether their talents and imagination—and thus their actions—are well or poorly suited to their times and to events." Different strategies may or may not be effective, depending on the circumstances. "If men could understand the nature of their times and of events, and change their behavior accordingly, then it would be true that wise men command the stars and their destinies."[2]

Machiavelli loved his work and the cachet his access provided. Although he was essentially a bureaucrat, his workhorse ethic and his shrewdness and writing skills earned the respect of Florence's ruling elite. He understood that he was not their political or social equal, yet he was gradually becoming more knowledgeable and experienced than most of his superiors. He in turn was entrusted with more and more responsibilities.

Machiavelli urged his councilors to recruit and train their own homegrown army. It was a proud moment for him when hundreds of these raw recruits paraded through the city. But this homegrown army would later prove to be disastrously inadequate. Overwhelmed by Spanish troops at the nearby battle of Prato (a protectorate), the Florentine Republic was soon defeated. "Machiavelli's own fortunes collapsed with those of the Republican regime. On 7 November [1512] he was formally dismissed from his post in the chancery."[3] Fortune's great and steely malice, he said, had suddenly been unloaded upon him.

Machiavelli married during his civil service years, and he and his wife, Marietta, had seven children. He seems to have been an indifferent and often absentee husband and father. Then in late 1512 he was unemployed as well.

Making matters worse, he was accused, probably falsely, of conspiring against the new Medici regime and was imprisoned and tortured for a few weeks in early 1513. He was later released as part of a general amnesty granted in celebration of a Medici family member (Giovanni de' Medici) becoming pope.

Machiavelli retreated to his father's Sant'Andrea in Percussina country farm. (The farm had an olive grove and a vineyard, among other crops, and these remain to this day.) He gardened and did some reading during the day, drank and played cards with locals at a nearby tavern in the afternoons, and read and wrote about statecraft at night.

The Prince (approximately thirty thousand words in length) was written in 1513, his first year of unplanned exile. Humiliated and nearly impoverished, he had every reason to be bitter. Indeed, some critics see *The Prince* as the work of a disillusioned and embittered outcast.

To his credit, Machiavelli attempted to place his nearly fifteen years of public service experience in a larger historical context. He read and reread the great classical writers on the histories of Greece and Rome and set out to join this large company of writers and philosophers. *The Prince*, in the tradition of "mirrors for princes," followed from Plato, Cicero, Aquinas, and many others, and had a virtual cousin in Erasmus's *The Education of a Christian Prince*, which was published in 1516. What makes for effective leadership—especially in turbulent times? How does a leader acquire power and then sustain a free, prosperous, and secure city-state? These were hardly new questions. Plato, Aristotle, Thucydides, Plutarch, and Cicero, among others, had wrestled with similar ones.[4]

The Prince was dedicated first to Guiliano de' Medici, and then, after Guiliano's death, to Lorenzo de' Medici, both members of the wealthy and autocratic banking family that had been recently reinstalled as rulers of Florence. Was *The Prince* a job application, a leadership essay intended to prove his bona fides to Florence's new rulers? Machiavelli had thoroughly enjoyed his responsibilities under the Florentine Republic. Was he celebrating the return of an autocratic leader? Did he want to get back into the game at any cost? Was he suggesting that Florence was not ready for a republican form of government? Did he believe that the city's very survival demanded a strong, ruthless, cunning prince?

One biographer suggests that *The Prince* was "one of the most ill-advised job applications of all time." The Medici would have viewed it as presumptuous. Its level of frankness and implicit praise for occasional cruelty and deceit might have handicapped the Medici, rather than helped them, in governing Florence.

The Prince seems less a how-to manual for the Medici than the product of Machiavelli's principled desire "to set down on paper his ideas" about what history and firsthand experience had taught him about leadership.[5]

Machiavelli was forty-four when he wrote *The Prince*. He may have started the essay as a form of job application, but it seems that he, like the great historian Thucydides, ended up setting his sights much higher, writing not just for contemporaries, whether in or out of power, but for a larger future audience. He declared his intention "to write something useful [based on reality, not imagination] to whoever understands it."

As he was writing *The Prince*, Machiavelli was also beginning to write his important treatise on the history of the Roman Republic, commonly called the *Discourses* (*Discourses on the First Ten Books of Titus Livius*). This is a sympathetic analysis of the Roman republican government and its innovative efforts to provide for both leadership and constitutional checks and balances.

Whereas *The Prince* is about the leadership needs for a city-state or principality whose existence is threatened by outside forces, the *Discourses* concentrates on governance arrangements and diplomacy needs for stable, long-standing republics. Machiavelli preferred a republican form of government, even though he understood that princely leadership—or "princing up"—was at times necessary. Machiavelli's hope, scholars suggest, was that princely leadership would eventually, under fortuitous circumstances, lead to a republican form of government. He also understood that republics can, after a time, unravel and then might require princely leadership en route to some form of refounding.

Machiavelli's prophetic epilogue chapter calls for leadership that would unify Italian city-states. Machiavelli apparently hoped his beloved Florence would be Italy's capital (which it briefly became in the nineteenth century). He exalts the coming of a unifying nation-state redeemer-prince to achieve this. And he expresses optimism that new developments in Rome were propitious omens for a new national covenant.

He was apparently hesitant to send the completed *Prince* to the Medici. He asked friends to read handwritten copies. He got mixed reactions. Some admired his masterful depiction of political realities. Others pointed out mistakes, faulted it for exaggeration, and noted that some of his themes, and even chapter headings, were borrowed from earlier writers.

He may have had second thoughts about the book as a job application. He still wanted to get back in the game, but the Medici then in power seemed unlikely consumers of his new treatise. And even Machiavelli himself might have wondered whether he had wandered too expressively and too boldly in his irreverence toward traditional notions of virtue and morality.

Neither the Medici in Florence nor those in Rome seemed to take much notice of *The Prince*. It did circulate, probably as much criticized as admired. It was formally published in 1532, five years after his death.

Machiavelli was not invited back into governing circles until very late in his life, and even this opportunity was brief. He continued to write in exile. In later years he wrote *The Art of War* (1521), a thoughtful if somewhat flawed treatise on military strategy and tactics. *The Art of War* builds on Machiavelli's own frustrating experience as an intermediary between Florence's general officers and the ruling elites. Machiavelli had learned from Florence's inability to defend itself. He remained an unapologetic and hawkish advocate for Florence having its own militia, with ample resources for its training and preparedness.

In his final years, he was commissioned to write a history of Florence. *Florentine Histories* is a ponderous, sometimes arthritic, pessimistic catalogue of the civic strife, endless feuds, and backstabbing that had characterized Florence's tumultuous past. As noted, he also wrote plays and poetry. His play *Mandragola*, a brilliant satire of marriage and intrigue, made him something of a celebrity in the arts community. Only some plays, plus *The Art of War*, were published before his death.

Machiavelli lived most of his post-public service days in near-poverty. He had no pension and little patrimony. Although he had an occasional writing commission or short-term assignments as a negotiator, he lived his last fourteen years highly marginalized. His most celebrated writings, as noted, were published and read only after his death. He also had to live with the stigma of having helped oversee a major military defeat for Florence. And he had to watch his beloved Florence lapse again into political strife.

His family and a few friends gathered for his funeral on June 21, 1527. They apparently considered him a man of modest means and modest achievements. Five hundred years later, however, we know Machiavelli as one of the world's most provocative and consequential political thinkers—hardly a modest achievement.

"Princing Up": What It Takes to Be an Effective Prince

The top priority of a prince, according to Machiavelli, is to master the art of war. Study the history of military battles. Learn which strategies work. Never demobilize. Always be prepared for war, and never be lulled into complacency. Understand the importance of deception and surprise. Learn the geography of your region and the physical terrain of possible battle sites. Understand, too, the liabilities of mercenaries. It is better to train your own citizens.

Now substitute the word "politics" for "war." Machiavelli's analysis of a prince's top priority also appears to be a useful description of how a political operative must act. Study the histories of past campaigns and learn which strategies work. Always be prepared for the next political skirmish.

Be realistic, Machiavelli urges his prince, about the weaknesses of human nature. He was despairingly uncomplimentary about human nature. Everyone has their own interest and self-preservation as their first priority. Every other city-state or nation will always act to further its own self-interest at the expense of your state, even if it has formed alliances with you. People and states will more often than not break their promises rather than subordinate their interests to yours.

At the heart of this pessimistic, realistic analysis is a notion we are familiar with today. It is the Darwinian idea that survival of the species is the first goal of any organism. We accept this notion—usually without moral qualms—as a scientific fact of life, one that holds true for every species. We may underestimate, however, how central this idea is in our political systems.

The American founding fathers faced a challenge that in many ways was similar to those Machiavelli's prince faced—how to create a nation-state that would be strong enough to maintain its independence from outside forces, yet also able to manage the competing self-interests of various internal factions. Transferring final authoritative power from a prince to a constitutional system, with elected representatives, was the founders' ingenious solution—a solution sometimes called "taming the prince."[6] Still, in times of war or threat, the president is a prince, exercising prerogative powers as commander in chief, declaring a state of emergency or issuing executive orders, and presiding, often secretly, over diplomatic and intelligence operations.

Machiavelli's next words of advice are more controversial. Effective leaders, he says, understand that there are two distinctive ways of competing: by law or by force. Law is the civilian temperament. Force is the province of beasts. A leader, Machiavelli suggests, has to be both man and, in part, beast. If possible, be virtuous, empathetic, and merciful, but know that you may sometimes have to use force, to lie, or be cruel.

An implicit doctrine of necessity calls on leaders to do whatever may be necessary to provide homeland security. A leader may sometimes have to bend civil laws and transgress normative rules of fairness to serve the larger interest of the state. Such a leader, in Machiavelli's argument, is granted greater moral leeway because he acts on behalf of the larger purposes of the state. This, some suggest, is Machiavelli's utilitarianism.

The necessity of maintaining the state, Machiavelli suggests, is a moral imperative in itself. Effective princes must have a finely tuned understanding of power. They must know what power is—hard as well as soft power—and how to acquire it and exercise it. They must know how to play one interest off against another. Their own success and the success of their state trump conventional pieties about moral character.

These words of advice are controversial. Machiavelli grants his prince greater moral leeway than most people might like. We can understand today the need for executive prerogative power to be exercised on rare occasions, but not for any lengthy duration.

A prince should act virtuously when possible, he says, but also realize that state interests may require the use of force, fraud, or cruelty. Such behavior—what today many call Machiavellian tactics—must never be excessive or continuous, and should be engaged in only as it enhances the purposes of the state. Do not, Machiavelli warns, love cunning and cruelty for their own sake.

Americans celebrate their revered presidents—Washington, Jefferson, Lincoln, Roosevelt—in large part because they believe these leaders acted on moral principles and the mutually shared hopes of society. On the opposite side, we condemn the world's most autocratic and toxic leaders—Hitler, Stalin, Idi Amin—for their unrestrained, egregious, and self-serving immoral actions, even though these leaders successfully seized power and controlled nations for a significant period.

History, Machiavelli suggests, teaches about both acceptable and unacceptable uses of force, violence, and betrayal. Moses and Romulus acted acceptably. Agathocles, among others, engaged in unnecessary or ill-suited killings and betrayals—methods that may temporarily have gained power but not lasting glory.

Students of American history acknowledge that American presidents have sometimes acted out of necessity and used Machiavellian tactics of brute force or deception. Washington became a cunning leader and a strict disciplinarian during the American Revolution. General Washington favored severe punishment for soldiers who deserted or shirked responsibilities. He effectively used deception and surprise as military tactics.[7]

Lincoln prized constitutionalism, but as a leader tested in the enormously divisive and costly Civil War, he assumed executive prerogative powers that exceeded literal Article II authority. He believed his supreme constitutional obligation—to preserve the Union—transcended lesser constitutional or moral obligations. "Are all the laws, but one, to go unexecuted and the government itself to go to pieces," Lincoln asked a special session of Congress on July 4, 1861, "lest that one be violated?"[8] One might see in this an uncanny echo of Machiavelli: the prince's first obligation is to establish the city-state and keep it secure.

In the early years of World War II, Franklin Roosevelt was faulted by isolationists for working with Churchill in secretive ways to assist Britain. FDR took risks and was threatened with impeachment. But as president, he acted in ways Machiavelli may have appreciated. Roosevelt also authorized a dozen internment camps for Japanese American citizens—an act that would later be viewed as unconstitutional as well as wrong.

At the end of World War II, Harry Truman was confronted by the decision of whether or not to use the newly developed atomic bomb. While this decision continues to be debated, Truman repeatedly said that it was an easy one for him to make. He believed the bomb would save countless American lives by ending the war with Japan sooner. He understood the tremendous precedent of using a weapon of mass destruction—that there would be tremendous civilian casualties—but the greater moral imperative for him was saving the lives of American soldiers and sailors, restoring America's national security, and bringing about an orderly transition in Japan. (He also probably believed that General MacArthur's proposed siege of Japan, which would likely have starved a wide swath of the population, would have produced a greater death toll than dropping the two bombs.) Machiavelli would have understood.

In short, most American presidents and kindred Western leaders share the view that "there will be times when nations, acting individually or in concert, will find the use of force not only necessary but morally justified."[9]

In the past half-century, American presidents have used undeclared war, preemptive war, or clandestine operations to try to bring about regime change in other countries. These tactics (which might be called Machiavellian) have not always been successful, sometimes resulting in weakening America's position.[10] And presidents such as George W. Bush and Barack Obama have been faulted when they pushed executive prerogative, executive orders, and similar strategies beyond what Congress, the courts, or legal scholars considered legitimate. Machiavelli would doubtless have questioned the effectiveness of long deployments of U.S. troops in places such as Vietnam and Afghanistan.

Yet presidents (and their advisers) understand the bottom line as stated by Machiavelli: "those republics which in time of danger cannot resort to dictatorship will generally be ruined when grave occasions occur." (This comes from his *Discourses* and is vintage Machiavelli.) Contemporary leaders who bristle at Machiavelli's blunt use of the word "dictatorship" may prefer to use the term "executive prerogative" or "state of emergency." Still, the Machiavellian injunction lives.

The troubling question remains: How are leaders held accountable?

If one can put aside this especially nagging question, much of what follows in *The Prince* is valuable advice for a would-be leader. His observations seem prescient for American business and political leaders.

A leader must understand the difference between Plato's imaginary philosopher-king—as well as Christian notions of the virtuous, forgiving "Prince of Peace"—and the clear-headed, realistic, and calculating power wielder who must sometimes do "wrong" things for the sake of his state. The prince must on occasion be like the surgeon who is prepared to sacrifice a limb to save a life.

A leader has to navigate the complicated chemistry between leaders and followers. Even in emergency times, followers can abandon their leaders. So a leader must cultivate allegiance and respect and try to meet not only the security needs but the social needs of a people as well. Private property rights and respect for women should be maintained. Bullies and tyrants eventually sever the bond of trust necessary for effective leadership. Machiavelli is famously quoted as saying it is better to be feared than to be loved. Yet he implicitly, if not explicitly, makes the case that the effective leader will do what is necessary to earn respect.

A leader must understand the mask of command and the theater of leading. People want their leaders to display not only prowess, but dignity, courage, steadfastness, and grace under pressure. As the military historian John Keegan later writes, "the leader of men in warfare can show himself to his followers only through a mask, a mask that he must make for himself, but a mask made in such a form as will mark him to men of his time and place as the leader they want and need."[11] A leader must act in ways that are not only compelling but also reassuring. Statecraft and stagecraft, Machiavelli implies, have overlapping requirements.

A leader needs to have the boldness and ferocity of a lion and the wily ingenuity of a fox. The leader needs to be able to fight within the law as well as by force, law being a quality of men, and force a quality of animals. The example that comes to mind is that of the mythological centaur (a creature with the head, arms, and torso of a human and the body and legs of a horse).[12] Leadership requires the ability to adapt to different situations, but youthful impetuosity will usually serve one better than cautious passivity. Success comes to the leader who is bold but also prepared—to the leader who challenges fortune. Machiavelli's leader understands that opportunity is the lifeblood that empowers a leader, and that the job of the leader is to steer the ship of state toward opportunities. A leader needs to embrace adversity and develop the resilience of a chameleon, who responds with different colors according to different environments.

The effective leader needs to understand distinctive factions within a community—most notably, the nobility as opposed to the common masses. While both haves and have-nots need to be served—and controlled—they have different needs and pose different challenges. Machiavelli's discussion of these issues (which Madison, Marx, and Thomas Piketty would later address more fully) is rather cursory. His general point is that princes have to understand the competing needs and aspirations of elites and masses, and learn to simultaneously serve, as well as control, all factions. Machiavelli, for purposes he discusses, would cater to the public rather than the elite.

Machiavelli advises a leader to be curious and skeptical, and to ask probing questions. A leader must have impartial advisers and never trust flatterers or those unwilling to confront brutal realities—especially the harsh realities that characterize relations between states. Most advisers, Machiavelli counsels, are inclined to tell a leader what they think the leader wants to hear. A leader will be judged by his advisers, yet the feckless leader can easily be undone by self-promoting flatterers.

The effective political leader, Machiavelli suggests, will celebrate artists and promote festivals and parades. The leader should seek a balance between trying to satisfy citizen aspirations and being willing to utilize hard power.

The effective leader should be known for frugality rather than for lavishness. Do not tax or spend excessively, as this can drain state resources that might be needed for national security and weaken a leader's legitimacy. National security preparedness, however, will always be a tax priority.

An effective leader should encourage good, orderly habits among the people and recognize, counsels the ever-pragmatic Machiavelli, the salutary role religion can play.

Above all, Machiavelli urges the leader to be a realist. The leader must recognize that military preparedness, the shrewd use of force, and the arts of surprise and deception are necessary in winning wars and instituting a stable government. Machiavelli admonishes a leader to face each challenge with a clear sense of strategic, brutal realities.

Why We Cringe at the Term "Machiavellian"

The adjective "Machiavellian" is used to refer to treachery, guile, double-dealing, cunning, scheming, murder, and every kind of villainy, especially in politics or in career advancement. An enduring complaint is that *The Prince* recommends that leaders have to practice evil. Thus it is, some critics charge, merely a handbook for thugs, gangsters, and dictators.

The constitutional scholar Scott Gordon, for example, contends that Machiavelli's "insistence that a successful ruler be totally unscrupulous, devious, and amoral, recognizing no loyalties or obligation that will not assist him to sustain and extend his power, is responsible for the pejorative adjective 'Machiavellian.'" Gordon pointedly concludes that there is "nothing in *The Prince* that requires a modern reader to revise this view."[13] Gordon is correct about the lasting use of the adjective. Machiavelli, however, does not propose that a successful ruler be *totally* unscrupulous—rather, Machiavelli insists, a successful ruler is unscrupulous only on occasion, as necessity dictates.

Critics emerged even among Machiavelli's earliest readers. Pope Paul IV placed *The Prince* and other writings by Machiavelli on the Church's index of prohibited readings (while at the same time some of the Church officials were practicing Machiavellian tactics). England later banned the book. A few of Machiavelli's friends chided him for provocative exaggeration, saying that most people actually want to be good, to do the right thing, to care for their neighbors and community.

Machiavelli had studied enough history to know that warfare was regularly based on surprise and deception and that wars inevitably produce collateral damage. He was a proponent of selective "shock and awe" tactics and using violence to instill dread in those who might become subversive to the state. His imagined prince, critics believed, would be an opportunistic and deceptive autocrat, in league with the devil.

Machiavelli seems to be celebrating top-down manipulative authoritarianism. The road to power he describes is occasionally paved with guile, cruelty, and casualties. His maxims are provocative:

> Know how to lie and do wrong, and use these tactics when strategically necessary.
>
> A leader who wants to maintain national security is often forced not to be good.
>
> Men will always do badly by you unless they are forced to be virtuous.
>
> For national security, a prince will often be compelled to work against humanity, religion, and mercy.
>
> Anyone who gains new territories and wishes to hold on to them must do two things: the first is to extinguish the ancient lineage of the previous ruler; the other is to alter neither their laws nor their taxes.
>
> Beware consistency, complacency, and stagnation. An effective leader must not only be a great dissembler and pretender: circumstances and changing situations will force him to change as fortune and context change.

Politics, for Machiavelli, was an unsentimental profession. Promises are merely that—they will not always be kept. Other nations will regularly ignore agreements and even moral understanding if it is in their interest to do so. Both men and nations, Machiavelli implies, will sometimes act like animals, and thus the effective prince must understand how to deal with inhumane or beastly behavior.

Machiavelli understands that governance requires political leaders to get their hands dirty. He accepts the occasional need for what today we might call "Godfather" vengeance. Moses, he points out, had to kill people en route to the promised land. Romulus, to unify Roman leadership, had to kill his brother. Philip of Macedon is condoned even though he engaged in what we would call ethnic cleansing. Hannibal is admired for instilling dread in his troops. Cesare Borgia shocked the citizens of Romagna with an extravagant public execution. Sometimes, Machiavelli says, such coarse acts must be imitated—but he would reject the connotation that this was "dirty work."

His examples of useful fraud and cruelty are offset by a few warnings of overreach. But the general tone makes Machiavelli appear heartless.

By nature irreverent, Machiavelli did little to hide his contempt for Church officials, who, he believed, were often corrupt. The selling of indulgences was merely one example. He also publicly chided the pious monks who retreated from the challenges of this life to concentrate on preparing for the next.

Machiavelli dismisses Christian teaching as of little help (even though his younger brother was a priest). Church fathers, he believed, preached too much about tenderness, humility, and forgiveness and were overly preoccupied with the salvation of the individual's soul. These qualities do not win wars, secure diplomatic victories, or achieve the exacting tasks of statecraft.

Turning the other cheek "may gain the kingdom of heaven but is likely to lose an earthly kingdom," writes the British political theorist Alan Ryan. Machiavelli believed that most of his hometown Florentines "were too willing to think they were under the peculiar protection of God, and were therefore lackadaisical about their political and military affairs."[14] Thus his blunt warning of the tension between Christian pieties and practical political truths.

Since Machiavelli's time, Enlightenment thinking has encouraged us to regard individuals as ends in themselves rather than as simply a means to maintain a successful state. For us, life, liberty, and the pursuit of happiness are foundational principles, the very justification for our state's existence. Machiavelli, of course, was writing before the idea of the "consent of the governed" had been well developed. His notion is of a top-down rather than bottom-up society: individuals must serve the state, rather than the state existing primarily to serve individuals.

Most political observers today hold that leadership can be effective and government can be efficient even when constitutionally constrained. To paraphrase Scott Gordon, effective government can derive from a structure of political institutions that enables executive power, and even executive prerogatives, to be controlled and properly directed without relying on Machiavellianism.[15]

The Prince also disturbs us because, while history has taught about emancipation and liberation leaders, it has also taught about tyrants, dictators, and toxic leaders. We recognize that Hitler, Stalin, Saddam Hussein, Robert Mugabe, and Kim Jong-Il all used "Machiavellian" tactics to entrench themselves in power and make their people dependent on them. Admirers of Machiavelli will cavil at the description of these dictators as Machiavels. These leaders, they note, acted as "strongmen" in establishing their regimes but ignored much of the governing advice outlined in *The Prince*. Machiavelli does not condone toxic cruelty, state ownership of property, or relentless demagoguery.

Still, the world has watched scores of liberation leaders become tyrants and dictators. The organization theorist Jean Lipman-Blumen speculates that "when our freedom unnerves us, we tend to gravitate toward any leader who will make us feel safe, protected and good about ourselves. Toxic leaders, who promise security and assure us that we are special or 'chosen,' become particularly powerful magnets for our unmoored egos."[16]

Machiavelli glosses over some of the irritating realities of leadership everywhere—that leaders with great strengths often have great liabilities or weaknesses as well. And with significant power comes a sense of entitlement and often a reluctance to let go of it.

Power holders and the privileged in general are reluctant to yield power or privilege. Indeed, the most corrupting part of holding power, for the power holder, is fear of losing power. Further, with power and privilege often comes a sense of indispensability.

Precisely because we accept Machiavelli's view of human nature, we yearn for safeguards against the abuse of power. For, if Machiavelli is even somewhat right about human nature—"ungrateful, fickle, liars and deceivers, . . . and greedy of gain"—will the prince not also be liable to some of these same human tendencies?

On the one hand, the effective exercise of power can lead to a free and independent state, and perhaps even to honor and glory. On the other, political power, lodged (as it must be) in human hands, is invariably subject to overreach and injudicious behavior. Machiavelli underestimates the role that pride and hubris often play in bad governance. Thus the widespread sentiment that while it may be necessary to consolidate power in order to build a successful state, power also has a tendency to corrupt its possessors.

This is why most of the world today favors constitutionalism and some form of leadership rotation or term limits. Americans, by a strong majority, support the Twenty-Second Amendment, which limits presidents to two four-year terms. The People's Republic of China limits its leader to a single ten-year term. Even Machiavelli, in the *Discourses*, favors such constitutional practices.

But he was an advocate for realpolitik centuries before the term came into common use. Realpolitik describes strategic thinking and especially a foreign policy based on military strength, preparedness, and blunt calculation of national interests. As a point of view, it is devoid of sentimentality, conventional ideology, morality, or appeals to world opinion. Machiavelli understood this perspective. He is, in some ways, one of the godfathers of such thinking, even though he was mostly elaborating on and embellishing views that went back to the Greeks and earlier.

Machiavelli believed it is impossible in the world of politics to consistently be good and to do good at the same time. Sometimes what must be done in the short term, he implies, is different from what will benefit a state in the long term. A leader or prince may on occasion have to do harm in the larger cause of national security.

Thus leaders live in a morally ambiguous world. Sometimes, in what scholars refer to as moral leadership paradoxes, the right thing to do may be ethically or morally wrong. We want, Machiavelli says, leaders who will understand the rules of civility, yet also be smart enough to know when to break such rules.[17]

Machiavelli's defenders say he was not advocating toxic leadership but was merely the product of his times. He was an unemployed diplomat who loved his country so much that he wrote an antiterrorist and anticolonial tract that would provide for the law, stability, and security his beloved Florence so desperately needed. He was a patriot who yearned for homeland security.

Nowadays we want leadership to be in service of explicitly stated and widely shared goals, such as liberty, equality, and justice, as well as national security. Looking back on Machiavelli's propositions, we fear that leadership, divorced from transcending enlightened purpose, can too easily become manipulation, deception, and repression. Leadership can become tyranny. Machiavelli would retort that *The Prince* explicitly deals exclusively with monarchical leadership and its challenges.

Post-Enlightenment notions of leadership emphasize that it involves a two-way engagement. Positive leaders, in this view, listen, educate, and empower their followers or constituents. Legitimacy must be earned—it is conferred on leaders by their constituents. Negative images of the term "Machiavellian" live on, especially as we place a high value on constitutionalism and checks and balances.

But a disproportionately negative view of *The Prince*, focusing mainly on Machiavelli's celebration of cunning and cruelty, detracts from its salutary analysis of power politics, human nature, and the strategies leaders may need as they try to establish new states or introduce new policies.

We still shudder at the term "Machiavellian" because most of what Machiavelli revealed is realities we often do not want to acknowledge. Deceit and manipulation crop up in every society. Machiavelli was merely reminding us that the art of governing ourselves is enormously challenging. We are all torn, for example, between the Greek, pagan, or Mafia code—*thou shall avenge the murder of thy father* (an eye for an eye)—and the Christian (New Testament) mercy code—*thou shalt not kill.* This is the dilemma that tormented Shakespeare's Hamlet and Melville's Captain Vere. Competing interpretations of right and wrong hover over us all the time. We do not like being confronted with such realities.

Ideals and ethics are important in governance, yet they alone may not lead to effectiveness. "The successful statesman," writes the historian Max

Lerner, "is an artist, concerned with nuances of public mood, approximations of operative motives, guesswork as to the tactics of his opponents, [and] back-breaking work in unifying his own side by compromise and concession."[18] Machiavelli lives on in our times because we are constantly challenged with how to adapt democratic constitutionalism to the demands of a world in which Machiavellian intrigue and machinations are an enduring reality.

The Prince was intended less as a theory of leadership and power (though it in many ways is that) than as a persuasive argument that desperate times call for a pragmatic and energetic opportunist. Securing order was more of a priority than achieving justice. Philosopher-kings and the virtuous "Christian prince" celebrated in Plato and Erasmus, respectively, are wonderfully idealistic, yet there are times when a society must rely on the leadership of a crafty strongman.

Machiavelli wanted a vital, robust, and civically healthy Florence, and in his epilogue chapter 26 he calls for a resilient and unified Italy. He wanted honor and glory for the state even more than for the prince. His chief goal was to save the life and liberty of the country—to build a prosperous yet secure polity that would combine the best features of Periclean Athens, Sparta, and his esteemed Roman Republic.[19]

Paradoxes of *The Prince*

Machiavelli understood that compromise and patience may be required in one situation, yet bold decisive action and the ruthless display of brute force in another. Leadership is a moving target, complicated and fraught with paradox. It is, as Machiavelli suggests, an art, not a science.

The Paradox of the Pessimistic Optimist

One of the most puzzling aspects of *The Prince* is that the author is simultaneously a pessimistic realist and an empowering optimist. One of his strengths is that he understands the weaknesses and imperfections of human nature.

He fully grasps that violence, corruption, and chaos are persistent challenges for most communities. He brilliantly exposes human and civic pathologies that must be taken into account.

Yet, "for all its pessimism," writes Miles J. Unger, "Machiavelli's philosophy is ultimately empowering. He insists that man has the capacity, indeed the duty, to shape the course of his destiny."[20] Individuals *can* create a favorable *fortuna*. Individual agency, even in a Tolstoyan world, is inherent in the quality of *virtù* (the strength and boldness that a prince must have).

Similarly, the Machiavelli scholar Maurizio Viroli downplays the view of *The Prince* as a bible of unscrupulous leadership tactics, preferring instead to view Machiavelli's treatise as a patriotic plea for an enlightened liberation activist leader, one who will help unify and consolidate the fragmented Italian city-states.[21]

Hobbes, Locke, and the American framer Alexander Hamilton would further develop the need for sovereignty and executive prerogative. These later theorists and practitioners wrote in the long shadow of Machiavellian realism. Yet they wanted, perhaps like the Italian, to channel any pessimism in ways that would promote the common good.

The "Curse of Machiavelli" Paradox

The "curse of Machiavelli" is the painful reality—one we are hesitant to acknowledge—that in a world governed by self-interest, greed, and clashing ambitions, leaders need to exercise hard power. Machiavelli pulls back the curtain and helps us see the stark realities of emergency leadership.

Machiavelli celebrates boldness and the exercise of hard power by such historical figures as Alexander, Caesar, Romulus, Hannibal, and Cesare Borgia. He justifies the violence and harshness of these leaders as a temporary expedient. "Judicious cruelty" can be dictated by a doctrine of necessity—to prevent the anarchy and untold misery that otherwise might result.

Historians who study Lincoln's presidency see him as both a moral standard-bearer and a fiercely resolved warrior—a warrior who presided over an enormously bloody war, and who bent the Constitution when he deemed it necessary, suspending habeus corpus, usurping civil liberties, ignoring some laws, and dissembling when he believed he had to.[22]

Those who look at the history of the U.S. Central Intelligence Agency, the National Security Agency, and U.S. Special Forces understand, albeit with ambivalence, the darker side of Machiavelli's message. A notable example is Attorney General Robert Kennedy's persistent prodding of the CIA to assassinate Fidel Castro.[23] Recent U.S. tactics in the war on terror, such as targeted drone strikes, extraordinary rendition, enhanced interrogation, and the massive Internet mining of personal communications, understandably trigger debate about constitutionality and the proper extent of executive prerogative.

Machiavelli seems to suggest that good sometimes comes from evil, foreshadowing Shakespeare's Hamlet, who explains, "I must be cruel only to be kind."

The "Machiavelli curse" is as endlessly debated as it is probably incurable. Is he advocating moral relativism? Is this not a slippery slope leading to abusive and toxic leadership? Who decides when cruelty or force is "necessary"? Are princes exempt from normal standards of human conduct? What are the limits to a prince's authority? For how long is this princely prerogative granted? And what about the role of a higher law or a natural law?

We want to believe it is not necessary to do evil in order that we may do good. But we understand that tough and sometimes tragic choices have to be made. The theologian Reinhold Niebuhr contends that there are situations when a choice must be made between reasonably valid principles where one value must be sacrificed to another.

The contest between Antigone and Creon, for instance (in Sophocles's play *Antigone*), was tragic because each from his or her own perspective—Creon from the standpoint of the state and Antigone from that of the family—was right. All rational resolutions of such tragic dilemmas which pretend that a higher loyalty is necessarily inclusive of a lower one, or that a prudent compromise between competing values can always be found, are false.[24]

Leaders must make choices not just between right and wrong, but sometimes between right and right, or between what may be wrong now but right tomorrow.

Niebuhr speculates that leaders can become handicapped if they fail to realize the ironic tendency that virtues may turn into vices when too complacently relied upon. And they also may become handicapped if they become "too blind to the curious compounds of good and evil in which the action of the best men and nations abound."[25]

The Prince exposes a fundamental paradox of leadership: even though a leader's legitimacy may ultimately derive from the consent of the governed, a leader must be able to wield hard power when necessary. We are simultaneously fascinated and unnerved by a leadership guided by a "whatever it takes" philosophy.

The Paradox of Virtue and Virtù

Machiavelli wants his prince to be virtuous, yet also capable of cruelty, deception, and manipulation. A prince should possess a kind of pugnacious strength or boldness—and this means being able to act in what we would call an "unvirtuous" or even "bestial" manner.

Machiavelli understands traditional virtue. But, he says, that kind of virtue is sometimes insufficient for his imagined prince to function effectively. Thus he develops a parallel notion of *virtù*, for which there is no simple translation. But scholars have come to define Machiavelli's notion of *virtù* as a largely military quality of inner strength and force of will, a steely discipline and virility, and an aggressive political willingness to confront challenge and adversity. A prince with *virtù* is capable of many qualities—being generous or cruel, faithless or compassionate, rapacious or miserly—as the situation warrants.

In today's colloquial terms, leaders need to "kick ass," "lean in," or "prince up." In other words, they may need to act in ways contrary to traditional conceptions of virtue.

Machiavelli suggests that a greater good sometimes comes from a leader's devious actions. While there may be times to show mercy or forgiveness—traditional Christian virtues—Machiavelli exalts the use of force and violence if required. The prince, Machiavelli suggests, must accept this aspect of his own character and even cultivate the ability to act this way. Ultimately *virtù* is a strength, a leadership ability that is essential if a prince is to be able to create and sustain a free and independent state.

In sum, paradoxically, be virtuous when possible, but exercise *virtù* when necessary.

The Paradox of the Villain as Celebrity/Hero

Machiavelli asks us to understand that the prince, at certain times, may do things that we may not admire or condone. His prince must transcend the law, or the conventional norms, in order that good results can be achieved. Machiavelli chillingly portrays his Cesare Borgia as an almost operatic heroic villain.

A long history of narratives celebrates those who lie, break the law, and resort to violence. Robin Hood steals from the rich to share his bounty with the poor. Huck Finn delightfully lies to protect his friend Jim. Abraham Lincoln dissembles about ongoing peace negotiations to help secure passage of the Thirteenth Amendment. The gunslingers of the American West—Billy the Kid, Jesse James, Kit Carson, Bonnie and Clyde—were at least occasionally cold-blooded killers, yet they became icons.

Popular culture provides countless examples of audiences cheering on law-breakers, criminals, and unsavory characters who compete for power. In the iconic *Godfather* films, audiences are fascinated with how the Corleone family goes about its businesses, using Machiavellian strategies. Murder, blackmail, and intimidation seem to be accepted. The Netflix series *House of Cards* focuses on a ruthless Machiavellian politician, Frank Underwood, who lies, cheats, steals, and commits murder. Yet his machinations are endlessly fascinating—we cannot look away. We sometimes celebrate "bad boys" in professional sports as well as in some styles of hip-hop music. In fact, we pay money to participate vicariously in the danger these bad boys represent.[26]

We cringe at the cruel tactics of Machiavelli's prince, yet cheer on mythic antihero villains and lawbreakers. Think of John Steinbeck's Tom Joad, Margaret Mitchell's Rhett Butler, Ayn Rand's John Galt, and Edward Abbey's Monkey Wrench Gang in American literary fiction. Part of the answer is an inherent American antipathy to established authority and a natural skepticism about government. We are generally cynical and suspicious about politicians and government.

Machiavelli may claim that when the prince breaks the law, it is for the greater good of the state. But having seen how politicians benefit themselves, how a Tammany Hall does business, how oligarchs and rent seekers profit, how once-admired liberation leaders become tyrants and despots, we have become skeptical about our leaders.

Why do we seemingly celebrate the Machiavellian tactics used by Vito Corleone, Tony Soprano, and Frank Underwood, cheering at their successes and conveniently ignoring that these characters are hungry for personal power and traffic in manipulation and cruelty?

Machiavelli's suggestion—that leaders sometimes need to engage in morally debatable behavior—is a complicated and messy position. Machiavelli would probably have replied that life *is* complicated and messy. "Man up," "power up," or "prince up." He might add too that ends equally valued sometimes collide with each other and a leader has to choose.

The Allegiance Paradox

Machiavelli is, as noted, secular, irreverent, and anticlerical. Yet he also seems to embrace many traditional or conservative views about property rights, respect for women, frugality, and, above all else, law and order. In a typical passage, he explains that it is okay to be feared, yet leaders need to act so that they do not become hated. A leader who is hated loses respect, allegiance, and, ultimately, legitimacy. No leader, he says, can survive the disaffection of his people.

Machiavelli does not explicitly discuss the role trust plays in his imagined principality, but he acknowledges that people will abandon leaders who lack this sensibility. He would probably agree with contemporary leadership analysts who emphasize the centrality of trust. "Trust is the emotional glue that binds followers and leaders together. The accumulation of trust is a measure of the legitimacy of leadership. It cannot be mandated or purchased; it must be earned. Trust is the basic ingredient of all organizations: the lubrication that maintains the organization, and . . . it is as mysterious and elusive a concept as leadership—and as important."[27]

The Reporter's Paradox

The Prince is an unmistakable call for a strong leader and a condemnation of vacillation and timidity. (Nevertheless, Machiavelli would cleverly remind us that if the ruse of appearing timid or cautious leads to victory, then the prince should "appear" to be so.) Still, Machiavelli's emphasis on bold "superhero" leaders is based on his reading of history as well as on his own experience in diplomatic service. For example, some of his dramatic encounters with "Italian" leaders informed his writing.

Machiavelli claims that he is just a realistic observer of human nature and the life of politics. Rejecting theology, idealism, and metaphysics, his goal is pragmatism. This, he says, is just how leaders behave, especially in troubled times. Effective leaders of the past sometimes used morally questionable tactics but were successful in maintaining their state.

While we can be disappointed in the way *The Prince* sometimes seems to celebrate violence and brutality, we need to be careful not to blame Machiavelli for creating these qualities. To fault Machiavelli for the actions of historical figures such as Romulus or Cesare Borgia is like faulting Shakespeare for the actions of his Richard III, Iago, or Macbeth.

Machiavelli shares with Shakespeare the notion that every leader—indeed, each of us—is a composite of good and evil inclinations. So while Machiavelli prioritizes national security and hard power, he also encourages civility and tolerance. Effective leadership, he says, requires balancing toughness with sensitivity, boldness with preparedness, and a tenacious self-confidence with the contextual and social intelligence of a servant-leader.

The need for force or hard power, Machiavelli claims, is just a historical given.

The Paradox of the Moral Leader yet "Bad Dude"/Enforcer

A final paradox suggested by *The Prince* deals with our contradictory expectations of a leader. It is sometimes said in the United States that we have one constitution for peacetime and another (less precise and more flexible) for wartime.

But this notion speaks far beyond the American political experiment. People everywhere generally want just, compassionate, and morally inspired leaders—except when they want tough, cunning, manipulative, and intimidating "bad dude" leadership.

"The challenge of politics," writes *New York Times* columnist David Brooks, often "lies in the marriage of high vision and low cunning." Brooks was writing about Lincoln, who, he said, had the courage "to take morally hazardous action in order to make that vision a reality."[28] Brooks's "courage" and "morally hazardous action" are, at least in part, what Machiavelli means by *virtù*.

People may deplore the ways and means Machiavelli's prince uses to gain and maintain power. Yet the same prince may earn grudging respect, if not full legitimacy, to the degree he diminishes "the amount of random, unpredictable, pointless violence and cruelty" a people might otherwise suffer.[29]

Concluding Note

"Ye shall know the truth and the truth shall set you free," says John in the Gospels. The British author and wit Aldous Huxley replies by suggesting, "Ye shall know the truth and the truth shall make you mad."

The Prince succeeds in doing both.

Machiavelli's insights, however borrowed or clichéd, help us today to understand the subtleties of acquiring and exercising power. But the implicit premise that the prince knows best and the sometimes cheerful celebration of treachery are bridges we are, of course, hesitant to cross. Also, *The Prince* and similar writings seduce us to place too much faith and unrealistically high expectations on single leaders to achieve what in reality has to be the work of large cohorts, movements, and teams of citizen-leaders.[30]

Machiavelli has provoked and challenged his readers for five hundred years. We read *The Prince* because it is a powerfully argued view that can be ignored, realistically, only at our own peril. Machiavelli reveals many of the ironies and realities of political life even as he leaves us uneasy and unsatisfied with the predicament of being dependent, for any length of time, on any one person who is the sole wielder of public power. As Machiavelli suggests elsewhere, and as the American political experiment aspires, the transcending goal of political architects is to design governing systems that create law and order yet also provide for checks against the abuse of power—whether by the leader or the led.

CHAPTER 8

The Riddle of Cesare Borgia and the Legacy of Machiavelli's *Prince*

CLIFFORD ORWIN

It is wrong to read Machiavelli as a political writer who composed his works having in view a close, visible purpose. His most important pages are written to indicate distant, difficult, almost impossible goals. . . . In all his major works he explicitly reveals to readers that he is writing for another time.[1]

The ancient miracles happened on the way from the house of bondage to the promised land: they happened immediately before the revelation on Mount Sinai. What is imminent, Machiavelli suggests, then, is not the conquest of a new promised land, but a new revelation, the revelation of a new code, of a new Decalogue. . . . Compared with this achievement, the conquest of the promised land, the liberation of Italy . . . can wait. The new Moses will not be sad if he dies at the borders of the land which he had promised, and if he will see it only from afar. For while it is fatal for a would-be conqueror not to conquer while he is alive, the discoverer of the all-important truth can conquer posthumously.[2]

You often read—because people often write—that Cesare Borgia was Machiavelli's "ideal prince." Among those who write this, year in and year out, are students sitting the final exam of my introductory course in the history of political thought. They write it not because they have heard it from me but because someone slipped it into their cultural baggage, left unattended at the airport as they jetted to Florida for spring break. Students may not know much about Machiavelli, but they figure that they do know that Cesare was his ideal prince. They thus see him as the embodiment of Machiavelli's intended legacy.

You cannot fault my students for finding Cesare *The Prince*'s most arresting figure. Machiavelli's treatment of him is far more detailed than that of any of his other actors, permitting the reader to come to know him as we do no other. Everyone else in the work is just an example (however lofty); only Cesare approaches the fullness of a *character*. Of all the actors in the work, moreover, he is the only one whose discourse Machiavelli repeatedly echoes, the only one, therefore, with whom he establishes a dialogue. Lastly, there is no other actor whom he praises so repeatedly and effusively. All of which marks Cesare as uniquely important to Machiavelli. The question is why.

One possible answer is that Cesare is indeed Machiavelli's model or "ideal" prince.[3] Such a view would imply consequences for our understanding of his legacy. It would skew that understanding in the direction of the lone wolf or the efficient despot. Popular Machiavellism vulgarizes this view in manuals on "power and how to get it."

Another possibility would be to acknowledge Cesare as the protagonist of *The Prince* while recalling that Machiavelli also wrote the *Discourses*, among other works promoting republicanism. Then you are left to reconcile Machiavelli the adviser of despotic thugs with Machiavelli the loyal republican. This thankless task preoccupies much of the secondary literature. The most extreme solution to this problem (if also the least plausible, although originating in the greatest mind) is Rousseau's claim at *Social Contract* 3.6 that *The Prince* is "a book for republicans." "Machiavelli's choice of his execrable hero (i.e., Cesare) is itself sufficient to make manifest his hidden intention."[4]

A third possibility is to accept something like the Cesarean model as Machiavelli's intended legacy but to argue that this diminishes the relevance of that legacy to us. As Harvey Mansfield has put this position at the end of chapter 1 in this volume, Machiavelli so understood seem[s] "simplistic and irrelevant to us today."

I will argue for a different view of Cesare's significance for Machiavelli. Important as Cesare is to him, it is not as his ideal prince. Almost the opposite, in fact. Cesare matters because of all the *failures* in *The Prince*, a work so rich in them,[5] Cesare is the one who most evokes Machiavelli's own situation. His is the failure that casts the most doubt on the possibility of Machiavelli's success. Rather than defining Machiavelli's legacy, the example of Cesare reveals the foremost obstacle to his transmitting one.

Cesare as Machiavelli's Double

By far the most remarkable feature of Machiavelli's presentation of Cesare is that he casts him as his double. The two mirror each other not, however, in what they do but in what they suffer. Each endures the malice of fortune, "great and continuous" toward Machiavelli, "extraordinary and extreme" toward Cesare.[6] No other character in *The Prince* is presented as thus afflicted, nor does Machiavelli cast any other as his double. Consider also that in calling the reader's attention to the example of Cesare, Machiavelli five times uses the emphatic personal pronoun *io* (as well as one additional instance of a verb in the first person singular), the greatest density of such occurrences in the work. Similarly, of the only two conversations in the work in which Machiavelli recounts having participated, one was about Cesare and the other was with him (chap. 3, p. 16; chap. 7, p. 32).[7] On the second of these occasions the topic of discussion (of which only Cesare's side is reported) was precisely the hostility of fortune. We are uniquely summoned to reflect on the parallel between Machiavelli's situation and Cesare's.

This is what explains the seeming disproportion between Cesare's achievements, which are so meager, and the attention that Machiavelli lavishes on him. The narrative exposes Cesare as a flash in the pan, no more than a noisy footnote to history. Having so recently as chapter 6 raised our sights to the millennial foundings of a Moses, a Cyrus, a Theseus, and a Romulus, the deadpan Machiavelli of chapter 7 urges us to marvel that after the death of Cesare's father, the Romagna—that wretched backwater for which he had done so much—remained loyal to him in his absence for "over a month."[8] Yet it is precisely as so great a failure that Cesare poses so great a problem for the reader—and for Machiavelli. Rather than distancing himself from this failure, Machiavelli embraces it. Cesare had found himself ten years before where the author of *The Prince* finds himself now: enduring the grim hostility of fortune. Posthumously he serves Machiavelli as canaries used to do coal miners: he provides him with a crucial test case. As has befallen so many canaries, this test had ended in failure. Is this the fate that awaits Machiavelli?

If Cesare was in fact as virtuous as Machiavelli claims, this merely sharpens the problem. How could someone who combined so privileged a situation with such great capacities have thus come to nothing? And if the malice of fortune was the culprit, would that not confirm its ascendancy over virtue—thereby confirming the hopelessness of Machiavelli's own plight? Of all the characters in *The Prince*, Cesare is thus the one whose relevance to Machiavelli is most urgent.[9]

Open Season on Unpleasing Prelates: Cesare and Giovampagolo

Machiavelli's focus on Cesare persists beyond chapter 7, the schematic account of his career. The celebrated final chapter of *The Prince* reads like an ironic paean to him. It is precisely in the wake of his failure to establish a princely dynasty independent of the papacy that Italy is in such dire straits that only a god can save it. Machiavelli obligingly invents one: the God not of Abraham (let alone the Gospels) but of the Italian nation. And although he has made it indubitably clear that reliance on the Christian God is responsible for Italy's servitude (chap. 12), he now relies on the comical presumption that the Church will abandon that God in favor of his new pasta-wreathed one. Having anticipated the anticlerical God of Mazzini and Garibaldi, he exhorts the clergy to desert to it. Lorenzo junior, that cipher of a prince, is called upon to succeed with the same strategy that has so utterly failed Cesare, dependence on the Church to found a principality to supplant the Church. Now, however, Machiavelli extends this incongruous scheme from central Italy to the "province" or country as a whole, while inventing a pan-Italian deity to suit.

That the Church might rally to this grand project of depriving it of its temporal power is not a serious suggestion but a reminder of Italy's grievous dilemma. Cesare's hectic efforts to free himself from the Church's clutches had only served to expand and entrench its power. If he is indeed the "glimmer of light" (*spiracolo*) to which Machiavelli refers here in chapter 26, that glimmer was faint indeed. As he repeats in this very place, the adversity of fortune had extinguished it. And by the adversity of fortune Machiavelli means above all the predominance of the Church.

On the question of the obstacle posed by the Church we might compare Machiavelli's seeming praise of Cesare with his seeming blame of Cesare's rival in notoriety, Giovampagolo Baglioni. In a memorable chapter of the *Discourses* (1.27) Machiavelli deplores Giovampagolo's failure to dispose of Pope Julius II, his attendant cardinals, and their rich baggage when Julius had rashly placed all three at his mercy. Giovampagolo "did not know, or to say better did not dare . . . to be the first to demonstrate to the prelates how little to be esteemed is whoever lives and reigns as they do." Instead he had tamely acquiesced in Julius's deposition of him, an armed man obeying an unarmed one.[10]

In a brilliantly provocative article Vickie Sullivan and John T. Scott have argued that Machiavelli's critique of Giovampagolo implies a parallel one of Cesare. Cesare too should have killed the reigning pope (at that time his own father) and the cardinals, thereby putting an end to the papacy. They adduce to this end Machiavelli's statement that on the death of Alexander VI, Cesare enjoyed a veto over his successor: "he could have kept anyone from being pope" (*e poteva tenere che uno non fussi papa*) (33). They take this to mean not just that Cesare could have blocked any particular candidate from becoming pope, but that he could have prevented anyone at all from becoming one, thus abolishing the papacy.[11]

Intriguing as this argument is, I am skeptical of these authors' reading of the line in question. While intrinsically possible—read on its own, the line is ambiguous—the context tells against it. Machiavelli introduces it with "as was said": what was said was that "if [Cesare] could not make Pope whomever he wanted, at least it would not be someone he did not want" (32). This because Cesare had done all he could to increase his influence among such Roman barons as might hold the new pope in check as well as among the College of Cardinals which would choose him. All this "for he had to fear, first, that a new successor in the Church might not be friendly to him and might seek to take away what Alexander had given him." Machiavelli thus seems to join Cesare in assuming that precisely because the papacy would continue, the question of its next incumbent was of crucial importance to him. Even after the statement cited above, on whose ambiguity Sullivan and Scott rely, Machiavelli proceeds to consider only which candidates for pope Cesare should have blocked and which he should have sponsored.

Nor should we overlook the ambiguities of Machiavelli's presentation of Giovampagolo. Certainly a bloodbath of the higher clergy would have tickled Machiavelli's fancy. Yet he does not exaggerate its likely consequences. He does not suggest that it would have succeeded in extinguishing the papacy. Its value would have rested in its exemplarity, Giovampagolo having been the first to show the prelates the contempt that they deserved. This would imply that he would also have been the first to show others how to show that contempt. Machiavelli admits, moreover, that far from winning Giovampagolo acclaim, this deed would have incurred great infamy. Whatever else a massacre might have taught the prelates, they would have learned fear and hatred from it. Even granting Machiavelli's judgment that Giovampagolo "would have done a thing whose greatness would have surpassed all infamy, every danger, that could have proceeded from it," this infamy and these dangers would have destroyed him. Whichever cardinals remained would have elected a successor to Julius who would spare no pains to hunt down Giovampagolo. While Machiavelli offers him the hypothetical consolation that he "would have left an eternal memory of himself," he fails to mention that it would have been one of the utmost infamy. Even the most lukewarm Christians—however receptive to Savonarolan blasts against papal corruption—would have shrunk in horror from Giovampagolo's deed. The rehabilitation of his reputation would have depended on something he could not possibly have foreseen, the writings of Machiavelli himself.

As confirmed by the cravenness of the actual Giovampagolo, the power of the Church did not rest on its temporal pomp, on popes, cardinals, and baggage trains. It relied on a spiritual dread that had succeeded in unmanning even him. Giovampagolo may have been almost comically wicked—openly incestuous and parricidal—but that is why his example is telling. It takes a really bad Christian to confirm the pervasiveness of Christianity's power. What Giovampagolo shrank from teaching the prelates in deed was left to Machiavelli to teach them through his writing; writing will succeed (eventually) where action is not yet ripe.[12] We may say much the same of the part that Cesare plays in *The Prince*.

That papacide is by no means foreign to Machiavelli's own mind will emerge from chapter 4 of *The Prince*. As the first chapter of the work that lacks Italian examples, it ipso facto calls on the reader to apply its lessons to Italy. In this chapter Machiavelli speaks of the rigors of acquiring a state in which all authority emanates from the center. Whoever assaults it must expect to confront the sum total of its power. Should you succeed in defeating it, however, you need only extirpate any surviving members of the royal family in order to govern your new realm in safety.

Machiavelli's examples of such highly centralized regimes are the safely distant (heathen) ones of the ancient Persian Empire and the contemporary Ottoman one. Still, it is easy to identify the one Italian regime conforming to this model.[13] Yet the parallel is an imperfect one. For the papacy, being the vessel of no one family, does not lend itself to extirpation.

Ultimately, then, papacide was insufficient; what was needed was ecclesiacide. For this, however, the time was not ripe. Sects have their shelf lives (cf. *Discourses* 2.5), and that of Christianity (while past its "best before" date) had not yet expired. In a world still dominated by Christianity, Giovampagolo could hardly have been expected to act as Machiavelli pretends to suggest.[14] This problem also frames Machiavelli's treatment of Cesare.

Machiavelli's Doubtful Praise and Cesare's Impossible Dilemma

We are now ready to examine more closely Machiavelli's ambiguous praise of Cesare. That praise is defensive: Machiavelli must explain Cesare's failure. It also displays a glaring contradiction. Machiavelli offers not one but two accounts of that failure. The first is highly favorable to Cesare. It casts him as the very model of a new prince who has risen through fortune, or even of the new prince simply. All that he did is worthy of imitation, and none of it contributed to his downfall. The maleficence of fortune (that is, the morass in which he found himself at his father's death) thwarted his exemplary efforts but in no way diminished them: "But Alexander died five years after he had begun to draw his sword. He left the duke with only the state of Romagna consolidated, with all the others in the air, between two very powerful enemy armies, and sick to death. And there was such ferocity and such virtue in the duke, and he knew so well how men have to be won over or lost, and so sound were the foundations that he had laid in so little time, that if he had not had these armies on his back or if he had been healthy, he would have been equal to every difficulty" (chap. 7, p. 31–32).

Now, that is impressive. We soon learn, however, that this flattering view of Cesare's failure is that of Cesare himself: "And he told me, on the day that Julius II was created, that he had thought about what might happen when his father was dying, and had found a remedy for everything, except that he never thought that at his death he himself would also be on the point of dying" (ibid.).[15]

There is just one thing wrong with Cesare's mournful scenario. In fact he did not die. Having without further comment resurrected him, Machiavelli must adduce a different reason for his downfall.

Machiavelli's new position is that Cesare failed because of his bad choice in permitting his enemy Giuliano della Rovere to be elected Pope Julius II. You should never grant power to anyone whom you have offended (as Cesare had offended Giuliano) or who will have reason to fear you. Since not just Giuliano but all the Italian cardinals of the day fell into one or both of these categories, Cesare (claims Machiavelli) should have acquiesced in the election of a Spaniard or a Frenchman (33). "And whoever believes that among great personages new benefits will make old injuries be forgotten deceives himself. So the duke erred in this choice and it was the cause of his ultimate ruin." Cesare's undoing, then, was not the malignity of fortune, prevailing over his flawless virtue, but an unforced and really quite elementary error.[16] Has Machiavelli completely reversed his position on the reasons for Cesare's failure?

Perhaps not entirely. As experienced readers of Machiavelli will know, he is not above giving bad advice to his characters. Such appears to be the case here. What were Cesare's actual options? Machiavelli has explained why no Italian cardinal would have been a better choice than Giuliano; what then of the prescribed French or Spanish one? As we have already learned, the French had soured on Cesare because of his double-dealing, whereas his hopes of consolidating his ties with the Spanish had depended on his now dead father (30, 31).

Yet it is a certain blank in the argument that Machiavelli not once but twice requires the reader to complete that proves the bombshell fatal to a sanguine reading of Cesare's situation. First he tells us of the "two very powerful enemy armies" between which Cesare found himself on Alexander's death, then confirms these a few lines later as no less an obstacle to Cesare's success than his illness. "Two very powerful enemy armies?" In Italy? Wherever might these have come from? Not from any of the Italian states. So who else was campaigning in Italy at the time?

Cesare was the prisoner of the Church not least due to that weakness of Italian arms that Machiavelli lays firmly at its door in chapter 12. This weakness had left him first dependent on foreign arms for his victories and later facing defeat at their hands. Both the French and the Spanish had decided it was time for Cesare to pursue other opportunities. At best he could have remained as the abject flunky of one of them. The only French or Spanish pope who might have offered continued support was the very one unavailable to Cesare, a second consecutive pope named Borgia.

Cesare then might well have defended his choice of Giuliano as the least of the various evils available to him. With Giuliano there was at least the hope that as Cesare's lifelong enemy he would be grateful to be chosen, a hope only to be expected of the Christian that Cesare remained. If he had clutched at a straw, it was because nothing else remained to him. Still, it was a wonderful irony: Cesare, of all people, reduced to loving his enemy in the vain hope that his enemy would love him.

Cesare's problem with Giuliano (now soon to be Julius), as with all other possible popes, was not personal but theologico-political. Had Cesare been a hereditary prince, the legitimate son of a legitimate father, he would in the natural course of things have inherited a domain that was rightfully his. Instead he was the illegitimate son of a father all of whose children were by definition so and whose principality was uninheritable. Neither Cesare nor any other Borgia could hope to succeed Alexander as pope. However corrupt the Church of those days, certain appearances had to be maintained. "Cesare Borgia as Pope! . . . all the deities on Olympus would have had occasion for immortal laughter."[17] The Church, however, had other priorities than amusing discarded pagan gods.

This hypocrisy so necessary to the Church was necessarily fatal to Cesare. No pope but a Borgia would have continued to drain power from the Church into the reservoirs of the Borgias. No other would have failed to place Cesare's ouster at the top of his to do list. Precisely because the papacy was not a family dynasty but an office charged with enduring until the end of time, it did not even matter whether the new incumbent had taken personal umbrage at Cesare or had personal reasons to fear him. He could not but take offense *as pope* at Cesare's ongoing project or fail to fear this growing cancer on the body of the Church.

Cesare's Place in the Argument of *The Prince*

Of what exactly are we to take Cesare as a model, and which account of his failure are we to credit? Just what are we to learn from his example?

There is one phrase of Machiavelli's praise of Cesare that states with precision both the scope of his achievement and its limits. Cesare is a model for "whoever in his new principality judges it necessary to renew old orders with new modes" (*innovare con nuovi modi gli ordini antiqui*). While other aspects of Machiavelli's praise of Cesare may echo the latter's bluster, the vocabulary of this one is distinctively Machiavelli's own (see, above all, chaps. 6 and 15 by way of comparison).

If Machiavelli praises Cesare's *nuovi modi*, he does not praise the *ordini antiqui*. In context that term can only refer to Christianity, which is as clearly the root pathology in *The Prince* as it will be declared to be in the *Discourses* (1.12). Earlier in the chapter, in his initial bouquet of praise for Cesare,

Machiavelli has lauded him for his *ordini* (implicitly, then, for Cesare's own *ordini* [27]). He has now conspicuously withdrawn that praise. We learn that for his *ordini* too Cesare had depended on others: to put it bluntly, that he was at bottom a creature of the status quo. We now read the statement at 27 differently: "And if [Cesare's] orders did not bring profit to him, it was not his fault, because this arose from an extraordinary and extreme malignancy of fortune." If not his fault, we now see, that is only in the sense that we can never expect profit from orders not our own.

Cesare, then, had not just failed to make things better; he had left them worse. By deploying his bag of unchristian tricks however unwittingly on behalf of the Christian pontificate, he had given it a new lease on life.[18] Julius, so pious in his worldly fashion, would collect all of Cesare's markers and play them with his usual audacity. We might therefore think of Cesare as a sanguinary successor to the Franciscans and Dominicans of *Discourses* 3.1. I leave it to better scholars of Machiavelli to parse fully the distinction between *rinovare*, Machiavelli's word for the contribution of the friars (whom he also credits with *nuovi ordini*), and *innovare ordini antiqui*, the achievement ascribed to Cesare. It seems clear, however, that the accomplishment of the friars was more fundamental and had bought Christianity more time than it was likely to gain from Cesare's antics.

As for the renovation of Italy, it would require new modes and orders (chapter 26), a foundation and a founder on the level of those of chapter 6. These were of course founders on whom their respective gods had depended (being but aspects of their new modes and orders), not servants of old orders (and hence old gods).

What Cesare showed, and what Machiavelli's contradictory verdict on him expresses, was the futility of building on old orders, even as renewed with new modes. Inevitably they and not the innovator would triumph. It was not the choice of Giuliano (just one bad option among others even worse) but Cesare's broader reliance on fortune (namely, on the *ordini antiqui* of the Church) that doomed him to failure. This was his fatal choice; the rest—which is to say the weakness of his arms and therefore the insufficiency of his virtue—followed from it. This is how we may reconcile the seeming contradiction in Machiavelli's presentation of his failure.[19] In chapter 11 ("On Ecclesiastical

Principalities"), when Machiavelli revisits the events of chapter 7, Cesare figures only as "Duke Valentino," a title obtained for him by his father,[20] and only as the instrument (*lo instrumento*) of his father.

This view of Cesare draws further support from the role assigned him in chapter 13 ("Of Auxiliary, Mixed, and One's Own Soldiers"). Here, he stands out in two ways from the chapter's other three examples: Hiero of Syracuse, David, and King Charles VII of France. He is both the only one of them who is Italian and the only one with personal experience of commanding each of the three types of soldiery mentioned in the title of the chapter—a fact that Machiavelli underlines by listing them there in just the order that Cesare would encounter them.

Of these four examples, two, the ancient and central ones of Hiero and David, were total and splendid successes. Both are presented as having ascended from an inferior form of arms ("a mercenary military" of "*condottieri* set up like our Italians" in Hiero's case; an unwanted auxiliary in David's) in order to rely only on their own. By contrast the more recent example of Charles figures as only a partial success. He had liberated the French from the English by upgrading their system of arms. His son Louis XI, however, following a pattern we have come to expect among Machiavelli's recent (that is, Christian) characters, had partially disarmed the kingdom by reverting to an inferior mode (the "mixed" arms of the title). "And the example given is enough, because the Kingdom of France would be unconquerable if the ordering of Charles had been expanded or preserved. But lack of prudence in men begins something in which, because it tastes good then, they do not perceive the poison that lies underneath, as I said above of consumptive fevers." The final reference, as Mansfield notes, refers us back to a celebrated metaphor in chapter 3: "where NM referred to diseases, not remedies" (57n). Unlike Hiero and David, Louis fails to grasp the harsh necessities of his situation. Blind to the need of expanding and preserving his father's achievement, he permits it to slip away. Unable to discern the weakness lurking beneath France's seeming strength, he prefers indolence to continued rigor. Yet not even Charles entirely escapes Machiavelli's censure, for by leaving his innovation in need of expansion he too had fallen into dependence on others, including his feckless son. Hence Machiavelli's ascription of Charles's liberation of his people from the English not to his virtue alone (the accolade reserved for the highest cases) but to the alloy of "his virtue and his fortune."

It will not surprise us that in this complex example (featuring, like that of David and Saul, two protagonists rather than one), Machiavelli's Christian characters fare less well than his pre-Christian ones (including David, whom Machiavelli rewrites as a paragon of pagan self-reliance). Yet what of Cesare, the first of Machiavelli's examples in the chapter, of whom (like his ancient examples and unlike his French *père et fils*) he offers nothing but praise?

In fact this praise is equivocal. In the end Machiavelli says nothing but that Cesare's repute was never higher than when he enjoyed his own arms. This repute was based on what "all saw"—but what "all see," according to Machiavelli, is never more than the appearance of the thing rather than its reality (chap. 18, p. 70: "Men in general judge more by their eyes than by their hands, because seeing is given to everyone, touching to few. Everyone sees how you appear: few touch what you are").[21] Is this another case of Machiavelli praising Cesare according to the latter's self-estimation?[22] Does the subsequent formulation concerning King Louis, restating the inferiority of Machiavelli's contemporaries at discerning hidden evils, subvert the seeming praise of Cesare? Had Cesare too failed to discern the worm gnawing at his succulent apple? Erica Benner notes drily of his slow ascent to reliance on his own arms that he "begins to sound like a slow learner."[23] Unlike Hiero and David, he has required experience of each defective mode of arms in order to grasp its defects, which is to say that he has demonstrated no capacity to foresee these. This much is clear: Machiavelli's Hiero (and by extension his David) dwells in the highlands of chapter 6, while his Cesare languishes in the mire of chapter 7. However impressive to himself and most others Cesare's semblance of self-reliance (which reached its peak just before his disaster), the outcome belies it: he "acquired his state through the fortune of his father and lost it through the same." Everywhere, it seems, Cesare's appearance of self-reliance masked his continued reliance on others.

Two examples of success (one past, the other future) illuminate Cesare's failure. The first is that of Francesco Sforza.[24] He is the sole instance of success in the very chapter of *The Prince* in which Cesare is the primary instance of failure. It is important to recognize, however, that he is not an instance of success drawn from the title characters of chapter 7, those who owe their principalities to fortune. The chapter offers no such instance. Rather, Francesco figures as a refugee from the preceding chapter 6, in which Machiavelli has presented the loftiest examples, those of the armed prophets. Not of course that Francesco qualifies as the equal of Moses and his peers, but rather as that of the "lesser" (sc. but otherwise identical) example of Hiero. Unlike Cesare, Francesco built on his own virtue rather than on the fortune of others, but turning away from Rome to Milan, he did not challenge the power of the Church. He also accommodated that power in a deeper sense: unlike Hiero (so fortunately pagan), he did not seek to free himself from the insecurity of relying on mercenary arms (chap. 12, p. 50–51). He is the most notable of those ambiguous figures in *The Prince*, the best *condottieri*, able commanders of mercenary troops so worthless except against each other (ibid., 49–50). He thus lives by those *ordini antiqui* that would deliver Italy into servitude. The reader will not be surprised to learn that Francesco's descendants disarmed themselves (14[58]), reverting to that unwarlike model common to both priests and citizens (chap. 12, p. 52–53). Francesco is the contemporary Italian success so sorely missing from chapter 6, but the scope of his success is necessarily limited. Machiavelli notes of Braccio da Montone, the founder of the rival mercenary troop of Bracceschi, that "[unlike Francesco] he [turned his ambition not against Milan but] against the Church and the Kingdom of Naples" (chap. 12, p. 51). He enjoyed no such solid success as Francesco, and the vengeful Colonna ope Martin V would order him buried in unconsecrated ground.

The second alternative to Cesare's bloodletting is Machiavelli's writing. Unlike Cesare, he neither relies on old orders nor confines himself to bringing new modes but offers new versions of both, as he affirms in chapter 15.[25] Given the abiding power of the old, however, he is restricted to waging a war of words. In chapter 14, the comprehensive chapter on war (note the title), half of which treats reading and writing, Machiavelli boasts of the progress already made. In the dedicatory letter that begins the book he had evoked an image of peaks and valley. There he had addressed the titled twit Lorenzo *de bas en haut*, as the hapless victim of fortune, abysmally weak and condemned to flatter and whinge. Now in chapter 14, however, and so just halfway through the book, he returns to (and rewrites) his landscape metaphor. He announces through his stand-in Philopoemen that he has now acquired an army. With them he discusses the best strategy for removing the enemy positioned on the hilltop which they eye from their valley. The enemy of course remains Lorenzo. Still chafing in the lowlands, but now bent on seizing the heights, Machiavelli composedly directs his army in that most comprehensive of studies, war. As with the mysterious troops that bedeviled Cesare at the death of his father in chapter 7, we must ask where these ones can have come from. The discussion in this very chapter of reading as practice for war supplies our answer: Machiavelli has assembled his comrades-in-arms from among his readers. This is of course but the first step. The enmity of fortune can be overcome, but it will take time. Happily, once dead—and *The Prince* would be published only posthumously—Machiavelli will have plenty.

Cesare then should not be mistaken for the legacy intended by Machiavelli. He figures in *The Prince* not as a model for the future but as a noisy ripple in the pond of the recent past. He remains the creature of those *ordini antiqui* which his frenzy of unchristian activity would only serve to renew (chap. 7, p. 32). Like Giovampagolo he is noteworthy primarily for what he has left undone: which is to say, left to be done by Machiavelli.

In this essay, the last in the volume, I have tried to bring it full circle. I have sought to clarify the question that all my colleagues have, in their different ways, addressed. Only once we recognize how far short Cesare fell of providing Machiavelli's solution to what he regarded as the most pressing problem, that of the *ordini antiqui*, can we ask how Machiavelli hoped to improve on him—and whether our modern way of life represents the realization of those hopes. Only if we recognize that mere ruthlessness, however successful, is not Machiavelli's teaching—but that neither does he preserve the slightest vestige of the morality of the *ordini antiqui*—can *we* come to see the subsequent evolution of modern thought not as an abandonment of his teaching but as a series of friendly amendments to it. Once we grasp his goal as a fundamental transformation of human understanding beyond the classical and Christian models of which Cesare was an incoherent relic, so we may grasp such innovations as the peaceful democratic commercial republic as variations on his comprehensive theme.

N O T E S

CHAPTER I. MACHIAVELLI'S ENTERPRISE

Chapter 1, Machiavelli's Enterprise, is developed from a shorter version published in *The New Criterion* 32, no. 2 (October 2013): 4–11.

1. Citations of this letter are from the appendix (107–11) to my translation of *The Prince*, 2nd ed. (Chicago: University of Chicago Press, 1998).

2. References to the *Discourses on Livy* are to book, chapter, and paragraph of the translation by Harvey C. Mansfield and Nathan Tarcov, University of Chicago Press, 1996.

3. References to *The Prince* are to chapter and page in my translation.

4. Jacob Burckhardt, *The Civilization of the Renaissance in Italy* (New York: Phaidon, 1950), 53–56, 104. For Burckhardt the rebirth of the ancients provided a transitional guide to "culture" (mistranslated "civilization" in the title) on its own way to modernity, and Machiavelli, "first of the moderns," contributed the notion that Burckhardt considers a fallacy of "the state as a work of art." Machiavelli must then have done so by replacing, more than reviving, the politics of the ancients.

5. For this summary view of scholarship on Machiavelli, still accurate, see Leo Strauss, *Thoughts on Machiavelli* (Glencoe, Ill.: Free Press, 1958), 9–14.

6. Quentin Skinner and J. G. A. Pocock are the maestri of the contextual view that I contend against. Their "republican interpretation" is a version of the patriotic excuse for Machiavelli's amusing moral lapses.

7. Of Italian editions of *Il Principe*, only that of Luigi Russo has anything to say of the phrase *verità effettuale*. Russo remarks on the word *effettuale* that it is a "creation of Machiavelli" celebrated "with the new intuition he was expressing." Other editors find contemporary references in the humanists to necessity and to Machiavelli's setting aside imaginary republics and principalities, citing what has sources rather than addressing what is new. This is true from the edition by L. Arthur Burd, *Il Principe* (Oxford: Clarendon Press, 1891), 202–3, to that of Mario Martelli, *Edizione Nazionale delle Opere di Niccolò Machiavelli* (Rome: Salerno Editrice, 2006), 1:215n3. See also Machiavel, *Le Prince*, ed. Jean-Louis Fournel and Jean-Claude Zancarini (Paris: Presses Universitaires de France, 2000), 406–7. For comment, see Pierre Manent, *Metamorphoses of the City*, trans. M. LePain

(Cambridge, Mass.: Harvard University Press, 2013), 7–8; Claude Lefort, *Le travail de l'oeuvre Machiavel* (Paris: Gallimard, 1972), 402.

8. Marsilius, *Defender of the Peace*, 1.1.3, 2.1.1, and the passage cited in the latter to Aristotle's *Metaphysics*, 994b32–995a1. In the first passage from Marsilius the enemy of truth is an opinion, in the second a habit, suggesting hope of change. Thanks to Gladden Pappin for these references.

9. Machiavelli, letter of December 10, 1513, 109–10.

10. The food that alone is his is, of course, for such as Guicciardini or Vettori as little as it is for the vulgar ordinarily understood. To the extent one puts credit in this statement in this letter one must subtract from all his other letters addressed to lesser minds than his.

11. Plato, *Republic* 379a–381e.

12. See John 8:32, 14:6.

13. From the first line of the first extant letter and throughout his correspondence, Machiavelli shows no reluctance to speak of "this world"; letter of December 2, 1497. *The Prince* and the *Discourses* have a special status as the only works of his in which he says at the beginning that they contain everything he knows; Leo Strauss, *Thoughts on Machiavelli* (Glencoe, Ill.: Free Press, 1958), 17–20.

14. Letter of April 16, 1527; see also *FH*, 3.7. *Patria* in the phrase is usually translated "native city," but "fatherland" preserves the ambivalence of Florence/Italy as well as earthly/heavenly. It also has the merit, though some would say the defect, of suggesting that there is no fatherland without a father.

15. See *D* 2.31 on how dangerous it is to believe the banished, who have been "thrown out of their fatherland," and "how vain are both the faith and the promises of those who find themselves deprived of their fatherland." This could refer to both priests and philosophers who, unlike Machiavelli, believe themselves entitled or required by their offices to leave the confines of the world.

16. Aristotle, *Politics* 4.12, 6.2.

17. Of the senses, Machiavelli prefers touching to seeing and hearing, both of which are subject to misrepresentation. What one sees can be either appearance or truth, and the voices one hears can be misunderstood, but touch is unconnected to imagination and hence certain. *P* 18.71; *D* 1.56.1, 3.14.1, 3.41.1.

18. Aristotle, *Nicomachean Ethics* 1.1094a1-3, 17–25.

19. Psalms 18.2; 62.2, 6; 71.3; 95.1. On the image of hunting, see Erica Benner, *Machiavelli's Ethics* (Princeton, N.J.: Princeton University Press, 2009), 116–24.

20. For another view of these frescoes, see Quentin Skinner, *L'artiste en philosophie politique* (Paris: Seuil, 2003).

CHAPTER 2. THE REDEEMING PRINCE

1. Niccolò Machiavelli, *Discorsi sopra la prima deca di Tito Livio*, 1.9, in *Niccolò Machiavelli, Opere*, ed. Corrado Vivanti, 3 vols. (Turin: Einaudi, 1997–2005); English

translation by Harvey C. Mansfield and Nathan Tarcov; Niccolò Machiavelli, *Discourses on Livy* (Chicago: University of Chicago Press, 1996). All subsequent references in the text to Machiavelli's works are from *Opere*.

2. Niccolò Machiavelli, *Discursus florentinarum rerum*, in *Opere*, 1:744; English translation from Allan Gilbert, *Machiavelli: The Chief Works and Others* (Durham, N.C.: Duke University Press, 1965), 114.

3. Niccolò Machiavelli, *Dell'arte della guerra*, 7.7.

4. Niccolò Machiavelli, *Istorie fiorentine*, 4.1.

5. Niccolò Machiavelli to Francesco Guicciardini, March 15, 1526, in *Opere*, 2:271; English translation from James B. Atkinson and David Sices, eds., *Machiavelli and His Friends: Their Personal Correspondence* (DeKalb: Northern Illinois University Press, 1996), 382–83.

6. Niccolò Machiavelli, *Discoursi sopra la prima deca di Tito Livio*, 1.58.

7. Niccolò Machiavelli, *Istorie fiorentine*, 7.6.

8. Niccolò Machiavelli, *Il Principe*, chap. 8.

9. Niccolò Machiavelli, *Discorsi sopra la prima deca di Tito Livio*, 1.2.

10. See my *Machiavelli's God* (Princeton, N.J.: Princeton University Press, 2010).

11. Hans Baron, "The *Principe* and the Puzzle of the Date of Chapter 26," *Journal of Medieval and Renaissance Studies* 21 (1991): 83–102; Sergio Bertelli and Piero Innocenti, introduction to *Bibliografia machiavellina* (Verona: 1979), xxviii–xxxvi; Mario Martelli, introduction to Niccolò Machiavelli, *Il Principe*, ed. Mario Martelli, Edizione Nazionale delle Opere, vol. 1 (Rome: Salerno Editrice, 2006).

12. See Martelli, introduction to Machiavelli, *Il Principe*, 39.

13. I agree with Gennaro Sasso and Giorgio Inglese's view that Machiavelli composed the "Exhortation" before early 1514. See Gennaro Sasso, "Del ventiseiesimo capitolo, della 'provvidenza' e di altre cose," in *Machiavelli e gli antichi e altri saggi* (Milan: Ricciardo Ricciardi, 1988), 277–349; and Giorgio Inglese, "*Il Principe (De Principatibus) di Niccolò Machiavelli*," in *Letteratura italiana: Le Opere*, ed. Alberto Asor Rosa (Turin: Einaudi, 1999), 1:891.

14. In another context, in chapter 13 ("Of Auxiliary, Mixed, and Citizen Soldiers") Machiavelli uses the adverb *ora* in reference to the king of France's military defeats in June and August 1513: "This error, followed by others, as we can *now* observe from events, is the cause of the threats to that kingdom"; Federico Chabod, "Sulla composizione de *Il Principe*," in *Scritti su Machiavelli* (Turin: Einaudi, 1993), 156–66.

15. Pasquale Stoppelli, *La Mandragola: Storia e filologia; Con l'edizione critica del testo secondo il Laurenziano Redi* 129 (Rome: Bulzoni, 2005), in particular 69–89.

16. Petrarch's text reads: "Ma tarde non fur mai grazie divine."

17. *Le cose volgari di messer Francesco Petrarcha*, 1504 a di X di marzo et nuovamente riueduto Deo gratias, impresso in Firenze, a petitione di Philippo di Giunta cartolaio; or *Le cose uolgari di messer Francesco Petrarcha*, impresso in Firenze, a petitione di Philippo di Giunta fiorentino, nel anno 1510 adi. 17 di Agosto. Another edition was the *Opera del preclarissimo poeta miser Francesco Petrarcha con li commenti sopra li Triumphi: Soneti &*

Canzone historiate & nuouamente corrette per miser Nicolo Peranzone con molte acute & excellente additione. Miser Bernardo Lycinio sopra li Triumphi. Miser Francesco Philelpho. Miser Antonio de Tempo. Hieronymo Alexandrino. Sopra Soneti & Canzone, 1508 adi xv febraro Stampadi in Venetia, per Bartholomeo de Zanni da Portese. I doubt Machiavelli could have had available this text.

18. "Quanto alla unione delli altri italiani, voi mi fate ridere: prima, perché non ci fia mai unione veruna a fare ben veruno; e se pure e' fussino uniti e capi e' non sono per bastare, sì per non ci essere armi che vagliono un quattrino, dagli spaguoli in fuora, e quelli per essere pochi non possono essere bastanti; secondo, per non essere le code unite co' capi"; Niccolò Machiavelli to Francesco Vettori, August 10, 1513, in *Opere*, 2:277–78; English translation from Atkinson and Sices, *Machiavelli and His Friends*, 249–50.

19. Niccolò Machiavelli to Giovanni Vernacci, June 26, 1513, in *Opere*, 2:264; English translation from Atkinson and Sices, *Machiavelli and His Friends*, 239.

20. Niccolò Machiavelli to Giovanni Vernacci, August 4, 1513, in *Opere*, 2:271; English translation from Atkinson and Sices, *Machiavelli and His Friends*, 244.

21. Niccolò Machiavelli to Francesco Vettori, June 10, 1514, in *Opere*, 2:325–60; English translation from Atkinson and Sices, *Machiavelli and His Friends*, 290.

22. Niccolò Machiavelli to Francesco Vettori, August 3, 1514, in *Opere*, 2:328–39; English translation from Atkinson and Sices, *Machiavelli and His Friends*, 292–93.

23. Niccolò Machiavelli to Francesco Vettori, January 31, 1515, in *Opere*, 2:351; English translation from Atkinson and Sices, *Machiavelli and His Friends*, 314.

24. Niccolò Machiavelli to Giovanni Vernacci, August 18, 1515, in *Opere*, 2:349; English translation from Atkinson and Sices, *Machiavelli and His Friends*, 314.

25. Niccolò Machiavelli to Giovanni Vernacci, November 19, 1515, in *Opere*, 2:352; English translation from Atkinson and Sices, *Machiavelli and His Friends*, 314.

26. Niccolò Machiavelli to Giovanni Vernacci, February 15, 1516, in *Opere*, 2:353; English translation from Atkinson and Sices, *Machiavelli and His Friends*, 315.

27. Niccolò Machiavelli to Giovanni Vernacci, June 8, 1517, in *Opere*, 2:354; English translation from Atkinson and Sices, *Machiavelli and His Friends*, 316.

28. Niccolò Machiavelli to Giovanni Vernacci, January 5 and January 25, 1518, in *Opere*, 2:357–59; English translation from Atkinson and Sices, *Machiavelli and His Friends*, 319.

29. I have discussed this issue at length in my *From Politics to Reason of State: The Acquisition and Transformation of the Language of Politics* (Cambridge: Cambridge University Press, 1992), 178–80.

30. Niccolò Machiavelli to Francesco Guicciardini, March 15, 1526, in *Opere*, 2:418–22; English translation from Atkinson and Sices, *Machiavelli and His Friends*, 380–83.

31. Roberto Ridolfi, *Vita di Niccolò Machiavelli*, 7th ed. (Florence: Sansoni, 1978); English translation from Cecil Grayson, *The Life of Niccolò Machiavelli* (London: Routledge and Kegan Paul, 1963). A genuine political realist like Gaetano Mosca was not prepared to list Machiavelli among his intellectual mentors. See *Elementi di scienza politica* (1896), in *Scritti politici*, ed. Giorgio Sola (Turin: UTET, 1982), 780–81.

32. Niccolò Machiavelli, *Istorie fiorentine*, 6.29.

33. "È necessario a uno principe, volendosi mantenere, imparare a poter essere non buono, e usarlo e non l'usare secondo la necessità," and that "uno principe, e massime uno principe nuovo, non può osservare tutte quelle cose per le quali gli uomini sono tenuti buoni, sendo spesso necessitato, per mantenere lo stato, operare contro alla fede, contro alla carità, contro alla umanità, contro alla religione. E però bisogna che abbia uno animo disposto a volgersi secondo ch'e' venti della fortuna e le variazioni delle cose li comandano, e, come di sopra dissi, non partirsi dal bene, potendo, ma saper entrare nel male, necessitato." *Il Principe*, chaps. 15 and 18.

34. "E benchè quelli uomini siano rari e maravigliosi; nondimeno furono uomini, ed ebbe ciascuno di loro minore occasione, che la presente; perchè l'impresa loro non fu più giusta di questa, nè più facile; nè fu Dio più a loro amico, che a voi. Qui è giustizia grande: 'iustum enim est bellum quibus necessarium, et pia arma ubi null nisi in armis spes est.'" *Il Principe*, chap. 26.

35. The main proponents of the view that *The Prince*'s perennial philosophical value is the theory of the autonomy of politics from ethics are Benedetto Croce, *Elementi di politica* (1925), in *Etica e politica: A cura di Giuseppe Galasso* (Milan: Adelphi, 1994), 292; and Federico Chabod, *Del "Principe" di Niccolò Machiavelli* (1925), in *Scritti su Machiavelli*, introduction by Carlo Vivanti (Turin: Einaudi, 1993), 99–100.

36. *Il Principe*, chap. 8.

37. Niccolò Machiavelli, *Discorsi sopra la prima deca di Tito Livio*, 1.9.

38. Ibid., 1.58.

39. Niccolò Machiavelli, *Discursus florentinarum rerum*, in *Opere*, 1:735.

40. Antonio Gramsci, *Quaderni del carcere*, ed. Valentino Gerratana (Turin: Einaudi, 2007), 3:1555; English translation from *Selections from the Prison Notebooks of Antonio Gramsci*, ed. and trans. Quintin Hoare and Geoffrey Nowell Smith (London: Electric Book, 2001), 316.

41. Gramsci, *Quaderni del carcere*, 3:1555; English translation from Hoare and Nowell Smith, *Selections from the Prison Notebooks*, 316.

42. Gramsci, *Quaderni del carcere*, 3:1556; English translation from Hoare and Nowell Smith, *Selections from the Prison Notebooks*, 318–19, 328–29.

43. Gramsci, *Quaderni del carcere*, 3:1556; English translation from Hoare and Nowell Smith, *Selections from the Prison Notebooks*, 319.

CHAPTER 3. MACHIAVELLI'S REVOLUTION IN THOUGHT

1. Page citations to Niccolò Machiavelli, *The Prince*, trans. Harvey C. Mansfield, 2nd ed. (Chicago: University of Chicago Press, 1998).

2. On the reception of Machiavelli's work, see Victoria Kahn, *Machiavellian Rhetoric* (Princeton, N.J.: Princeton University Press, 1994).

3. E.g., Alastair Murray, *Reconstructing Realism* (Edinburgh: Keele University Press, 1997), 38–40; Ashley Tellis, "Reconstructing Political Realism," *Security Studies* 5, no. 2

(1995): 25–31. For a more nuanced view, see Steven Forde, "International Realism and the Science of Politics: Thucydides, Machiavelli, and Neorealism," *International Studies Quarterly* 39, no. 2 (1995): 142–43.

4. David Brooks, "Florence and the Drones," *New York Times*, February 8, 2013, A27.

5. Aristotle, *Politics* 2.1267b5–7.

6. Leo Strauss, *Thoughts on Machiavelli* (Glencoe, Ill.: Free Press, 1958), observes, "Machiavelli was the first philosopher who questioned in the name of the multitude or of democracy the aristocratic prejudice or the aristocratic premise which informed classical philosophy" (127). And Louis Althusser, *Machiavelli and Us* (London: Verso, 1999), affirms: "Machiavelli condemns definitively not only the *edifying* religious, moral or aesthetic discourses of the court humanists . . . but also the entire tradition of Christian theology and all the political theories of antiquity. . . . It is evident that Machiavelli considered himself the founder of a theory without any precedent" (7–8).

7. Isaiah Berlin, "The Originality of Machiavelli," in *Against the Current*, ed. Henry Hardy (New York: Viking Press, 1980).

8. Few commentators have noticed that, according to Machiavelli, as the culminating act of his bringing "good government" to the Romagna, Cesare established a civil court before he had the body of his cruel minister cut in two and displayed in the town square. Like the people, these commentators seem to have been left "at once satisfied and stupefied" by "the ferocity of this spectacle" (*Prince* 7.29–30). John M. Najemy, "Cesare Borgia and Machiavelli: A Reconsideration of Chapter Seven of *The Prince*," *Review of Politics* 75, no. 4 (November 2013): 539–56, shows that Cesare did not actually do what Machiavelli claims that he did in *The Prince*; Machiavelli attributes to Cesare actions he thinks a "new prince" should take.

9. Clifford Orwin, "Machiavelli's Unchristian Charity," *American Political Science Review* 72, no. 4 (December 1978): 1217–28, presents a similar analysis of Machiavelli's redefinition of the virtues of "liberality" and "mercy" (*pietate*). But Orwin takes Machiavelli's comment that conquering generals constitute exceptions to what he has said about both virtues, in general, to mean that he endorses an expansive, imperialistic policy of seizing the goods of other peoples. I argue, on the contrary, that the "liberal" behavior of generals constitutes a temporary exception to Machiavelli's general advice. He sees that it is not possible to maintain popular support by conquering ever more people and seizing their goods, because the people conquered become one's own subjects. And, as Machiavelli argues in chapter 19, a prince cannot continue to seize the property of his subjects and remain in power unless he uses an army to suppress them; and if he uses armed force to maintain his empire, that army may well come to control him by threatening to depose and replace him if he does not support their rapacious desires, rather than serving merely as his instrument.

10. Machiavelli has frequently been seen as the first modern proponent of realpolitik, that is, the cynical understanding of politics which not merely recognizes that nations always act on the basis of their self-interest, but argues that they should do so openly and unapologetically. As Ruth W. Grant, *Hypocrisy, and Integrity: Machiavelli, Rousseau, and the Ethics of Politics* (Chicago: University of Chicago Press, 1997), points out, how-

ever, Machiavelli "*recommends* hypocrisy." He sees that "the actions of states take place within a particular moral horizon and are always subject to ethical judgment. Rulers must attend to the way their actions will appear, they must speak a moral language, and they should exploit the opportunities to advance their aims that public moral discourse offers" (41). As Grant also observes, "hypocrisy is an extremely useful tool when you depend on the cooperation of others to further your aims. You must persuade them not only that it is in their interest to cooperate, but that you can be trusted" (50). This need is especially strong in democracies where "politicians, unable to take their support for granted and subject to frequent elections, must continually cultivate the public as well as actual and potential coalition partners" (44).

11. In his *Discourses* (where he is addressing young Florentines with republican sympathies and ambitions, and not a sitting prince), Machiavelli states the difference between what the prince desires and what the people desire more explicitly. "If a prince wishes to win over a people that has been an enemy to him," Machiavelli explains in *Discourses* 1.16, "he should examine first what the people desires; and he will always find that it desires two things: one, to be avenged against those who are the cause that it is servile; the other to recover its freedom. The first desire the prince can satisfy entirely, the second in part." Like Clearchus, tyrant of Heraclea, a prince can satisfy the people's first desire and thus win their support by enabling them to destroy the aristocrats or oligarchs who have oppressed them. "But as to the other popular desire, to recover freedom, since the prince cannot satisfy it, he should examine what causes are those that make (peoples) desire to be free. He will find that a small part of them desires to be free so as to command, but all the others, who are infinite, desire freedom so as to live secure. For in all republics, ordered in whatever mode, never do even forty or fifty citizens reach the ranks of command; and because this is a small number, it is an easy thing to secure oneself against them, either by getting rid of them or by having them share in so many honors . . . that they have to be in good part content. The others, to whom it is enough to live secure, are easily satisfied by making orders and laws in which universal security is included, together with one's own power" (46).

Later in the *Discourses* (2.2) Machiavelli makes the difference between the people's desires and those of the prince even clearer when he observes that "without doubt this common good is not observed if not in republics, since all that is for that purpose is executed, and although it may turn out to harm this or that private individual, those for whom the aforesaid does good are so many that they can go ahead with it against the disposition of the few crushed by it. The contrary happens when there is a prince, in which case what suits him usually offends the city and what suits the city offends him" (130). Machiavelli concludes by emphasizing that "all towns and provinces that live freely . . . make very great profits. For larger [populations] are seen there, because marriages are freer and more desirable to men since each willingly procreates those children he believes he can nourish. He does not fear that his patrimony will be taken away, and he knows not only that they are born free and not slaves, but that they can, through their virtue, becomes princes. Riches are seen to multiply there in larger number, both those that come from agriculture and those that come from the arts. For each willingly multiplies that thing and seeks to acquire those goods he believes he can enjoy once acquired" (132). Quotations and page citations are from Niccolò Machiavelli, *Discourses on Livy*, trans. Harvey C. Mansfield and Nathan Tarcov (Chicago: University of Chicago Press, 1996).

In *Prince* 21 Machiavelli limits himself to urging a ruler who wishes to become esteemed to encourage his people to labor by showing "himself a lover of the virtues, giving recognition to virtuous men, and . . . honor[ing] those who are excellent in an art. Next, he should inspire his citizens to follow their pursuits quietly, in trade and in agriculture and in every other pursuit of men, so that one person does not fear to adorn his possessions for fear that they be taken away from him, and another to open up a trade for fear of taxes. But he should prepare rewards for whoever wants to do these things, and for anyone who thinks up any way of expanding his city or his state. Besides this, he should at suitable times of the year keep the people occupied with festivals and spectacles. And because every city is divided into guilds or into clans, he should take account of those communities, meet with them sometimes, and make himself an example of humanity and munificence, always holding firm the majesty of his dignity" (91). By implication, this means of acquiring esteem would appear to be more desirable, both safer and in the long run more effective, than the examples of Ferdinand and Bernabò Visconti Machiavelli presents earlier in the chapter.

12. In *Discourses* 3.1 Machiavelli states even more clearly: "Kingdoms also have need of renewing themselves and of bringing back their laws toward their beginnings. How much good effect this part produces is seen in the kingdom of France, which lives under laws and under orders more than any other kingdom. Parlements are those who maintain these laws and orders, especially that of Paris. They are renewed by it whenever it makes an execution against a prince of that kingdom and when it condemns the king in its verdicts. Up until now it has maintained itself by having been an obstinate executor against the nobility" (212).

13. Cary J. Nederman and Tatiana V. Gómez, "Between Republic and Monarchy? Liberty, Security, and the Kingdom of France in Machiavelli," *Midwest Studies in Philosophy* 26 (2002): 82–93, point out that "many major contributions to Machiavelli scholarship in English have largely overlooked his remarks about the governance of France" (83). They list Hannah F. Pitkin, *Fortune Is a Woman* (Berkeley: University of California Press, 1984); Harvey Mansfield, *Machiavelli's Virtue* (Chicago: University of Chicago Press, 1996); Quentin Skinner, *Machiavelli* (New York: Hill and Wang, 1981); Maurizio Viroli, *Machiavelli* (Oxford: Oxford University Press, 1998); and Markus Fischer, *Well-Ordered License: On the Unity of Machiavelli's Thought* (Lanham, Md.: Lexington Books, 2000), as examples (83n4), and note that Mark Hulliung, *Citizen Machiavelli* (Princeton, N.J.: Princeton University Press, 1983), 85, explicitly denies the importance of Machiavelli's comments on the "well-ordered kingdom" of France (84n5). Nederman and Gómez also observe the increased emphasis Machiavelli puts on the king's obeying his own laws in his *Discourses*, but note that such a monarchy still falls short of the *vivere libero* described in *Discourses* 2.2, because the king cannot satisfy the people's desire to recover their freedom without relinquishing his own rule. He can, however, make them feel secure.

14. See Althusser, *Machiavelli and Us*: "Machiavelli formulated, in masterly fashion, the political question of the Italian nation's constitution by means of a national state. More precisely, Machiavelli grasped that as soon as the history of the initial development of the mercantile and capitalist bourgeoisie posed the problem of the constitution and definition of nations in specific geographical, linguistic and cultural zones, it imposed the solution: a nation can be constituted only by means of a state—a national state" (11).

15. Vickie B. Sullivan, *Machiavelli, Hobbes, and the Formation of Liberal Republicanism in England* (Cambridge: Cambridge University Press, 2004), 57–79, emphasizes the danger such a popular prince (like Cesare) poses to the preservation of a republic.

16. For a fuller description of the new form of republic Machiavelli envisioned, see Catherine Zuckert, "Machiavelli's Democratic Republic," *History of Political Thought* 35, no. 2 (Summer 2014): 262–94.

17. Harvey Mansfield, "Strauss on *The Prince*," *Review of Politics* 75, no. 4 (November 2013), 665, thus writes of "the enterprise against nobility" that Machiavelli "called his own."

CHAPTER 4. MACHIAVELLI'S WOMEN

1. Throughout I use Niccolò Machiavelli, *The Prince*, trans. Harvey C. Mansfield, 2nd ed. (Chicago: University of Chicago Press, 1998), and *Discourses on Livy*, trans. Harvey C. Mansfield and Nathan Tarcov (Chicago: University of Chicago Press, 1996). Citations to *The Prince* appear in the text according to chapter; those to the *Discourses* according to book, chapter, and paragraph.

2. All quotations from Machiavelli's letters are from James B. Atkinson and David Sices, eds. and trans., *Machiavelli and His Friends: Their Personal Correspondence* (DeKalb: Northern Illinois University Press, 1996). Citations in the text are according to the date of the letter and the number assigned to it (e.g., L 75) in the Atkinson-Sices edition.

3. There could be evocations here of the Socratic cave from the *Republic*, but that is for another time and another place.

4. Niccolò Machiavelli, *Clizia*, trans. Daniel T. Gallager (Long Grove, Ill.: Waveland Press, 1996), 58 (act 5, scene 3).

5. Arthur O. Lovejoy, *The Great Chain of Being: A Study of the History of an Idea* (Cambridge, Mass.: Harvard University Press, 1936), 10.

CHAPTER 5. MACHIAVELLI AND THE BUSINESS OF POLITICS

I am grateful to Robert Black for discussing this topic with me.

1. Henry Neville, in the first translation of the *Discourses* into English (1675, with later reprints and revisions), resolves this contradiction by simply omitting the first paragraph of the introduction to book 1.

2. On the idea of the state in the Renaissance, see (in order of publication) Jack H. Hexter, "'Il Principe' and 'lo Stato,'" *Studies in the Renaissance* 4 (1957): 113–38; Federico Chabod, "Alcune questioni di terminologia: Stato, nazione, patria nel linguaggio del Cinquecento," in *Scritti sul Rinascimento* (Turin: Einaudi, 1967), 625–61; Nicolai Rubinstein, "Notes on the Word 'Stato' in Florence Before Machiavelli," in *Florilegium Historiale*, ed. J. C. Rowe and W. H. Stockdale (Toronto: University of Toronto Press, 1971), 313–36; Harvey C. Mansfield Jr., "On the Impersonality of the Modern State: A Comment on Machiavelli's Use of 'Stato,'" *American Political Science Review* 77 (1983): 849–57; Quentin Skinner, "The State," in *Political Innovation and Conceptual Change*, ed. T. Ball, J. Farr, and R. L. Hanson (Cambridge: Cambridge University Press, 1989), 90–131; David Wootton, "The True Origins of Republicanism: The Disciples of Baron and the Counter-Example of Venturi," in *Il repubblicanesimo moderno: L'idea di repubblica nella riflessione storica di Franco Venturi*, ed. M. Albertone (Naples: Bibliopolis, 2006), 271–304.

3. William Baldwin, *A Myrrour for Magistrates* (London: T. Marshe, 1563), cx(r); Plutarch, *The Lives of the Noble Grecians and Romanes*, trans. Thomas North (London: J. Wight, 1579), 777; John Ponet, *A Shorte Treatise of Politike Pouuer* (Strasbourg: W. Köpfel, 1556), A5r: "And these diuerse kyndes of states or policies hade their distincte names, as wher one ruled, a Monarchie: wher many of the best, Aristocratie: wher the multitude, Democratie: and wher all together, that is, a king, the nobilitie, and commones, a mixte state."

4. Robert Black, *Machiavelli* (London: Taylor and Francis, 2013), 84, 97, 100–101.

5. Ibid., 81, 83–84; John J. M. Najemy, *Between Friends: Discourses of Power and Desire in the Machiavelli-Vettori Letters of 1513–1515* (Princeton, N.J.: Princeton University Press, 1993), 102, 108–9, 114, 122–23, 128–30, 140, 143–46, 149, 155–56, 172, 247, 282, 285.

6. Ernst H. Kantorowicz, *The King's Two Bodies: A Study in Mediaeval Political Theology* (Princeton, N.J.: Princeton University Press, 1957).

7. Maurizio Viroli, *From Politics to Reason of State: The Acquisition and Transformation of the Language of Politics, 1250–1600* (Cambridge: Cambridge University Press, 1991).

8. Giovanni Botero, *The Reason of State* (New Haven, Conn.: Yale University Press, 1956), 223 ("modern policy"); Giovanni Botero, *Della ragione di stato* (Milan: Pietro Martire Locarno, 1596), 316 ("moderna politica").

9. Noel Malcolm, *Reason of State and the Thirty Years' War: An Unknown Translation by Thomas Hobbes* (Oxford: Clarendon Press, 2007), 94, notes that there has been no study of the early history of the word—and makes the mistake of thinking it was new in 1588.

10. Russell Price, "The Theme of 'Gloria' in Machiavelli," *Renaissance Quarterly* 30 (1977): 588–631.

11. John A. W. Gunn, "'Interest Will Not Lie': A Seventeenth-Century Political Maxim," *Journal of the History of Ideas* 29 (1968): 551–64.

12. Traiano Boccalini, *Ragguagli di Parnaso e scritti minori*, ed. Luigi Firpo, 3 vols. (Bari: Laterza, 1948), 1:95–97; 2:17–35, 131–32; 3:93–94; Friedrich Meinecke, *Machiavellism: The Doctrine of Raison d'État and Its Place in Modern History* (New Haven, Conn.: Yale

University Press, 1957), 70–89; Peter Burke, "Tacitism, Scepticism, and Reason of State," in *The Cambridge History of Political Thought, 1450–1700*, ed. J. H. Burns and Mark Goldie (Cambridge: Cambridge University Press, 1991), 477–98 at 490; Alexandra Gajda, "Tacitus and Political Thought in Early Modern Europe," in *The Cambridge Companion to Tacitus*, ed. A. J. Woodman (Cambridge: Cambridge University Press, 2009), 253–68 at 264–65.

13. Meinecke, *Machiavellism*, 46. Despite its title, Alberto Tenenti, "Dalla 'ragion di stato' di Machiavelli a quella di Botero," in *Botero e la 'ragion di stato': Atti del Convegno in Memoria di L. Firpo (Torino 8–10 marzo 1990)* (Florence: Olschki, 1992), 11–21, is particularly helpful on the idea of reason of state before Machiavelli.

14. Francesco Guicciardini, *Dialogo e discorsi del reggimento di Firenze* (Bari: G. Laterza, 1932), 163.

15. Artemio A. E. Baldini, "Tempi della guerra e tempi della politica tra Quattro e Cinquecento: Alle origini del 'realismo politico' di Machiavelli e Guicciardini," in *La 'riscoperta' di Guicciardini: Atti del Convegno internazionale di studi, Torino, 14–15 novembre 1997*, ed. A. E. Baldini and M. Guglielminetti (Fiesole: Casalini, 2006), 79–93.

16. Meinecke, *Machiavellism*, 47–48; Giovanni della Casa, *Rime et prose: Riscontrate con i migliori originali* (Venice: Domenico Farri, 1565), 41v; Kenneth K. C. Schellhase, *Tacitus in Renaissance Political Thought* (Chicago: University of Chicago Press, 1976), 218n114, errs when he says this text was unknown to Meinecke. He is also wrong when he says (124) that the term was not used between della Casa and Botero: see, for counterexamples, Antonio Scaino da Salo, *La politica di Aristotile ridotta in modo di parafrasi* (Rome: Nelle case del popolo romano, 1578), 44; Girolamo Ruscelli, *Lettere di principi, le quali ò si scrivono da principi, ò à principi, ò ragionan[o] di principi*, 3 vols. (Venice: G. Zeletti, 1570), 3:246; Giovanni B. Adriani, *Istoria de' suoi tempi* (Florence: Giunti, 1583), 669, 874, 940; Giovanni B. Leoni, *Considerationi sopra l'Historia d'Italia di messer Francesco Guicciardini* (Venice: I. Gioliti, 1583), 13, 83, 121, 137, 172; Giouambatista Ubaldini, *Istoria della casa de gli Ubaldini e de fatti d'alcuni di quella famiglia* (Florence: B. Sermartelli, 1588), 12, 20. Indeed, the term had already reached English before the publication of Botero: the *Oxford English Dictionary* gives 1585, but there is an earlier usage in Robert Parsons, *A Defence of the Censure, Gyuen upon Tuuo Bookes of William Charke and Meredith Hanmer Mynysters* (Rouen, 1582), 10.

17. Raymond De Roover, *The Rise and Decline of the Medici Bank, 1397–1494* (Cambridge, Mass.: Harvard University Press, 1963), 78 and note 7; *Vocabolario degli Accademici della Crvsca* (Venice: Iacopo Sarzina, 1623), s.v. "ragione."

18. David Wootton, "From Fortune to Feedback: Contingency and the Birth of Modern Political Science," in *Political Contingency: Studying the Unexpected, the Accidental, and the Unforeseen*, ed. S. Bedi and I. Shapiro (New York: New York University Press, 2008), 21–53.

19. Which is not to say that he believes that normative issues are irrelevant: see the classic essay by Isaiah Berlin, "The Originality of Machiavelli," in *Studies on Machiavelli*, ed. M. P. Gilmore (Florence: G. C. Sansoni, 1972), 149–206.

20. On Machiavelli and Hobbes, see David Wootton, "Thomas Hobbes's Machiavellian Moments," in *The Historical Imagination in Early Modern Britain: History, Rhetoric, and Fiction, 1500–1800*, ed. D. R. Kelley and D. H. Sacks (Washington, D.C.: Woodrow Wilson Center, 1997), 210–42.

21. Niccolò Machiavelli, *Selected Political Writings* (Indianapolis, Ind.: Hackett, 1994), 3; Quentin Skinner, "Classical Liberty, Renaissance Translation and the English Civil War," in his *Visions of Politics*, vol. 2, *Renaissance Virtues* (Cambridge: Cambridge University Press, 2004), 308–43.

22. For Hobbes and Galileo, see Thomas Hobbes, *Critique du "De Mundo" de Thomas White* (Paris: J. Vrin, 1973), 178. On Galileo and Lucretius, see David Wootton, *Galileo: Watcher of the Skies* (New Haven, Conn.: Yale University Press, 2010), 167–68, 194, 219, 242–45; and Michele Camerota, "Galileo, Lucrezio e l'atomismo," in *Lucrezio, la natura, la scienza*, ed. F. Beretta and F. Citti (Florence: Olschki, 2008), 141–175.

23. Stephen Greenblatt, "Martial Law in the Land of Cockaigne," in his *Shakespearean Negotiations*, 129–64 (Berkeley: University of California Press, 1988), 129–98.

24. Alasdair MacIntyre, *After Virtue: A Study in Moral Theory* (London: Duckworth, 1981).

25. Alison Brown, *The Return of Lucretius to Renaissance Florence* (Cambridge, Mass.: Harvard University Press, 2010).

26. In saying this I am defending the sort of enterprise embodied in Quentin Skinner's *The Foundations of Modern Political Thought*, 2 vols. (Cambridge: Cambridge University Press, 1978), an enterprise since disowned by Skinner.

CHAPTER 6. MACHIAVELLI AND MACHIAVELLIANISM

1. Friedrich Meinecke, *Machiavellism: The Doctrine of Raison d'État and Its Place in Modern History*, trans. from German by Douglas Scott (1924; 1957; New York: Praeger, 1965), 36.

2. Frederick of Prussia, *The Refutation of Machiavelli's Prince; or, Anti-Machiavel*, ed. Paul Sonnino (1740; Athens: Ohio University Press, 1981).

3. John Hale, *The Civilization of Europe in the Renaissance* (New York: Scribner's, 1995), 190.

4. See Guicciardini's reflections in his "Considerations on the *Discourses* of Machiavelli": "It is advanced too absolutely [by Machiavelli] that men never do good except when forced to, and that anyone organizing a republic should assume them all to be wicked, for there are many who, even when they could do ill, do well, and all mankind is not wicked. It is true that in organizing a republic, or anything else, one should take care to prevent anyone harming it who might wish to, not because all men are always wicked, but as a precaution against those who are." Francesco Guicciardini, *Selected Writings*, ed. and intro. Cecil Grayson, trans. Margaret Grayson (Oxford: Oxford University Press, 1965), 66–67. This edition contains both the "Considerations on the *Discourses*,'" written in 1530, after

Machiavelli's death, and the last version of his "Ricordi" or "Reflections," a set of short observations and maxims he worked on at various times in his life.

5. Friedrich Schlegel, *History of Ancient and Modern Literature* (1815), quoted in Jean-Pierre Barricelli, ed., *Machiavelli's "The Prince": Text and Commentary* (New York: Barron's Educational Series, 1968), 286.

6. Adam Smith, *The Theory of Moral Sentiments* (Philadelphia: Anthony Finley, 1817), 350–51.

7. J. G. A. Pocock, *Barbarism and Religion*, vol. 2, *Narratives of Civil Government* (Cambridge: Cambridge University Press, 1999), 370.

8. David Hume, "Of Civil Liberty," in *Essays Moral, Political, and Literary*, ed. Eugene Miller (Indianapolis, Ind.: Liberty Fund), 88–89.

9. Daniel Deudney, *Bounding Power: Republican Security Theory from the Polis to the Global Village* (Princeton, N.J.: Princeton University Press, 2007), 130.

10. Montesquieu, *The Spirit of the Laws*, bk. 21, chap. 20, pp. 389–90.

11. See Russell Price, "The Theme of *Gloria* in Machiavelli," *Renaissance Quarterly* 30 (1977): 588–631. In no writer of his times, Price notes, "is the theme of glory more prominent" than in Machiavelli (631).

12. I have used the edition of the *Discourses* available at Liberty Fund's Online Library of Liberty, http://oll.libertyfund.org/titles/1866. This is the Christian E. Detmold translation, published as *The Historical, Political, and Diplomatic Writings of Niccolo Machiavelli*, 4 vols. (Boston, 1882). Subsequent quotations in the text are from book 2, chapters 1–4, of the *Discourses*.

13. The incapacity of those who were subdued to anticipate their subjection also astonishes Hume, in his essay "Of the Balance of Power," in *Essays: Moral, Political and Literary*, ed. Eugene F. Miller (Indianapolis, Ind.: Liberty Fund, 1985), 336. See also discussion in Thomas Pangle and Peter Ahrensdorf, *Justice Among Nations: On the Moral Basis of Power and Peace* (Lawrence: University Press of Kansas), 1999.

14. Montesquieu, *The Spirit of the Laws*, ed. Anne Cohler, Basia Miller, and Harold Stone (1748; Cambridge: Cambridge University Press, 1989), bk. 9, chap. 2, p. 132.

15. Machiavelli's expectation reflects a common delusion among great thinkers, especially marked the greater they are. First, there is no guarantee that many people will read them seriously; second, the more widely read they are, the more misunderstood they are likely to be. T. S. Eliot remarked that "Machiavelli has been called a cynic; but there could be no stronger inspiration to 'cynicism' than the history of Machiavelli's reputation. No history could illustrate better than that of the reputation of Machiavelli the triviality and irrelevance of influence" ("Niccolò Machiavelli," *Times Literary Supplement*, June 16, 1927, cited in Barricelli, *Machiavelli's "The Prince,"* 295). At the time of his death, Machiavelli had no earthly consolation that he had been understood, and no expectation of a divine one. At the end, he was commonly reputed in Florence as "an evil man, a heretic, and an advisor to tyrants." The common people, said one contemporary, "hated him because of *The Prince*; the rich thought his *Prince* was a document written to teach the duke 'how to take away all their property, from the poor all their liberty; the

piagnoni [followers of Savonarola] regarded him as a heretic; the good thought him sinful; the wicked thought him more wicked or more capable than themselves—so they all hated him.'" Maurizio Viroli, *Niccolò's Smile: A Biography of Machiavelli*, trans. Antony Shugaar (New York: Hill and Wang, 2002), 257, citing Ridolfi, *Vita*.

16. Guicciardini, "Considerations on the *Discourses* of Machiavelli," 113.

17. Ibid., 92.

18. That lay in the future, as even Guicciardini, who wrote about the Italian balance of power with the most sophistication, was not recommending it as "a formula of general policy" but as "a historian diagnosing a situation that seemed unique." Machiavelli, notes Herbert Butterfield, is a disappointment for diplomats, with little conception of the general balance: "He repeatedly deals with the question whether a state should remain neutral when its neighbors are at war, and he is aware that the result of the war itself may be the aggrandizement of one of the belligerents. If he presses the policy of intervention, however, this is not out of consideration for the balance, but because in his view the neutral loses the respect of both sides—he treats the problem as a question of prestige." Only in the late seventeenth century, Butterfield argues, does the balance of power emerge as a coherent and well-thought-out doctrine. Herbert Butterfield, "Balance of Power," *Dictionary of the History of Ideas*, vol. 1 (New York: Scribner's, 1973), 180–81.

19. In practice, as Maurizio Viroli shows, Machiavelli did recognize the disease of excessive self-regard that made the Italian states incapable of effectual opposition to foreign invasion and occupation. Viroli presents an illuminating portrait and argument, but I am not sure that Machiavelli's biography can be successfully invoked against his books. That Viroli suggests there is a difference here—two different paths to understanding Machiavelli's political thought—makes his work intriguing. Viroli, *Niccolò's Smile*.

If Machiavelli's biography is to be invoked against his books, it would seem proper to admit as evidence at the bar all the salacious details of Machiavelli's sex life that are sprinkled throughout Viroli's biography. Machiavelli, it appears, was not unfamiliar with the splendid orifices of Florence, and seems to have explored them top to bottom and front to back. "Every day," notes Viroli, Machiavelli "and his friends would visit some girl to recover their vigor." The evidence suggests that he loved his courtesans more than his wife, and that men would do when women were not around. Viroli offers a simple defense and explanation: "where passions, desires, and pleasures were concerned, he listened only to nature, his own nature, and paid no attention to the views of moralists and prudes." However, I imagine Niccolò today as the object of one of those all-points bulletins—mothers beware—warning that a man convicted of a sex crime has moved to your neighborhood.

As Viroli shows, Machiavelli was a great lover of women, in both their earthiness and their divinity—"to think that he hated and scorned women shows appalling ignorance." But though "fascinated by the power of love," Machiavelli was also certainly transgressive in his complete indifference to conventional norms of sexual morality. Is that relevant? I think it may be. Both the allowance and control of the sex impulse (like that of impulses toward power and greed) are part of the business of every decent society. Given what Machiavelli said about politics, it would have been impossible for him to be a prude;

and had he been a prude, he would likely not have gone as far as he did in relaxing conventional restraints in politics that forbade lying and the breaking of oaths. I do not deny the obvious objection that people can put these things into separate compartments: the same man who is a rat in one context can be righteous in another. But there seems to me a relation here in how Machiavelli treats this trinity of appetites (the big three of Augustinian demonology). It may help explain Machiavelli's perambulations in chapter 25 of *The Prince*, where he compares the mastery of fortune to the thrashing of a woman. This is not only offensive; it is also untrue, as any gentleman knows. Only a barbarian would think of mastering a woman by beating her up.

20. G. John Ikenberry, *Liberal Leviathan: The Origins, Crisis, and Transformation of the American World Order* (Princeton, N.J.: Princeton University Press, 2011).

21. Richard Tuck, "Grotius, Hobbes, and Pufendorf on Humanitarian Intervention," in *Just and Unjust Military Intervention: European Thinkers from Vitoria to Mill*, Stefano Recchia and Jennifer M. Welsh (Cambridge: Cambridge University Press, 2013), 98.

22. Thomas Hobbes, *On the Citizen*, ed. and trans. Richard Tuck and Michael Silverthorne (Cambridge: Cambridge University Press, 1998), 3.

23. This contrast between Machiavelli and Hobbes runs in parallel with the contemporary distinction in international relations theory between offensive and defensive realism.

24. William Robertson, *The Progress of Society in Europe: A Historical Outline from the Subversion of the Roman Empire to the Beginning of the Sixteenth Century*, with an introduction and historical notes by Felix Gilbert, was published by the University of Chicago Press in 1972. The extract comes from the beginning of Robertson's *History of the Reign of the Emperor Charles V* (1769). Machiavelli's forecast of perpetual war: "For as long as I can remember, people have always been either making war or talking about going to war; it is now being talked about and in a short while it will be declared; when it is over, people will start talking about it again, so that there will never be any time to reflect about a thing." Machiavelli to Guicciardini, January 3, 1526, in James B. Atkinson and David Sices, ed. and trans. *Machiavelli and His Friends: Their Personal Correspondence* (DeKalb: Northern Illinois University Press, 1996), 378. Professor Mansfield's slighting reference to Guicciardini in this volume is quite unfair. Machiavelli *loved* Francesco Guicciardini and did not put on airs in his friendship with him. Mansfield's conceit is that Machiavelli was engaged in a dialogue with Plato and Aristotle that Guicciardini would not have understood; in fact, as is intimated in Viroli, Machiavelli would have surrendered the delightful though illusory prospect of chatting with Plato and Aristotle in the afterlife if he could have joined with Guicciardini in saving his country in the here and now.

25. Desiderius Erasmus, *The Education of a Christian Prince* (1516). I hope someone somewhere celebrates the five hundredth anniversary of that. Even more likely to fire me with anticipation is the homage due to the quincentenary, in 2017, of *Querela Pacis*, Erasmus's *Complaint of Peace (Peace Speaks in Her Own Person)*.

26. Mark Hulliung, *Citizen Machiavelli* (Princeton, N.J.: Princeton University Press, 1983), ix–x, 28.

27. See the long introductory essay by Noel Malcolm exploring the reason of state literature in Malcolm, *Reason of State, Propaganda, and the Thirty Years' War: An Unknown Translation by Thomas Hobbes* (Oxford: Oxford University Press, 2007), 95–98, 100–101.

28. Denis Diderot, "Machiavelism" (1773).

29. Jean Bodin, *The Republic* (1576); Innocent Gentillet, *Discourse . . . Against Machiavelli* (1576), quoted in Barricelli, *Machiavelli's "The Prince,"* 283, 278–79.

30. Malcolm, *Reason of State*, 100–101.

31. Henry Wheaton, *Elements of International Law*, 8th ed., ed. Richard Henry Dana Jr. (Boston: Little, Brown, 1866), xv–xxiii.

CHAPTER 7. MACHIAVELLI'S *PRINCE*

Special thanks to Tania Cronin, Michael A. Genovese, Addis Goldman, James Earl Kiawoin, Robert D. Loevy, Norman W. Provizer, and several Colorado College students for their suggestions.

1. Max Weber, *Politics as a Vocation* (Philadelphia: Fortress, 1965). First published 1919.

2. This was what Machiavelli was learning on the job, according to biographer Maurizio Viroli, *Niccolò's Smile: A Biography of Machiavelli* (New York: Hill and Wang, 2000), 94.

3. Quentin Skinner, *Machiavelli: A Very Short Introduction* (Oxford: Oxford University Press, 1981), 22.

4. Countless authors have penned "advice to rulers" books or pamphlets over the centuries. Most of them encouraged wisdom, humility, and compassion. One of the most intriguing "mirror-for-princes" or kindred tutorials for would be princes was written at virtually the same time as *The Prince* (see Desiderius Erasmus, *The Education of a Christian Prince* [1516]). An earlier example is the thirteenth-century mystic Persian Sunni philosopher and poet widely known to his followers as Saadi, whose advice on leadership is summarized, in translation, in Afsaneh Nahavandi, *Ancient Leadership Wisdom* (Shelbyville, Ky.: Wasteland Press, 2012). Most of Saadi's advice encourages listening, kindness, and chess-master astuteness. But Machiavelli might have appreciated at least part of this proposition: "An intelligent person will submit to an unworthy person who is enjoying good fortune and has power. . . . Wait until fate ties his hands, and then rip out his brains to the delight of your friends" (74).

5. From Miles J. Unger, *Machiavelli: A Biography* (New York: Simon and Schuster, 2011), 215–16.

6. See Harvey J. Mansfield Jr., *Taming the Prince: The Ambivalence of Executive Power* (New York: Free Press, 1989).

7. See David McCullough, *1776* (New York: Simon and Schuster, 2005).

8. James M. McPherson, *Tried by War* (New York: Penguin, 2008), 29–30.

9. Barack Obama, remarks in Oslo, Norway, 2009, www.whitehouse.gov/the-press -office/remarks-president-acceptance-nobel-peace-prize.

10. Stephen Kinzer, *Overthrow* (New York: Times Books, 2006).

11. John Keegan, *The Mask of Command: Alexander the Great, Wellington, Ulysses S. Grant, Hitler, and the Nature of Leadership* (New York: Viking, 1987), 11.

12. This idea is suggested by Corrado Vivanti in *Niccolo Machiavelli: An Intellectual Biography* (Princeton, N.J.: Princeton University Press, 2013), 98. Three generations after Machiavelli's *The Prince*, Shakespeare has his Henry V rally the troops at Agincourt by urging them to "imitate the action of the tiger," disguise "fair nature with hard-favored rage."

13. Scott Gordon, *Controlling the State: Constitutionalism from Ancient Athens to Today* (Cambridge, Mass.: Harvard University Press, 1999), 161.

14. Alan Ryan, *On Politics: A History of Political Thought From Herodotus to the Present* (New York: W. W. Norton, 2012), 359.

15. Gordon, *Controlling the State*, 361.

16. Jean Lipman-Blumen, *The Allure of Toxic Leaders: Why We Follow Destructive Bosses and Corrupt Politicians—and How We Can Survive Them* (New York: Oxford University Press, 2005), 35.

17. Michael Walzer, *Thinking Politically: Essays in Political Theory* (New Haven, Conn.: Yale University Press, 2007). Deciding what is moral or not is the subject matter of a huge intellectual field. See, for example, David Edmonds, *Would You Kill the Fat Man? The Trolley Problem and What Your Answer Tells About Right and Wrong* (Princeton, N.J.: Princeton University Press, 2014).

18. Max Lerner, introduction to *"The Prince" and "The Discourses"* (New York: Modern Library, 1950), xliv.

19. See Isaiah Berlin, "The Question of Machiavelli," *New York Times Book Review*. November 4, 1971, 30–32; Ross King, *Machiavelli: Philosopher of Power* (New York: HarperCollins, 2007); and Ryan, *On Politics*.

20. Unger, *Machiavelli*, 228.

21. Maurizio Viroli, *Redeeming "The Prince": The Meaning of Machiavelli's Masterpiece* (Princeton, N.J.: Princeton University Press, 2014).

22. See the examination of why leaders lie (sometimes wrongly, but sometimes justifiably) by John J. Mearsheimer, *Why Leaders Lie: The Truth About Lying in International Politics* (New York: Oxford University Press, 2011).

23. Discussed at length in Evan Thomas, *The Very Best Men: Four Who Dared; The Early Years of the C.I.A.* (New York: Simon and Schuster, 1995).

24. Reinhold Niebuhr, *The Irony of American History* (New York: Scribner, 1952), 157.

25. Ibid., 133.

26. *House of Cards* writer Michael Dobbs based much of his original British TV series on Shakespeare's *Richard III* and Iago (from *Othello*). These characters doubtless were derivative from Machiavelli. But why did people enjoy the Frank Underwood character? Actor Kevin Spacey speculates that viewers are fascinated because, unlike the then

Congress in Washington, D.C., the fictional Congress of the TV series actually got things done. "True," Spacey adds, "[Underwood] crosses the line. He's not the best role model. But we look back in history and see a lot of political figures who were Machiavellian bastards, who were incredibly tough. It is interesting to see how audiences have dug it." Spacey, interviewed in Elysa Gardner, "Kevin Spacey Relishes His Audience of 'Co-conspirators,'" *USA Today*, April 28, 2014, D2.

27. Warren Bennis and Burt Nanus, *Leaders: The Strategies for Taking Charge* (New York: Harper and Row, 1985), 153.

28. David Brooks, "Why We Love Politics," *New York Times*, November 27, 2012, A27.

29. This is a point made by Alan Ryan, who is elaborating on an observation by political theorist Sheldon Wolin, in Ryan, *On Politics*, 376.

30. See, for example, Thomas E. Cronin and Michael A. Genovese, *The Paradoxes of the American Presidency*, 4th ed. (New York: Oxford University Press, 2013); and Archie Brown, *The Myth of the Strong Leader* (New York: Basic Books, 2014).

CHAPTER 8. THE RIDDLE OF CESARE BORGIA AND THE LEGACY OF MACHIAVELLI'S *PRINCE*

My thanks to Ryan K. Balot, Timothy Fuller, Damon Linker, and Diego von Vacano, for their adroit midwifery, and to John T. Scott and Vickie Sullivan for reigniting my interest in Cesare.

1. Maurizio Viroli, *Machiavelli's God*, trans. Antony Shugaar (Princeton, N.J.: Princeton University Press, 2010), xvii–xviii.

2. Leo Strauss, *Thoughts on Machiavelli* (Glencoe, N.Y.: Free Press, 1958), 83.

3. For a particularly sophisticated rendition of Cesare as a positive model, see Claude Lefort, *Machiavel: Le travail de l'oeuvre* (Paris: Gallimard, 1972), 369–72. These pages are now available in English in a recent partial translation of Lefort's great tome: *Machiavelli in the Making*, trans. Michael B. Smith (Evanston, Ill.: Northwestern University Press, 2012), 128–33. Among other recent writers, Alan Ryan sees Cesare as flawed but accepts Machiavelli's praise of him at face value; see Ryan, *Machiavelli: The Search for Glory* (New York: Liveright, 2014), 63–64. Maurizio Viroli, who characterizes Machiavelli as a "realist with imagination," sees the Cesare of *The Prince* as a mythic representation of some of the qualities required in an eventual redeemer of Italy. See Viroli, *Redeeming "The Prince": The Meaning of Machiavelli's Masterpiece* (Princeton, N.J.: Princeton University Press, 2014), 66–67, 72–75. Other leading recent scholars who subscribe to the view that Cesare was Machiavelli's model or ideal include Gennaro Sasso, *Machiavelli e Cesare Borgia: Storia di un giudizio* (Rome: Edizioni dell'Ateneo, 1966); Gian Mario Anselmi, "Machiavelli, i Borgia, e le Romagne," in *Machiavelli senza i Medici (1498–1512): Scrittura del potere / potere della scrittura*, ed. Jean Jacques Marchand (Rome: Salerno Editrice, 2006), 221–30;

Jean-Jacques Marchand, "L'évolution de la figure de César Borgia dans la pensée de Machiavel," *Schweizerische Zeitschrift für Geschichte* 19 (1969): 327–55.

4. Rousseau, *On the Social Contract*, ed. and trans. Roger D. Masters and Judith R. Masters (New York: St. Martin's Press, 1978), 88. Recent variations on this interpretation include Mary Dietz, "Trapping the Prince: Machiavelli and the Politics of Deception," *American Political Science Review* 80 (1986): 777–99; and James O. Ward, "Reading Machiavelli Rhetorically: *The Prince* as Covert Critique of the Renaissance Prince," *California Italian Studies* 2, no. 2 (2011): 1–31, http://escholarship.org/uc/item/4sc5s550#page-1.

5. "*The Prince* is a study of failed princes and of the many ways they fail." John M. Najemy, "Machiavelli and Cesare Borgia: A Reconsideration of Chapter 7 of *The Prince*," *Review of Politics* 75 (2013): 555.

6. Machiavelli, *The Prince*, trans. Harvey C. Mansfield, 2nd ed. (Chicago: University of Chicago Press, 1998), dedicatory letter, 4; chap. 7, p. 27. I have cited this translation throughout; in-text citations indicate the chapter followed by brackets enclosing the page number in this edition. These not quite parallel formulations suggest that while the malice of Fortune toward Machiavelli has been more continuous, her malice toward Cesare has been more severe. Its characterization as *straordinaria* is the more striking given the centrality of the term *ordini* to Machiavelli's treatment of Cesare.

7. Nathan Tarcov, "Niccolò Machiavelli in *The Prince*," in *Political Philosophy Cross-Examined: Essays in Honor of Heinrich Meier*, Thomas Pangle and J. Harvey Lomax (New York: Palgrave Macmillan, 2013), 109, 110. This suggests the following question: When Liverotto baited his trap (chap. 8, pp. 36–37), would Machiavelli have fallen into it?

8. Ward, "Reading Machiavelli Rhetorically," 13, notes the "cognitive dissonance" between chapters 6 and 7. According to John Najemy, even the pitiful bouquet that Machiavelli offers here is ironic, as in fact disorders broke out in Romagna immediately upon Alexander's death. Najemy, "Machiavelli and Cesare Borgia," 544–49.

9. One should also consider, given Machiavelli's insistence on Cesare as the example for imitation par excellence, that one of Cesare's roles in the argument is as a stand-in for the figure previously held by Machiavelli's readers to be such. That Cesare is the placeholder for Machiavelli's preeminent (and necessarily unmentioned) example of an unarmed prophet is not at first apparent, yet we must acknowledge that the work progressively discloses the emptiness of Cesare's claim to arms. "Could Cesare Borgia, with his two names (called Duke Valentino by the vulgar), represent Machiavelli's portrayal of the most successful unarmed prophet who nonetheless erred in such a way as to cause his ultimate ruin?" Harvey C. Mansfield, "Strauss on '*The Prince*,'" *Review of Politics* 75 (2013): 659. Consider also that Machiavelli himself would seem to fall into the category of unarmed prophet, which, just like his calling our attention to the parallel between himself and Cesare, raises in most emphatic fashion the question of how he can possibly succeed.

10. Cf. *The Prince* chap. 14, p. 58: "For there is no proportion between one who is armed and one who is unarmed, and it is not reasonable that whoever is armed obey willingly one who is unarmed and that someone unarmed be secure among armed servants." Cf. the comment of Nathan Tarcov, "Arms and Politics in Machiavelli's *Prince*,"

in *Entre Kant et Kosovo: Études offertes à Pierre Hassner*, Anne-Marie Le Gloannec and Aleksander Smolar (Paris: Presses de Sciences Po, 2003), 119: "In saying that it is not reasonable for the armed to obey the unarmed, Machiavelli is not saying that it is not possible; on the contrary, he has shown that armed soldiers and princes obey unarmed priests and popes, however unreasonably and unreliably."

11. Vickie Sullivan and John T. Scott, "Parricide and the Plot of *The Prince*: Cesare Borgia and Machiavelli's Italy," *American Political Science Review* 88, no. 4 (1994): 887–900.

12. For a contrary reading of Machiavelli's critique of Giovampagolo, see Patrick Coby, *Machiavelli's Romans: Liberty and Greatness in the Discourses on Livy* (Lanham, Md.: Lexington Books, 1999), 231. Coby does not sufficiently consider just who it was that the supposedly impious Giovampagolo balked at being the first to show both themselves and others the deserts of those who lived as they did, and why it was regarding them in particular that he proved himself incapable of showing himself "all bad."

13. Cf. Sullivan and Scott, "Parricide," 892–93.

14. Cf. the somewhat different treatment of Giovampagolo by Sullivan and Scott, ibid., 890–91. It underscores the main disagreement between us: that they see Machiavelli as indicating the possibility of ending Christianity in his lifetime, whereas I see him as laying the foundations for this accomplishment by a future generation.

15. Najemy, "Machiavelli and Cesare Borgia," 549–54, argues persuasively that this pattern pervades chapter 7, and that those aspects of Machiavelli's account seemingly most flattering to Cesare repeatedly reflect both Cesare's self-serving excuses for his failures and his self-deluded estimations alike of his present power and his future successes. This he ascribes to Machiavelli's "ironic mimicry." Erica Benner, *Machiavelli's Prince: A New Reading* (Oxford: Oxford University Press, 2014), also presents Machiavelli's treatment of Cesare as ironic. See also Michael McCanles, *The Discourse of "Il Principe"* (Malibu, Calif.: Undena, 1983), 70–85.

16. Thus Erica Benner, *Machiavelli's Ethics* (Princeton, N.J.: Princeton University Press, 2009), 371–72.

17. Friedrich Nietzsche, *The Antichrist*, sec. 61, trans. Walter Kaufmann, in *The Portable Nietzsche* (New York: Viking Press, 1954), 653–54.

18. "Cesare's successes ultimately benefited only the Church, and thus increased the obstacles to the conquest or liberation of Italy." Strauss, *Thoughts on Machiavelli*, 68. Cf. Sullivan and Scott, "Parricide," who clearly recognize what most of the literature on Cesare does not, that the issue his failure poses is that of Christianity. Cf. also Ronald Beiner, *Civil Religion: A Dialogue in the History of Political Philosophy* (New York: Cambridge University Press, 2011), 21–22.

19. Here I can hardly improve on the excellent formulation of Najemy, "Machiavelli and Cesare Borgia," 553.

> In this light, Machiavelli's allegedly contradictory explanations of Borgia's
> failure—"the extreme and exceptional malice of fortune"—and the error in

allowing Julius's election—are not mutually exclusive and need not be understood as alternative explanations for his collapse. Borgia no doubt lamented fortune's "extreme malice" as uncontrollable fate, but Machiavelli wants his readers to understand that Borgia failed to understand that his "error" resulted from the lack of autonomy that forced him to depend on the conclave to give him a friendly pope and then to rely—foolishly—on the mistaken notion that "recent favors would make Julius forget former injuries." The "error" is not separate from the "malice of fortune." It is the culminating example of how fortune—dependence—shackled him. He committed the error because he lacked the autonomy and arms that would have allowed him not to depend on the College of Cardinals to provide him with a friendly pope. Machiavelli reproduces Valentino's misunderstanding of the "malice of fortune" in his failure to recognize that "fortune" is not external to one's choices and actions. Cesare had chosen the easy route to the acquisition of a state and was now paying the inevitable price.

Cf. the similar verdict of Benner, *Machiavelli's Prince*, 108, and the parallel (if much more "literary") assessment of McCanles, *Discourse of "Il Principe,"* 82–85.

20. Cf. Benner, *Machiavelli's Prince*, 96. So too Ryan K. Balot, "Machiavelli's Military Advice," unpublished manuscript.

21. On this passage, cf. Viroli, *Redeeming "The Prince,"* 85–87.

22. Such is the conclusion of Najemy, "Machiavelli and Cesare Borgia," who argues forcefully that Cesare never escaped his primary dependence on mercenaries, that Machiavelli had underlined this in his diplomatic dispatches at the time, and that this dependence helps explain the rapid collapse of Cesare's position. Najemy thinks that here too Machiavelli ironically adopts Cesare's typical boastfulness and overestimation of both his accomplishments and the strength of his position.

23. Benner, *Machiavelli's Prince*, 166.

24. On Francesco as the counterexample to Cesare, see Erica Benner, *Machiavelli's Ethics* (Princeton, N.J.: Princeton University Press, 2009), 371–72; and *Machiavelli's Prince*, 94ff.

25. Nathan Tarcov has reminded me that in chapter 8 Machiavelli credits Liverotto da Fermo with having brought new orders (p. 37), thereby implying his superiority to Cesare. Perhaps we may take Liverotto's highly successful reign of terror in Fermo as a model on a very small scale of what would be required on a great one. At the very least he freed himself, unlike Cesare, of his initial dependence on his relatives, not one of whom remained alive. That Liverotto's orders are confined to little Fermo and that he so soon falls prey (in the blackest of Machiavelli's black comedies) to a trap of Cesare's hardly distinguishable from the one he had so recently sprung on his kinsmen underscores the narrow limits of his accomplishment.

Thomas E. Cronin is McHugh Professor of American Institutions and Leadership at Colorado College, and president emeritus of Whitman College. Among his books are *Leadership Matters: Unleashing the Power of Paradox* (2012) and *The Paradoxes of the American Presidency* (2013). He is the recipient of the American Political Science Association's Charles E. Merriam Award (1986) and the Outstanding Leadership Book Award (2013).

Timothy Fuller is professor of political science at Colorado College, where he teaches political philosophy and has served as both chief academic officer and acting president. He is the recipient of several NEH awards as well as awards from the Colorado Endowment for the Humanities. He writes on modern political philosophy, especially British thought from Hobbes to Oakeshott, whose work he has edited and commented on extensively, including *The Voice of Liberal Learning: Michael Oakeshott on Education* (1989) and *Religion, Politics, and the Moral Life* (1996). He has also written numerous essays on Leo Strauss and Eric Voegelin, among others. He served as president of the Michael Oakeshott Association from 2003 to 2006.

David C. Hendrickson is professor of political science at Colorado College, where he teaches American foreign policy and international relations. He is the author of seven books, including *Union, Nation, or Empire: The American Debate over International Relations, 1789–1941* (2009); *Peace Pact: The Lost World of the American Founding* (2003); and, with Robert W. Tucker, *Empire of Liberty: The Statecraft of Thomas Jefferson* (1990), which was nominated for the Pulitzer Prize. He has received awards from the Lehrman Institute, the

Olin Foundation, and the NEH, and has served as a book review editor for *Foreign Affairs.*

Harvey C. Mansfield is the William R. Kenan Jr. Professor of Government at Harvard University. He is the recipient of Guggenheim and NEH fellowships and of the National Humanities Medal from President Bush. He has written many distinguished works in political philosophy, including his acclaimed translation of Machiavelli's *The Prince* (1998) and other major works of Machiavelli and, with Delba Winthrop, a celebrated translation and commentary on Tocqueville's *Democracy in America* (2000).

Clifford Orwin is professor of political philosophy at the University of Toronto and also serves as chair of the Munk Centre's Program in Political Philosophy and International Affairs. He has received Guggenheim and NEH fellowships. He writes extensively on both ancient and modern political thought. His books include *The Humanity of Thucydides* (1994) and *The Legacy of Rousseau* (1997), edited with Nathan Tarcov.

Arlene W. Saxonhouse is the Caroline Robbins Collegiate Professor of Political Science and Women's Studies and an adjunct professor of Classics at the University of Michigan. She is the author of numerous works of political philosophy, including *Free Speech and Athenian Democracy* (2006) and *Women in the History of Political Thought: Ancient Greece to Machiavelli* (1985).

Maurizio Viroli is currently professor of government at the University of Texas, professor of politics emeritus at Princeton, and professor of political communication at the Italian University of Switzerland. He is an internationally acclaimed scholar of Machiavelli's political thought. Among his many publications are *Redeeming "The Prince": The Meaning of Machiavelli's Masterpiece* (2013) and *Niccolò's Smile: A Biography of Machiavelli* (2000).

David Wootton is anniversary professor of history at the University of York. He has published a wide range of works, and has edited numerous collections of writings, on intellectual and cultural history and early modern political theory in England, France, and Italy in the period 1500–1800. He also writes on the history of science in this period. Among these works is *Galileo: Watcher of the Skies* (2010). He is a fellow of the Royal Historical Society and has served on its council.

Catherine Heidt Zuckert is Nancy Reeves Dreux Professor of Political Science at the University of Notre Dame. She is also editor in chief of *The Review of Politics*. She is the author of numerous award-winning books, including *Natural Right and the American Imagination: Political Philosophy in Novel Form* (1990) and *Plato's Philosophers: The Coherence of Dialogues* (2009), and is currently finishing a major commentary on Machiavelli's politics.

INDEX

ACKNOWLEDGMENTS

To mark the five hundredth anniversary of Machiavelli's composing of *The Prince*, seven leading scholars decided to address the question of Machiavelli's legacy in our time. This work was made possible through funding from the McHugh Family Endowment, which supports the department programs of the Political Science Department at Colorado College, with additional support from the Manning Endowment. Special thanks are also due to my assistant, Jackson Porreca, for his help in the technical preparation of this work.

—Timothy Fuller